D0820763

# THE PROMISE

BOOK PUBLISHING INFORMATION
*traitmarkerbooks.com*
*traitmarker@gmail.com*

ATTRIBUTIONS
*Foreword: Jon Stewart*
*Introduction: Rosie Torres*
*Editors: Robbie & Sharilyn Grayson*
*Cover Design: Robbie Grayson III*

PUBLICATION DATA
*Paperback: 979-1-888862-623-8*
*Hardcover ISBN: 978-1-08808-114-3*

*Interior Title & Text Font: Minion Pro*
*Interior Text Font: Minion Variable Concept*
*Interior Title Fonts: Ink Free*

*Printed in the United States of America.*

# THE PROMISE

*The Stories of Four Burn Pit Survivor Families Who Found Friendship in Their Fight to Win the Largest Veteran Medical Bill in American History*

**KIMBERLY HUGHES | KEVIN HENSLEY**
**TIM HAUSER | GINA CANCELINO**

*Traitmarker Books*

**988**

**SUICIDE &**

**CRISIS LINE**

## Group Dedication

*We dedicate this book to the more than 3.5 million Iraq, Afghanistan, Gulf War, Vietnam Veterans, and their families for whom the Honoring Our Promise to Address Comprehensive Toxins (PACT Act) of 2022 will cover the medical care and benefits that they deserve. To the surviving spouses, children, and family members: may all the advocacy and actions of so many involved in this historical law bring you peace.*

Kim | Kevin | Tim | Gina

*December 2022*

# TABLE OF CONTENTS

# by Jon Stewart

The passage of the PACT Act, which will bring much needed medical help and care for veteran survivors of burn pits and their families, is a victory that means a lot to me. Just like the first responders on the scene during the September 11 attacks, these veterans were harmed in the process of doing their jobs. Since Congress hired them to do those dangerous jobs, it's only right that Congress continues to support their medical care and expenses.

A lot of people fought side by side to get this historic piece of legislation passed. We needed every single voice, every single story. Everyone, from members of huge veteran organizations to volunteers with smaller ones, played a vital part in helping Congress do the right thing.

When Le Roy and Rosie Torres from Burn Pits 360 called me about veterans that were sick and dying from toxic exposure, I knew I had to get involved. These veterans took an oath to protect our country, and Congress took an oath to take care of these veterans when they returned home. Congress failed them.

I worked closely with Rosie and Le Roy Torres and Burn Pits 360 during the fight to pass the PACT Act. In that time, I got to know some of the volunteers who showed up to tell their stories. Four of those volunteers were Gina Cancelino and Kimberly Hughes, two widows fighting for veterans and survivors, and Kevin Hensley and Tim Hauser, two veterans sick from their toxic exposure fighting for their brothers and sisters. They showed up faithfully and frequently to keep the pressure on Congress. They walked the halls of our legislature and told the truth to powerful people without backing down. They brought energy, enthusiasm, and much needed hope to this fight.

As they continued to advocate over time, the bond they formed turned into one akin to a family. They looked out for one another, supported each other during the difficult times and ensured that each of their stories were heard. They knew that by pushing each other to continue on, they'd help so many others in the end.

I'm pleased that they've collected their stories here in *The Promise*. I can say based on my relationship with these four individuals that they are compassionate, dedicated, and honorable. And what you're about to read will give you an insider's take on burn pits, military service, family, and fighting for what you believe in.

JON STEWART
*American Comedian | Activist*

## INTRODUCTION
### by Rosie Torres

For thirteen years, my husband Le Roy and I have been fighting for the survivors of burn pits and their families to get the life-changing and lifesaving medical care and benefits that they have earned and desperately needed. During that time, we would talk to men, women, mothers, and fathers every day who were telling us, "We have nowhere to turn. We don't know who to go to. There is nowhere. There is no one." Before the PACT Act, there was nowhere to turn to.

We attended so many funerals and said goodbye to so many amazing men and women who didn't survive, some of whom actually were compensated right before they died—some even hours before they died— through our advocacy. Through our organization, Burn Pits 360, we literally were carrying the DOD and VA on our backs for thirteen years, doing their job. We were helping these veterans who had no one else in their corner to carry the burden of proof placed on them by a system that made not believing them a policy. Prior to the PACT Act, that was exhausting.

Not only were we actively helping veterans, but we

were also advocating for legislation to change the way the VA and the DOD worked. Every time a version of what would soon become known as the "PACT Act" would come to a vote, it was always up in the air. I never felt, "This is the time it will pass."

And in the beginning, we were by no means a powerhouse advocacy group at Burn Pits 360. If advocacy were high school, we weren't the popular kids. We weren't the jocks and cheerleaders. We weren't the true leaders of the school. We took a very nontraditional way of doing things.

The real leaders of advocacy high school were the "Big Six," which are the largest six veteran lobbying organizations in Washington: the Veterans of Foreign Wars (VFW), American Veterans (AMVETS), Vietnam Veterans of America, Paralyzed Veterans of America, The American Legion, and the Disabled American Veterans (DAV). Working with them is the way that Congress traditionally has prioritized legislation for veterans.

When we went to Congress, I was just this little, five-foot-one Hispanic woman, advocating on behalf of my husband. I perceived their reactions to be, "Why are you here? What is it that you would like us to do? We don't care about this issue. It's not a priority. No one's talking about it." To them, I guess, we were the rejects who knew nothing about how to get a bill passed.

Burn Pits 360 showed up as a group of families and advocates, leading the movement for justice for burn pit survivors. These individuals who served in the military or in civilian professional capacity had a de- termined passion and drive for justice. We would not have had a bill had it not been for everyone contrib- uting what they had from their grassroots organizing ability to military experience to civilian experience and to their experience as military families. That alone was powerful. Eventually, the bigger organizations re- alized how late they were to the game. But to be fair, we also realized how much we needed them.

While we were all negotiating the space, Jon Stew- art entered the picture. That was a game changer. He joined shortly after I asked and said "yes" because he cares for America's Warfighters and their families. Jon made sure that everyone understood why he was there: "I'm here because Rosie and Le Roy asked me to be."

With Jon Stewart, in his interviews about the issue, he always mentions Rosie and Le Roy. When he did Joe Rogan or when he was talking about burn pits on CNN—it didn't matter what the situation was—he di- rected people to us. Some people might have wanted to push us aside so that they could call victory on their own (things got very political). But Jon was so humble and always made it so clear why he was helping.

Jon is a genuine person, too. When I met him for the first time in D.C., I asked him to do a PSA for Burn Pits 360. He agreed, so I flew to New York and went to his office. He did a quick PSA about burn pits and what he did for the 9/11 first responders. I told him about Le Roy going through a rough time and losing hope. Jon said that he wanted to speak to Le Roy.

I got Le Roy on FaceTime, and Jon talked to him. He said, "Hey, brother, I don't know you. I've just met Rosie. And I want you to know that she told me about your story. And I promise you that we're going to get this done. So don't give up on me. Don't give up on us. Give me an opportunity to help you." And Jon kept his promise.

The first time that the PACT Act officially passed in the House, there were a few reporters asking us, "Hey, how do you feel?" I remember telling Le Roy later, "I don't really feel anything. I'm not excited. I'm not crying." I didn't feel anything because it didn't resonate. It wasn't gut wrenching. It was what it was. For some reason, it just didn't feel like it was real, even though it passed the House unanimously. Maybe my heart was just telling me what was coming.

Then the Senate voted it down, and we decided later on to peacefully protest on the steps of our nation's capital. History was in the making as we announced the PACT ACT Firewatch to the world. We slept outside for five nights and six days, keeping a constant presence in front of the Senators and Congressmen. Sometimes, I would stay all night until the next morning.

After hour 56, however, we took shifts. We finally got it down to where the guys would stay at night, and the women would sleep during the day. I would leave at midnight or at one in the morning. Then the Grunt Style team would take over the night shift. They slept during the day, as it was safer for them to be out at night. Then we'd go to sleep at night for at least four or five hours.

During Firewatch and some other press conferences, we always positioned the families and advocates to have the front row. In every photo and in the press coverage—you'll always see our advocates right there in the front.

On day six when we finally got the bill passed, one of the reporters asked Jon, "Jon, why are you here?" He pointed at me and said, "I'm here because of her. I'm here for Rosie and Le Roy." They asked me about Jon's statement, and I told them, "He made me a promise. He made my husband a promise."

The final time the bill went up for a vote, which was the second time, my knees buckled when it passed. I sort of fell on someone. Those six days of sleeping on the steps and then that thirteen years of work hit me emotionally all at one time, and I just buckled. I felt like finally—after all the people, all the years, all the time away from my family, away from our children, all the sacrifices—we had achieved something. That just hit me really, really hard.

When it did pass, we were in the gallery, and I broke down crying. The staffers had told us that we could have no reactions, no response. We couldn't make noise. And I said to myself, You know what? I don't care. I don't care if they get mad at us. I don't care if they kick me out. How am I going to hold back on this?

The PACT Act saves lives. It extends help to survivors and widows. It's life changing. Knowing that the burden of proof won't be on these men and women that served our country is just emotional. There's so much to this journey, and the advocates and their sacrifice. Each one brings some special quality to the work ahead of us.

I think of Gina Cancelino being willing to open up her journey and bring her children to share her story on national television at a press conference in a moment's notice. She captured America and really got them to understand the depth of the issue. And she was also showing up during COVID.

Kevin Hensley is just a powerhouse. And Tim Hauser, being as sick as he is, was utilizing his military skill set in the civilian world. With Tim and Kevin, I really saw their military careers shine through their leadership and organizing in their areas. I mean, I never heard, "Well, I'll think about it." It was always, "I'm on the phone with my Senator tomorrow." They both have a skill set that you can't buy or find anywhere, and they brought all that military experience to this cause.

Kimberly Hughes would bring life back in. She would always tell me, "I'm arriving late. But I promise you'll know when I arrive!" Kim would walk in, and we would know she was there. How could we not know? When she showed up, it was really to refuel people if they were feeling depleted already. She would comfort other people when she should have been the one comforted. The beauty of her presence was that here was this widow survivor, who really never showed her emotion and very rarely ever cried until we were at a point of victory. There are a lot of layers to her.

I think the nation and Congress underestimated what we could bring to the table and how we could get our stories out there. We wouldn't have a bill without these advocates who worked so diligently on getting the bill across the finish line. I know each of these four advocates, and I value their stories and their experiences. In the following pages, I know you will come to like and respect them the same way that I do.

ROSIE TORRES
*Executive Director | Burn Pits 360*
burnpits360.org

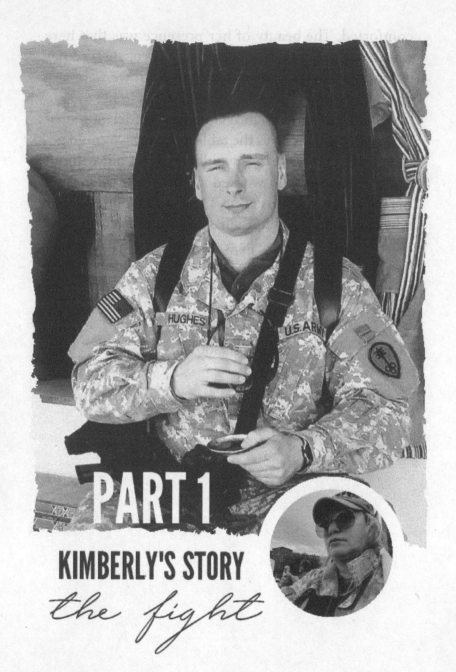

# PART 1

## KIMBERLY'S STORY
*the fight*

DEDICATION

*To my beloved Gary in Spirit:*

*I kept my promise, and I fought this.*
*I miss holding your hand.*

*To our son Justin and our daughter Kaylee:*
*continue to honor your father's legacy,*
*fight for what you believe in,*
*and always keep moving forward.*

*To the veterans, their families, and the survivors:*
*We did this for you.*

*And to all our friends, families, and neighbors:*
*We thank you for all your support.*

*And a shoutout to all the loving people*
*on the southwest side of Chicago.*

INTRODUCTION

# Military Injustice
## A History of Broken Promises
## to Warfighters

There are certain things we agree should come out
of the public purse as Americans. We all need streets
to drive, bridges to cross, schools to educate the next
generation of voters, and safety at home and work.
That last one, safety at home and work, has a lot of
different layers to it. It's one of the reasons cities pay
police officers, to protect and to serve.

But at its foundation, that public safety comes from
the US Military. The Army and Marines secure our
land, the Navy and the Coast Guard our seas, and the
Air Force our skies. Their presence and their work is a
public good, just like our roads, bridges, and schools.
In fact, the armed forces predate all those other public
works.

The preamble of the Constitution says, "We the People of the United States, in Order to form a more perfect Union, establish Justice, insure domestic Tran-
quility, provide for the common defense, promote the
general Welfare, and secure the Blessings of Liberty to
ourselves and our Posterity, do ordain and establish

this Constitution for the United States of America."

Providing for the common defense is in our DNA as a nation. But from the very beginning, before those words appeared on paper, America had a hard time fulfilling that intention. Just look at our soldiers in the Revolutionary War. Later wars, more recent wars, carry the feelings about the political justifications for fighting them. But every American supports the Revolutionary War. We know we were right to fight it, and we're glad we won. Do we know how we treated our soldiers way back then?

These were citizen soldiers, pulled from farms and shops by their hope for independence. The organization and infrastructure of our modern army was absent. Troops depended on what they could bring from home, forage along the way, or gain from the prototype congress cobbled together out of necessity. You can see how that imperfect arrangement led to difficulties.

Still, the Revolutionary War soldier wasn't operating on dreams and moonbeams. He needed food, clothing, horses, wagons, bullets and other ammunition, and the machinery to fire them from. And the United States in its early stages promised to provide those materials and pay the men who fought.

Any child studying history in a school classroom could tell you how those early soldiers froze and starved at Valley Forge. They may not know why. They may not have heard how future president James Madison, aide to future President George Washington, begged the congress for basic food, shoes, and weaponry. They may not have heard how that ramshackle collection of wealthy southern planters and parsimonious New England shopkeepers cited strained budgets and political arguments instead of answering the need.

Some of the first American casualties died on our soil because congress left them to drill in the snow without shoes or coats, to boil hay or leather to fill their stomachs, or to take their last breaths under the stars, without a tent to block the weather. And what about their families back home? What were they to do when the breadwinner was gone?

Those first American Warfighters who survived to see the constitution written, the government formed, and the first president sworn to serve the people, not to rule them, had a bitter disappointment in store. Their wages, promised for good service and the hazard of their lives, were delayed and delayed. In March of 1783, George Washington had to quiet the unrest of officers in Newburgh, New York who feared they would not be paid. In June 1783, unpaid soldiers rioted, holding congress hostage in Philadelphia. In 1786, unpaid and overtaxed Massachusetts veterans rose in armed rebellion against the wealthy merchants and government leaders out east.

Those early conflicts taught the American government that those who fought must be paid, though they didn't learn the lesson well. In the Great Depression, the US government still had not paid promised bonuses of $500 to those who fought in World War I. Times were tight in Washington, perhaps. How much tighter were they, then, for ordinary citizens, some of them wounded? When Congress told the veterans to wait for their bonuses until 1945 and have them as an old age pension, veterans marched on Washington. What good was $500 in the future (if it was even paid then), when their children were starving now and when they were losing their homes now?

Veterans camped on the national mall, casting eyes up to the Washington Monument from the doors of their tents. But President Herbert Hoover treated the people protesting as if they were gangsters or pirates, not honest servicemen. He sent the US Army with tear gas, guns, and sabers to clear the protestors from government property.

Uncle Sam was an ungrateful customer. As Jon Stewart has said, Uncle Sam was the kind of customer who ate the steak down to the bone and then complained to the kitchen about the check. And as he began, so he has gone on. Yes, pay became regular. The military established infrastructure so that American warfighters could work on full stomachs with adequate materials. But that lack of care for the returning veteran was forged into the government disposition.

General JM Wainwright wrote to returning World War Two veterans to embrace civic duty at home, to shoulder the responsibility for shaping their communities. But those inspiring words failed to acknowledge the toll of warfare on the body and the soul, a toll many warfighters medicated with alcohol, the only treatment available to them.

Still, those words were much better than the relative silence that met veterans from the Korean War or the public shame heaped on veterans of the Vietnam War. And in the Vietnam War, as medical science progressed alongside military science, the nation saw survivors of strange new illnesses. But Uncle Sam failed to connect the dots that would lead both to culpability and the payment of that ever-present check. He denied that the amazing new chemicals he ordered warfighters to use were causing the cancers and other illnesses and deaths that were increasing.

By the time of the Gulf War, it was common practice to deny service connection to illness. With the Reagan-era focus on balanced budgets, any savings was a good savings. Gulf War veterans like Tim Hauser faced decades of denial from Uncle Sam, who heaped medical bills on people who were unable to pay them. Veterans of the War on Terror, like Joseph Cancelino, Gary Hughes, and Kevin Hensley faced that same culture, and Joe and Gary paid the ultimate price for that national negligence.

Finally, though, following in the tradition of veterans from the Revolutionary War and World War One, this generation of warfighters is calling congress to account. They're reminding our elected officials that there are some expenses that are not so much a line item on a budget as a sacred obligation, and an honor.

Congressional infighting almost tanked the PACT

Act—the Promise to Address Comprehensive Toxins—just as it had the fourteen previous versions of that bill. The government wanted to prevent the possibility of spending future money on veterans not covered in the language of the original bill.

But if all those years of fighting for unpaid wages and fair healthcare had taught warfighters anything, it was that they had to prepare for the unforeseen, the unexpected. Apparently, no one thought that lighting computers, building materials, expired medications, human waste, and body parts on fire with jet fuel in a burn pit could cause cancer and respiratory disease. What a surprise to find that it did!

The implementation of the PACT Act was going to need a unique responsiveness and adaptability. As medical science discovered new connections and further illnesses, the veterans suffering from them would need to be covered. Their widows and orphans would need care. After all, had Uncle Sam not ordered that steak, no one would have to pay the check. The PACT Act was going to make sure that no veteran had to pay the bill alone for Uncle Sam's appetite.

And no future congress was going to reply to modern warfighters the way the original one did to James Madison over a Valley Forge campfire, with a shrug. This was a chance to write a new chapter in American history, one in which Uncle Sam did the right thing, paid the check—which is the cost of war—and said thanks. With the PACT Act, that's just what's happening.

*Kimberly Hughes*

As Kim Hughes, widow of Gary Hughes, said: "It's not about red and blue. It's about red, white, and blue."

## CHAPTER 1

# Chosen Family

I met Gina for the first time at a press conference. Rosie asked Gina to say a little bit, and she did. Gina is a really good public speaker. She talked about her late husband, Joe. She had her beautiful daughters with her, and I wanted to say hi to the kids.

Afterward, even though we didn't know each other or anything, we started talking a little bit. It was just, "Hey, I'm one of you," and then of course, "Are you service connected?"

She said, "No, I'm not."

And I said, "You started getting that paperwork together?"

She told me, "Yeah, I'm working on it."

We bonded over that, because it's a horrible feeling when you aren't service connected although you know you should be.

One memory that sticks out to me is seeing the Gold Star license plates on vehicles. Those license plates signal that someone has lost a loved one in the military and that their loved one driving that vehicle has also made the ultimate sacrifice. It isn't a plate that anyone wants to have. But to those of us who have sacrificed a spouse, and kids who have sacrificed a parent, that license plate is a badge of honor.

I met Kevin Hensley and his wife Theresa at a hotel meeting before attending a press conference in Washington, D.C. Rosie and Le Roy Torres were there, and we all introduced ourselves. Meeting in D.C. became routine, and so our friendships began.

Later, I met Tim Hauser at a press conference also in D.C. We were just about to start another press conference, and I asked him, "Are you ready to be a part of history?"

He nodded yes. Once the press conference was over, Tim said, "I didn't think I was going to get emotional, but I am."

I understood what he meant. "Yep, welcome to Burn Pits 360," I told him.

Later, in Tim's hometown of Ohio, he went on to have a rally and a press conference of his own. He's fought for so long and come such a long way.

In a short period of time, Gina, Kevin, Tim, and I all became close friends. We began talking regularly and bonding over our struggles. Sometimes, Tim and Kevin would drive together to D.C. while I'd fly out.

Washington, D.C. is an expensive city, and our expenses came out of our own pockets. Airfare, gas, parking, hotel, food, Ubers—it all added up! Each time we would show up, we'd ask, "Hey, you wanna just split a room?" or "Can you pick me up from the airport?" We'd stay at the Red Roof Inn, and I would never mind sleeping on the floor.

One time, Kevin drove all night from Michigan and only slept for three hours. On that same day, with oxygen in tow, he walked the floors of the Senate building advocating for what would become known as the Promise to Address Comprehensive Toxics (PACT) Act. I'd meet him at lunch and bring him something to eat. Exhausted, he'd rest a while and check in with Theresa.

We took turns buying breakfast and booking Ubers. We cut corners every chance we could. The guys would drop me off at the airport, and on their way back home, they'd share the cost of gas. Every sacrifice was worth it because we were passionate and because we believed in what we were doing. We have no regrets.

There were some people that would show up, and then you would never see them again. Cancers and other illnesses would take their toll. We would go for them or in their memory. Time and time again, we'd come back and get on what we called the "Advocacy ship." We were determined and always stayed on board all the way to pass one of the most historic bills in U.S. history.

## CHAPTER 2

# *Love at First Sight*

I lived on the southwest side of Chicago my whole life, and while I was on a mini break from college, I met Gary. It was December of 1996. I was working at a club on an off day because I had put myself on the schedule to make some extra money for Christmas. That's when Gary walked in.

It's hard to describe. But it was love at first sight. I knew. I can't even explain what that flash of intuition felt like, but I just felt I had finally found the one. And I was right.

Gary was the oldest of three boys. His parents divorced when he was seven; so, he was very protective and a strong leader. He joined the Army when he was eighteen and got his GED. He then went on to Officer Candidate School and became an officer. In the early 1990s he was deployed to the Persian Gulf, but it was all breaking up as soon as he arrived.

We were together almost exactly two years before we got married. And while we were engaged, we bought a house together. You guessed it: it was on the southwest side of Chicago right by Midway Airport.

Gary wanted a wedding, and we picked August 22, 1998, because it worked best with his military schedule. And we liked the "two twos" because they were even numbers. It was beautiful. That day, I became a military wife, and I couldn't have been more proud.

That day was also special because my dad, who had stage 4 throat cancer, walked me down the aisle. We were happy that he was well enough to do the honor. He did everything he could to keep himself well enough to be there, which made his presence very special.

Have you ever heard about new brides getting tunnel vision when they walk down the aisle? It's a real thing. I just saw Gary, and it was like nobody else was in the room. Instead of saying, "I do" after our vows, we decided to say, "I promise." It felt more solid.

At the reception, as Gary looked on, my dad and I danced together. We both knew it was his last dance. It was emotional, and I knew it meant the world to him. So, I smiled and talked him through it.

Dad died from cancer two and a half months later. He had just turned 50.

Gary and I had our son Justin, and then 2 years, 2 months, and 22 days later, our daughter Kaylee arrived. Gary was overjoyed! He loved being a daddy!

Everybody has their 9/11 story. That morning the phone rang. All I heard was, "What? What channel? Okay, I'm turning it on right now."

I thought, "That was weird." I heard the cartoons shut off and a news station go on. So, I got up, and I walked down the hall. Gary was watching the burning buildings on TV. And I said, "Oh, what the heck is that — some airplane?" The buildings had fallen, and at that moment as a military family, you think, "deployment."

Gary had to go to work that day. At that time, he was working for the Chicago Police Department (CPD). Before Gary left, I said, "You think you're going to get called up for a war?"

He said, "Yes."

And I told him, "Okay, we'll just deal with that when that time comes." We knew it was just a matter of time. Since we lived right by the airport, the silence in the neighborhood was something that I had never experienced. It was so quiet; it was eerie.

I was a substitute schoolteacher, and because the school was right across the street from the airport, people were apprehensive to send their kids back to attend classes. Everything felt like it stopped, like it was frozen.

But I'll never forget that night of 9/11. I was watching the sunset through the kitchen window. I tucked in Justin and carried our new little baby Kaylee to her crib where I laid her down.

I remember kneeling down and saying, "I wonder what kind of world this is going to be like for you. Because it's completely changed." Kaylee was just a little baby. And I'll never forget that moment.

The kids were six and eight in 2007 when Gary, who was a 1st Lieutenant with the 327th Battalion, told me, "I have to go to Iraq and teach them how to police."

We had time before he had to go, and so I made plans for us all to go to Washington D.C. I wanted to show the kids the monuments and explain to them why Daddy had to go away for a while. We wanted to educate them by showing them how important our country is. We hoped they would understand that Daddy was leaving to protect the freedoms we have.

While he was gone, I kept the kids busy, and we leaned on each other for comfort. At that time, we were the only family in the neighborhood that had someone deployed. We didn't live on base; so, we would go visit the nearest base around, which was Great Lakes Naval Base. People there understood us and our lifestyle. There was a beach, a USO, a movie theater, and a commissary; we would spend a day there feeling connected to Gary. There were always people there that we could talk to and who could help us cope if we needed.

When I would work, the kids got to go to my grandma's house who they called Busha. And we also were fortunate to have great friends and neighbors to help out and do activities with. We'd go to Great America, roller skating, White Sox games, or the zoo, stuff like that.

The kids and I would make "Daddy boxes." We'd fill them with coloring pages, schoolwork, and crafts. When they were full to the top, we'd close them, kiss them, and take them to the post office. There wasn't a whole lot of technology back then. We had phone calls, but not often. And I always had a phone with me; I'd sleep with the cordless phone next to me just in case it would ring.

When Gary would call, I would ask him if he could see the sun or the moon. I would tell him we can send them back and forth to each other every day and every night. Justin would talk to Daddy, too. But Kaylee didn't. She just chose to shut that part of herself off. She wasn't mad. She wasn't upset. That's just how she dealt with Gary's absence. I would say, "Kaylee, come and talk to Daddy. Daddy wants to talk to you." And she would run away down the hall. I never pushed her. I just wanted him to be able to hear her little voice.

Sometimes when I'd hear the Blackhawk helicopters getting louder in the distance, I would hurry up, saying "Okay, well, we love you, we miss you, and we'll talk to you soon." I would feel so close to him. The Blackhawks would blow out the signals, and the phone would just go completely silent and still. I hated when that happened. The distance, again, was a reality.

Gary was a Military Police Officer, and one of his jobs there was being the Provost Marshal; it's like the superintendent of a police department. He would interview witnesses after situations, like when an improvised explosive device (IED) from a suicide bomber would explode. He'd have to investigate and ask the witnesses questions like, "What did you see? Who was there?" It was like detective work. So, it was a whole lot of responsibility. And not everybody could do a job like that. It was like Gary was picked especially for his ability to handle aftermath work like that.

Gary was around burn pits during this deployment 24/7. He moved around a bit, but burn pits were always nearby. He was in Ramadi, Taji, and Baghdad, all burn pit toxic exposure locations. He even took pictures of how close they were to the camp and complained to me about how hard it was to breathe there. This went on for a full year.

In that year, he got to come home for two weeks. But there was something very profoundly different about him. He didn't want me to tell anyone he was visiting. He didn't want to attend any gathering. He didn't want to go anywhere. He just wanted me to keep everything normal, like it was when he left; so, I did.

He was really quiet, more quiet than usual. I don't know if depressed is the proper word, or if it's just no emotion. He wanted to be home and still. We knew he had to go back, and we supported him. He liked to be outside by himself a lot and just sit in the sun. It was hot, 80-something degrees outside. And he said he was cold.

I'd go talk to him, but he would just say "Get away from me."

I called him an alligator because the alligator likes to sun himself and be alone. So, I told the kids, "We're going to let Daddy just be an alligator. He's alligating." I always found a way to twist things and make things a little bit lighter.

I once asked, "Do you think you have PTSD?"

He lashed out at me, saying, "Don't ever mention that again! I have to work and take care of us! What don't you understand?"

He went back and finished his tour.

Everyone else was coming home, but he wasn't. He told me he had to wait a while. "Don't worry about anything; I'll get home when I get home."

It was 2008, and right at the airport, Kaylee was Daddy's girl again. She jumped in his arms, and there she was happy. Justin was happy to have his hero, his dad, home. Gary told me shortly thereafter that he had tuberculosis; so, the holdup was that he was on meds. Why didn't they check for cancer or for any toxic exposures?

After that deployment, Gary stayed with his job at the Chicago Police Department. I stayed with my job. I was working for Homeland Security at Midway Airport at the time. There, I was actively involved with the Safety Team. That led me to be a member of the National Advisory Committee IV, which generally consisted of members from all 50 states and then some. We would meet at the headquarters in Washington D.C. and work a few times a year. So, when I started advocating for Burn Pits 360, I already knew the lay of the land over there. And I already had friends all over the United States.

I asked Gary why he left the television on all the time. He grumpily told me that he suffered from tinnitus and hearing loss from all the bombs and explosions in Iraq. He said that the constant background noise made it more bearable.

Gary had worked for the Chicago Police Department

for fourteen years when he got called up again. He finished his bachelor's degree and was promoted to Captain. In August of 2013, he was asked to go to Afghanistan with the 416th. He had 30 days to get ready and leave. He was asked to work with the North Atlantic Treaty Organization (NATO) team, alongside military allies like the Italians, the Germans, and the French. He had five guys who followed him around wherever he went, and no matter where he went, the burn pits were there.

Skype was available, and so we actually got to see him quite regularly, at least once a week. He would be able to Skype while he was in his tiny little room where he had a little laptop. He was able to communicate with us pretty well. Then the iPads came out, and we got those. Now, the kids and I were able to carry him around and show him things. You know, stuff like, "Look at the snow we got outside! Look, I've been keeping my room clean!" Things like that.

He was always by those damn burn pits. He would talk about the soot that fell down from the sky, the ash. He was telling me how they would fire them up late at night, burning a whole lot of stuff with jet fuel.

It was disturbing to me when he told me that because now we know the truth. Burning them late at night, they couldn't see how much of the toxic cloud they were breathing in while they slept. Now, we know that so many soldiers, even from other countries, were also being poisoned as they slept. It makes me sick to know they were inhaling those toxins all day and every night—that's hard.

As we would have our Skype chats. Gary started clearing his throat from time to time. He was always asking about the kids, and I would tell him all sorts of good things to make his stay out there bearable. Once, I asked him about why he was clearing his throat because he did it a lot. That's when he would talk about the different ways that the wind would blow and how it was bothering him. He would say things like, "Well, it's not any different than any other day. I can't just take a break from breathing out here."

Later on, when we'd talk more in detail about all the equipment that he was responsible for, a lot of that equipment—like the machinery and vehicles—was burned.

Gary told me, "Anything that the enemy could possibly get was burned. If they could get something that they shouldn't get their hands on, it was gone. You know what I mean?" He wouldn't risk letting the enemy get anything, especially if it could compromise the mission.

Nearing the end of this deployment, Gary was standing on a platform when a loud explosion occurred. It was so powerful that it threw him off the platform, and he fell down quite a distance. He had torn the meniscus in his knee. However, he said he was fine, that nothing was wrong. He didn't want to abandon his battalion and knew that he was going to be home soon. That occurrence was filed, but Gary didn't like to talk about it.

And then his battalion came stateside. I know that the military would check these soldiers out post deployment, but why didn't they check for toxin exposure? Respiratory disease? Cancer?

CHAPTER 3

# In Sickness and in Health

This deployment was a little shorter, about 10 months. Gary came home on my birthday, Valentine's Day. It was late, about 11 p.m., and it was snowing like crazy. I had the house clean and a hot meal on the stove, and the kids and I just hugged him together.

Soon after his return home from Afghanistan, he casually told me that he fell and that he needed knee surgery. So, I set up an evaluation and the surgery for him, which was another missed opportunity to discover his cancer.

Once recovered, he wanted to buy a hair salon. Now, I don't do hair. And I mean, he was a cop. He didn't do hair. But it was something he always talked about. He invested our savings and investments and put up our home as collateral for it. He was very excited about having his own business.

Gary called it our retirement plan, and I supported his dream. And it wasn't just for us. Opening that business meant that we would have something to hand down to our children.

38

Again, he started showing signs of PTSD: constantly
locking things and then checking and rechecking that
they were locked. He'd get upset if I would walk down
the hall at the same time he wanted to. He'd get furious if I didn't know the exact location of my keys at all
times. He was detached from emotions and very hy-
pervigilant. He'd constantly be looking out windows,
closing curtains and blinds, and not wanting to go out
at all. He struggled to have a normal sleeping pattern.

About two months later, he went to his Annual Military Physical Fitness Training test. He worked out regularly and always did very well. However, this time he
was very discouraged about his running time. That's
when he told me that he was losing weight. Didn't the
Army notice that his running time was not consis-
tent? Why didn't they encourage testing then?

We all thought his throat clearing was just temporary. We thought it would clear up. Why wouldn't it?
If we asked him about it, he would get angry. Living
in a home with someone that has untreated PTSD is
like a progressive disease. Sadly, the kids and I were
infected from living with this secondary trauma. We
noticed that we were mimicking his behavior. We
were closing blinds. We became more antisocial, and
we were all getting worse.

I didn't know Gary went to the doctor, but suddenly
he had an inhaler next to him on the living room end
table. He told me the doctor told him he had asthma.
And I asked him, "When did you get that?"

He told me, "Oh, the doctor says I got that and acid

reflux, too. I'll be fine; don't worry about it."

That's definitely military guys; they're so tough. They don't want anybody to worry about them. They don't want anybody knowing they're going to the doctor, and they're always fine.

Kaylee and I were supposed to go to Nashville on some cheap airfare tickets. Kaylee had a lot of school-work and decided not to go. That's when Gary piped up, saying, "I'll go with you". I was shocked because he never wanted to go anywhere. I was excited and surprised that he wanted to go.

We went to Music City, and it was amazing. It was during the week; so, there weren't big crowds. We got to see the Broadway lights, the Country Music Hall of Fame, and the Johnny Cash Museum. The last night we were there, we went out to a nice dinner. I noticed that Gary hardly ate anything. He told me that his stomach hurt.

Two weeks later, we found out how serious his health problems were from a phone call. The phone rang one evening around seven or eight o'clock. All I heard was Gary saying, "What? What's a hemoglobin? I gotta do what? Right now? Okay, okay. Okay. Yeah, I'll tell my wife, Kim." Then he hung up the phone.

In a full panic, he said, "Kim, you got to take me to the emergency room. That was the doctor. You gotta take me." He was just frantic. He said, "Something's wrong with me. I don't know what's wrong with me. But he said there's something wrong with my blood, and I need to go to the emergency room right now."

And I said, "Okay. Justin, take care of your sister." And we jumped in the car and went to the ER. We were talking on the way there, about what, I don't know. I just wanted to talk to him and keep him calm. We didn't know what was going on.

The staff at the hospital were already waiting for Gary, and they started a blood transfusion. They said his blood count was so low that he was lucky he didn't have a heart attack or a stroke already.

At this point, we were scared and worried. But I am a positive person. I thought, "This is just a blood transfusion. Everything's going to be fine. This guy's a tough guy. He's only 48 years old. And we'll figure this out. This will be fine."

As the third bag of blood was dripping, I remember looking up at it and wondering who was so kind as to donate their blood? Who took the time to do that? In my mind I was praying for Gary and thanking the kind stranger. I started talking to the doctors.

They said, "We're going to put a scope down his throat to find out what's going on." They were going inside to take pictures.

I said, "Well, he's been clearing his throat and coughing, but his doctor said it was acid reflux and asthma."

The next day, October 5, 2016, they put the scope down his throat, and I was in the little waiting room. After the procedure, the doctor came in and said, "We're done with the procedure, and he's in the recovery room. He's doing just fine." I was relieved. "But we got some pictures," the doctor said, "and we're not quite sure. But it's possible it could be cancer."

I was confused and shocked. So, he showed me these pictures, and they were bad. I saw black. This was something that didn't belong in somebody's body. I believe that the doctor was preparing me for the worst by sharing the pictures with me the way that he did.

I looked longer at the picture, and after what he had just said, I put two and two together. I knew. But at this point, I thought, "Okay, we can deal with this. It's just a little bit. Let's see what we can do to fix this." I was positive again. Gary never smoked. Cancer wasn't a factor in his family. He worked out regularly.

I thought about how my dad was Gary's age and a big smoker. His cancer was understandable. This just didn't make sense. This news with Gary was out of the blue. It didn't seem like it was even happening. The thought of where it originated never occurred to me.

When the doctor came in while Gary was recovering from the scope procedure, he told both of us, "It looks like you've got some cancer. Now we're going to have to take more tests to figure out how much and what we're dealing with."

Gary was very emotional. He was very scared. I was concerned. I was thinking, "This doesn't make sense." Then I thought, "Let's go ahead and do chemo. Let's do radiation."

The doctors came back to us after they did more tests in the hospital, and they told us that it was stomach and liver cancer. It had already spread, and it was already stage 4.

And this was only 16 months after Gary came home from Afghanistan. So, he got it out there, without a doubt. He was perfectly healthy when he left, or they wouldn't have taken him. But nobody was really talking a whole lot about toxic air, carcinogens, or burn pits at that time.

We eventually got Gary home and set up chemotherapy treatments right away. And of course, I was on the computer, learning about what kind of beast we were dealing with, how we could mitigate it, and how we could handle it. So, I put into the computer "military cancer." And Burn Pits 360 came up.

Yep, I remembered Gary would talk about burn pits when we were on Skype calls, but it wasn't till I started researching burn pits, the locations of them, their size, and what was really going on that it all made sense. And all roads led to Rosie Torres and her husband Le Roy, the founders of Burn Pits 360.

I looked over at Gary sitting on the couch and said, "Gary, were those burn pits around you all the time?"

He said, "Yeah, ALL the time." That was exactly what he said. Then he asked, "Why?"

I said, "I think I figured this out."

I messaged Rosie on Facebook Messenger, right then and there, and we went back and forth a little bit. I was just intrigued by everything. Everything was making sense. All his symptoms were aligning with the symptoms of other soldiers that I found on the internet who were in the areas he had been. Even the times and who was getting sick matched.

Gary started chemotherapy the very next week, and doctors started giving him all kinds of medications. The doctor suggested that Gary get a port implant to make it easier for injections. He did. We met with his oncologist, and Gary and I both asked her to look into toxic air overseas. She said, "I've never even heard of burn pits."

Gary was happy that he wasn't getting too sick from the chemo. He wasn't losing his hair— it was thinning, yes—but he was happy he had it. Gary always took pride in his appearance, in looking clean and having his hair neat. It was a military thing.

Because Gary was a police officer, he had good insurance. But that didn't mean we weren't getting bills left and right. Some of Gary's medications were not covered by insurance; we had to pay for them. The kids had tuition and needed things. We had home costs, and there were co-pays, and so much more. Gary wanted to try different diets because we heard about certain foods and liquids that were helpful. He was interested in holistic approaches and supplements, too. Those weren't cheap, either. Not to mention all the bills coming from the salon: that was killing us.

Gary wasn't able to work his job or his overtime shifts that we relied upon. I kept researching the burn pits and discovering more about them and sharing this info with Gary. He tried to help and filed a claim with Veteran Affairs (VA), asking them to recognize his cancer from the toxic air because of the burn pits. Because I was driving a school bus, being a mom, helping Gary run the salon, and taking care of him, I was very busy every single day.

In 2016, we filed that VA paperwork for burn pit exposure.

Christmas came and went. Gary loved Christmas. It was his favorite holiday; he secretly told me he hoped that it wasn't his last. And then it was a new year, 2017. Gary had chemo every other week, doctor appointments, and medications, but we were excited because he started gaining a little bit of weight. Even one pound, two pounds, or three pounds meant so much.

Just into the new year, we were still adjusting. One day Gary wasn't looking very well at all. He started walking down the hallway, and he was just really wobbly. I scooped next to him to assist him, and he passed out. I pushed his body up against the hallway wall, and we slid down.

Luckily, Justin was home and called 911.

Gary was just lying there on me in the hallway. We thought that it was possible that he had passed away right there. Then his eyes quickly opened.

He said, "What happened?"

I told him, "You passed out. The ambulance is on the way."

He told me, "I don't need an ambulance."

But the ambulance was already on the way. So, we got him up and sat him down on the couch. The EMTs came and checked his vitals, offering to take him in. He didn't want to go, but the paramedics encouraged him. At the hospital, it was discovered that he had internal stomach bleeding; so, they did an Interventional Radiology procedure to stop the bleeding. They gave him more blood transfusions, and he got to come home.

But Gary said, "I'm going to get better. Everything's going to be fine." At the oncology appointments, he would say, "I just want to get this cancer out of me." We would always mention that he served overseas and talk about burn pits, but the doctor never wrote any of that down.

I was still constantly following Burn Pits 360. It was like I couldn't get enough information. I started reaching out to make connections with others on the internet. It was so hard because I felt like I was screaming for someone to do something. Help him! Fix him!

One day, Gary said to me, "Remember when Kaylee couldn't go to Nashville with you and I told you I'd go?"

I said, "Yes."

He replied, "I thought something might have been really wrong with me; so, I wanted to go just in case this was really bad." The memories we made there became that much more precious.

We had to consider filing for bankruptcy, but Gary didn't want to. He wanted to get better, and he wanted our business to be successful. Besides, our home was on the line, and he knew it. It was so embarrassing. We didn't want to tell anyone that we were having problems with money. But this was when our neighborhood friends said, "Hey, let's have a fundraiser."

Now, Gary didn't like a whole lot of attention, but he knew that they wanted to do this for him and that it would help our kids keep attending their private school. And he did like the idea of the community coming together.

The neighbors graciously started collecting items to make baskets to raffle off. They hung up fliers all over. This was a small neighborhood of mom-and-pop shops like little pizza places and sandwich shops which were generously donating gift cards and other items. The neighbors sold tickets and crafted the baskets. There were autographs from athletes for a silent auction and stuff like that.

Driving the school bus was a great job to have because I worked in the morning, took care of Gary, and then drove the afternoon route. In March, I remember work calling me on my radio. I said, "Yeah, go for Kimberly." They told me to call my daughter. And I thought, "That's not good." She'd only call me if she had to. She knew not to call me at work because she knew I was driving and wouldn't pick up.

When I was done driving the kids, I called her and said, "What's the matter? Is there something wrong?" She said, "Yes, it's Daddy. Something's not right. He's not making sense."

I said, "All right. I'll be there as soon as I can." When I walked in the house, I saw Gary just struggling to stand. He wasn't making any sense at all. Kaylee had to call the ambulance.

Kaylee was only fifteen years old. She was so scared

and worried. She wanted to know if she did the right thing by calling. I told her she did. "You did good. Things like this happen, but honestly, you really, really did good."

Gary was repeating words and struggling to function. I told him that he had to get checked out and that help was on the way. He made it clear that he didn't want help and was angry.

Gary's odd behavior that day was one of the clues that told the doctors that the cancer was in his brain. And he had his first brain surgery. He was in the ICU for eight days because they didn't have any other beds available on the other floors. I checked every day.

"This cancer is from burn pits overseas," I was telling doctors and nurses. "It's toxic air exposure." Gary and I both would tell people, but no one ever even listened, looked into it, or wrote it down.

In the ICU, there was a little window, but it was blocked so that it didn't let in a lot of light. It was like a cave. Also, there were really sick people nearby. A lady died right next door, and a chaplain was giving last rites in another room. Gary was disturbed because he could hear all this going on. I was asking to get him outta there and stayed with him to calm him at night while I slept on chairs.

The kids would come and visit for a while, but Gary didn't like them staying long. He didn't like them seeing him sick. He was worried and stressed about everything. And his recovery was slow.

I became aggravated. The whole situation was nerve

wracking. A social worker came in for a visit and talked to Gary. She asked him about PTSD, did a few mind exercises, and asked a few questions. She wrote some things down. I just wanted to go home and take Gary out of there.

The fundraiser was in April, and I didn't know if Gary was going to be well enough to attend. But he made it. And the outpouring of love that you could feel in that room was overwhelming.

The whole time, we had this secret, that we were losing everything. And we didn't want to tell anybody. It was a great thing that the neighbors did. It was beautiful how they came together for him. There were people who came that Gary hadn't seen in a while. Entertainment was provided by my brother who played the guitar while his friend played the violin.

Kaylee's friends were there, and Justin's Rugby team came to show support. Gary saw people who loved him and cared about him. He jokingly said, "I didn't know anyone would show up." And that amazing day I truly feel helped him heal. For a guy that didn't show much emotion, he talked about how special that day was for him. It gave him encouragement when he was feeling bad. People were praying for him, and he was on an upswing.

Just after the fundraiser, Gary was on the couch opening his mail. I was on the computer. Out of the blue he said, "Fight this. You gotta fight this." It seemed that he was holding back tears. I went to him, looked at the paper in his hand, and saw that the VA denied his cancer. Service Connection Denied. Looking at that great man's eyes and hearing his voice crack was heartbreaking. He realized right then and there that bankruptcy was our only option.

*2017 VA Paperwork Denied*

I'll never forget when he said that. "Fight this." It was as if time stood still. "Fight this." I promised him that I would.

Now that he had some time to heal from the brain surgery, Gary had some radiation and went back on medications but with a much more aggressive chemotherapy. The nurse said that it was the strongest one. Gary always said he was fine. So, if there was any pain or discomfort, he didn't tell me about it. He was a tough guy.

But he was on a lot of medications. You name it, and he was on it. There were liquids, powders, big pills, little pills, everything. Both Justin and Kaylee were dealing with Gary's illness in their own ways. I worried about them all the time. We had great people around us who would check in on them and make sure they were okay. I'd call them, talk to them, and spend time with them when I could. We were all struggling, trying to function in whatever way that meant for us at the time. Everything was touch and go. Each day was different, and you didn't know what to expect. We just did the best we could.

Still, the stress was always building. I was handling everything Gary did when he was well, all the things I was originally doing, all the medical stuff, working, trying to take care of the kids, dealing with the salon, managing all the bills, making sure there was food to eat, and keeping the house clean. It was way too much. Even though we all pitched in, it was hard.

One day, I got a call that the electricity had been cut off at the salon. And of course, that affected the wi-fi and the phones, too. I had to hurry and figure out a way to get the electricity back on.

He poured everything into that salon. Gary's American dream of having his own business was slipping away, crumbling along with everything he'd worked for and put his life on the line for. Our stake in that business represented over twenty-five years of his life along with his time away from us during deployments. We could never get that back. Our investments, life savings, and home were on the line. And so was his life.

And I was wondering what kind of future we were going to have. The kids were wondering if and/or where they were going to college. We were living moment by moment. I prayed all the time.

Justin was going to graduate high school in May. I remember him asking me if Dad was going to attend his graduation. Even though Gary was doing a bit better, I didn't really know how to answer him because I didn't know the answer. I was always honest with him and Kaylee; so, I just told them both, "I don't know."

Gary was well enough to attend the graduation. And it was really, really special to him. Everyone at the school knew what was happening, and they were so kind with the way they greeted him and encouraged him.

Kaylee was now sweet sixteen, and over the summer, Gary continued to be well. It was nothing short of a miracle that he was doing so well. He felt well enough in August to go on light duty at the Police Department. He helped out in the office. I knew he felt good, putting on his uniform and going to work. I liked that it got his mind off the cancer, even if for a while, and that he was around people. His tumors were actually shrinking! The treatments were doing a really good job. The doctors were amazed. We were all so excited. We were happy, and Gary was very hopeful.

He was going to recover and get the cancer out of him. There were a lot of prayers. He believed in prayer. And he found a church that he was comfortable attending. He enjoyed being there and found peace in praying and reading the Bible.

Gary wanted to participate in a MATCH study program where they took a biopsy and sent it to a lab in Texas to analyze it and find out what kind of cancer it was. If the program would help him or anyone else, he was willing to do it. He was hoping to be a match. The results came back as "unusual."

I kept in touch with Rosie. I was always looking for updated information for people in my situation. I wanted to know how she and Le Roy were doing along with how others were managing their situations. Rosie made sure that I told Gary about the Burn Pit Registry. I told him about it, and he submitted his name to it.

Justin was working full time, and in the fall, he went to community college. We felt bad because he couldn't go away to college as planned. We had looked at colleges before Gary was sick. Strong like his dad, Justin understood. We all just wanted to be together, and time was precious.

When we had to make the decision to close the salon, it was sad because the salon was in its infancy. It had only been open for a year. As the end of the year was approaching, the salon was barely in operation. We tried to sell it but were unsuccessful. Gary finally accepted that he had to let it go.

Gary took pride in how hard he worked and his accomplishments. After we closed the salon, Gary had to stop his short stint at work. He rapidly grew depressed, and the bills were coming in from all directions. They were just constant reminders of things he couldn't control anymore. I actually hated when he would check the mail because it would trigger him. He felt like a failure. When he would start a downward spiral, I would pick him back up and remind him of good things.

As autumn was now upon us, we as a family didn't do as much anymore. We were all getting detached from things like any home activities or entertainment. It just didn't exist for us. We were falling apart. We were different people.

Although Gary was very apprehensive, we signed the bankruptcy papers.

He was also very nervous because he was losing weight again. So, from that point on, I learned how to be a caregiver. I learned how to take his vitals, and I wrote everything down to keep track in case we needed to call the ambulance again. If we ever had to call again, I could give the EMTs one piece of paper with a list of all medications and a recorded history of everything.

He had a potential blood clot; so, I had to give him injections on his stomach. I'd alternate each day from one side to the other side. He said it felt like a bee sting. The chemotherapy sessions continued, and from time to time the blood transfusions did also.

I was finding that the cancers from soldiers around the burn pits were rare. I would check in with Rosie, but I felt bad that I wasn't able to help her out very much. There was a documentary in the works about burn pits: Delay, Deny, Hope You Die. Rosie and I shared some info that they used in that documentary. Gary said, "If the info will help someone else, then use it." Rosie continued to tell me to collect paperwork. She was always gearing me up for a battle. She knew that eventually I was going to get a hearing and that I would need all the information I could get.

Because Gary had developed neuropathy, the oncologist decided to take him off chemotherapy. It was taking a toll on his body. She wanted him to take chemo pills instead. Still, we were given no information or research about toxic exposure.

On Gary's birthday at the end of November, we all

went to his favorite pizza place, Vince's. And he was in good spirits. I remember thinking how incredibly amazing he was and what a good dad he was. Gary told me on his birthday, "I never wanted to turn 50, but I sure am glad that I have."

About a week later, I made him a sandwich and served it to him as I normally had. But that day he snapped, "No more white plates! Get them away from me!" He started pacing the floor very upset. You never knew when his PTSD would flare up.

It took him a while to calm down from that one. I knew he was referring to the military "Missing Man" table setting which symbolizes and honors those who died in combat. Seeing him out of control was difficult, to say the least.

Sometimes Gary would say things like, "I don't want to die," and then he would say, "I wish all this would just go away." So, I locked up the guns and hid the key. It felt like I paralyzed him when I did that.

A couple of days before Christmas, he and I went to Cafe 63, our favorite neighborhood cafe. The people that own it were just wonderful to us and always happy to see Gary. I was happy he felt well enough to go and wanted to eat, even if just a little.

And I remember Gary telling me there, "I think it's back."

I said, "What do you mean?"

And he said, "I can't remember which one the fork is."

So, I told him, "Okay, well, we'll talk to the doctor

about that."

He said "No," really firmly.

And I said, "You know if you wait, it's just going to get worse."

"I'll wait until after Christmas. I want to be home for Christmas," he said sharply and unshakably.

In that tone, I knew that it was his choice, his holiday, and it was non-negotiable. If he didn't want to go to a doctor, no one could force him. He had made up his mind and wanted to be home.

So, Christmas morning, the kids started opening their presents. Gary was not well. He had a hard time walking. And when he sat down, we noticed that he had a hard time lifting his right arm. He was holding it close and kind of babying it.

I said in his ear, "After the kids are done opening their presents, I'm going to take you to the hospital."

He said, "I'm fine. I'm fine." But he wasn't. He looked really, really drawn. He wasn't even making eye contact.

I said, "No, I don't think you are."

The kids and I decided to call 911.

"No, I'm fine," he told ambulance paramedics. I gave them the paper I kept, so they knew what meds he had and when he had them. They already knew our name and address. "I'm okay," he told them over and over again. But he was showing signs like slurred speech and being unable to stand up. The paramedics took him.

I packed a bag, and I asked the kids if they wanted to

go. I said, "I know it's Christmas. What do you guys want to do?" I never forced them to do anything they didn't want to. And Gary didn't ever like the kids to see him in a vulnerable state.

So, they decided to stay.

I got to the emergency room, and there wasn't very much staff. I could see that Gary was about to have a seizure. So, I started yelling for nurses and doctors to come. They came in just as he started to have a seizure.

I stepped out. The hospital had a counselor there, and he approached me. He had one of those funny Christmas sweaters on. And in the strangest way, it made me laugh a little bit, in a funny, sad, crazy, weird way. How could I laugh? And then I felt guilty. The reality of where I was and what was happening was again so stressful and overwhelming that I just couldn't compartmentalize. I felt like I couldn't move. I just didn't know how to react.

The counselor talked to me, and it was good to tell someone the truth. I told him, "It's Christmas. He's dying, and we're losing everything. And I just don't know what to do anymore. I'm done." I remember apologizing to him and saying, "I wish you were at home with your family instead of being with me. It's Christmas, and that's where you should be."

The next day, we were told the cancer was back on the other side of his brain. Gary agreed to have another brain surgery, which would also include more blood transfusions.

My one thought was, "I've got to get Gary home; how

can I get him home? I want to take him home." He was in recovery and was complaining about the walls closing in and feeling claustrophobic. I was trying to get him a bigger room to be moved to and the nurse said she was trying to find one. I tried to calm Gary down, but he was very emotional.

He was in the hospital for almost a week. During that time, I had to leave the hospital and go downtown to meet with our bankruptcy lawyer to see the trustee. It was snowing out, blizzard conditions. And it was terribly cold.

I kept wondering, "Why the heck is this building even open?"

When I got there, it was obvious that I was in a shambles. Our lawyer and I went into the office, and I asked the trustee in tears, "Can't we just finalize this bankruptcy right now?" It had been about three months.

They told us no. Our lawyer and I knew they were waiting for Gary to die so that I would open up funds from his pension and life insurance. Then the trustee would take all that away from us. They were also interested in our home. That's why they wouldn't settle right then and there.

Some of our investments and obviously the business had already gone. And I knew our house was on the line. Feeling crushed by my lack of mental energy to argue with the trustee broke me down. My lawyer argued for me, but even he knew the trustee wasn't going to budge. I was worried about Gary.

I was determined to get Gary outta there. He had

some tests done, a brain screening, and then I got to bring him home just in time for the new year.

He had memory issues and processing issues. And he would complain about this crunching sound in his head; it bothered him. I think it was just his skull trying to heal. They cut a hole in his head not once but twice: one on each side.

But I was so happy to have him home because sometimes I was afraid that I wasn't going to be able to get him home. He didn't want to pass away in the hospital, and I was going to do everything in my power to make sure that didn't happen.

The kids were still doing their best to be strong, and I knew it. But I was worried because I had focused so much time and energy on Gary, work, and everything else that I felt like I was neglecting them. They would reassure me that they understood.

After the second brain surgery and after Christmas break, I went back to work. I had to. That's when I got a phone call from the doctor looking for Gary. They said they needed to talk to him. I told them that I'd give him the message, and he'd call. I thought, "This is weird."

So, I called Gary to call his doctor. Soon after, I got a text message back from him saying, "It's not good."

I called him. I asked, "What's the matter?"

He told me, "It's just not good. It's not good. It's bad."

I said, "Where are you?"

He said, "I'm just sitting at a gas station."

I said, "Okay, I'm leaving work right now. I'll meet

you at home." And I hung up.

Then I walked down the hall and told my boss, "It's back." I was trembling. "I can't work right now." And it broke my heart to say that because I really loved my job. My boss lady told me to take as much time as I needed.

When I got home, Gary was just sitting in his car. So, I got out of my vehicle and sat down next to him in his car. We didn't say anything. We were just there, silent, together. I held his hand. That's when he told me that the cancer was back. It was in his brain, in seven different places. That was the last time he ever drove.

Two weeks later Gary asked Justin to drive him to Jos. A. Bank. There, Gary bought Justin a black suit. He helped his son pick out a suit because he knew that his son was going to need something nice to wear for his funeral. I don't know where he got the strength to do that. But he did.

Two weeks after that Kaylee drove him to her high school, junior year, father daughter dance. Gary was really sick, but he wasn't going to miss that dance for anything. He got dressed as best he could. Gary danced with her because he knew that he wasn't going to dance with her on her wedding day. I recalled how similar that was when my dad danced with me on my wedding day.

Gary never went back to the hospital. He was at home, getting home care. Then nursing staff started doing little homecare visits. He was doing okay one day and then he wasn't. Then he was just declining,

declining, declining. The nurses told me, "You're going to have to consider hospice." So, the kids stopped going to school to spend what time was left with him. We knew that hospice was inevitable. The cancer was taking its toll, and it was quickly getting worse. And so, the nurses would come to visit every day regularly.

Actually now, Gary didn't mind all the people over. So, I opened the doors for people to come to visit. I felt that people had a right to come see him if they wanted.

It was my Valentine's birthday. This time when the nurse came, she placed papers on the table. We knew what they were for before she explained them. The room was still as I stared at them. We all knew what I needed to do as whimpers, tears, and sadness filled the room. It was all up to me. So, with Justin, Kaylee, and everyone surrounding me, I said, "I know I'm doing the right thing, because there's not one person in this room telling me not to." I signed the papers.

After I signed those papers, I felt like I was playing God, deciding Gary's life for him. It was awful. I felt so guilty, even though I knew I had to let him go.

I turned 45 years old that day.

The Army contacted us and asked the kids and I if the Chaplain from Gary's Unit (along with SFC Luke Matheisen) could visit. We knew Gary knew them and so we welcomed them. They both provided comfort for Gary and ultimately us, too.

We just wanted Gary to be comfortable. And I told the kids, "Talk to him. Anything that you might want to know in your life, talk to him now, and remember what he says."

Months prior, the Army had approved the paperwork for Gary to be promoted. The General himself personally came over, and we had a ceremony right there in the living room. I pinned Gary's rank of Major on him. Again, he was emotional.

He wanted to stand up. He kept saying, "I wanna get up, I wanna get up, I wanna get up." So, Justin and I assisted him on each side and helped him. And when he rose up, he locked his knees, stuck out his chest, and pushed back his shoulders, while his hands made fists at his sides. We didn't know it at the time, but we later realized that he just wanted to stand at attention and salute, one last time. It took the last of his strength. Pure courage.

It was the last time he stood.

It was a cold February morning the day he died. The sun was rising as I opened the curtains. I blessed him and prayed beside him.

We asked Luke to come to the house. He arrived in full uniform and made sure everything was handled with dignity and respect. Gary had actually gotten his own uniform ready because he wanted it to look good. Polished and shined. He hung it where I could find it easily. To this day, I can't even imagine what that must have been like for him to do. When Gary left our home for the last time, Luke was his escort and went with him so that he didn't leave alone.

If it had been mandatory when Gary came home

from the war to be tested and get screened for toxin exposure, the doctors would have caught this cancer in time. Gary would still be alive. Why wasn't he tested? Our men and women deserve the best care possible. I always say that Gary never lost his battle because we kept fighting for him.

Those goddamned burn pits! And he was young! He had just turned fifty, the same age as my dad when he died. The military stepped up to honor his funeral. They honored him in the way we knew he would have wanted, with lots of respect.

Gary served the Chicago Police Department for nineteen years. He had many accolades, including a Life Saving Award and over 100 Honorable Mentions. CPD did a prayer at his wake and provided a squad car for his funeral. Then they were done.

CHAPTER 4

## CHAPTER 4

# *Keeping the Promise*

The first fight I had on my hands was with the CPD about insurance. At Gary's wake, they gave me a small check and offered to let us purchase health insurance, which would have taken up the amount of the whole check they had just given us and then some. How could I maintain that with a school bus driver's income? I couldn't touch any benefits or insurance because of the ongoing bankruptcy. CPD told us we had two months of medical care before we'd lose insurance, even though Kaylee was underage. So, while mourning the loss of their father, Justin and Kaylee had to get any medical and dental attention they needed quickly, and they did.

The forced living arrangement within Chicago's city limits, which I always thought was profoundly unconstitutional, was now null and void for me and the kids. Americans should have a right to live freely where they want, but not if you work for the CPD. If you marry an officer or have children with one, then all are forced to live there. That freedom is taken away.

I was ashamed of the way the CPD treated us after

Gary died. We were always told that the Chicago police were a family. They look out for each other, and they won't let you down. As a family, we sacrificed a lot for the city. It was hurtful for my kids to experience the disrespect when Gary died. The CPD turned their backs on us. The kids had always looked up with pride to their father for being in law enforcement, and now they were shattered. The Chicago police have a lot of room for improvement, to say the least. After the funeral, we never heard from them again.

In 2018, we filed VA paperwork for burn pit exposure.

Another fight on my hands was the bankruptcy. We had to wait for a closing date; until then, we were on our own. If any finances were touched, the Trustees could take everything away. They were forcing the kids and me into poverty. And the Trustees knew it. It was a horrible, horrible waiting game.

Kids were out of school; so, there was no more school bus driving. I told the kids to be extremely careful with everything they did because we had no insurance. I got a job with a caretaking service to make ends meet, and it wasn't working. Because we weren't service connected, we didn't get burial benefits. So, I couldn't pay for Gary's funeral. We qualified for state aid but had to wait for that to be approved; eventually that helped. It was embarrassing.

All this time, we were living on the funds from the fundraiser. Thank God for the great people in the neighborhood. We will forever be grateful for them.

They had no idea how much they helped.

I discovered the Tragedy Assistance Program for Survivors (TAPS). It's a great organization that offers seminars and assists with grief. I went to my first seminar just a few months after Gary passed away, and I met a whole bunch of people like me. When I mentioned burn pits, I found other people who were struggling, too. I had learned a lot. There were about 150 of us at the seminar, each dealing with different types of loss.

Some survivors had heard of burn pits; some also had spouses that had died from toxic exposure. And some told me, "I'm service connected." I asked them how they got service connected, and they said, "Oh, you need to be like a doctor and a lawyer."

I said, "Do you know Rosie Torres from Burn Pits 360? I've been talking to her." All of a sudden, we spouses started to become empowered. We were connecting with each other and becoming friends. So, the more I met people, the more information we were sharing. We were learning about the burn pits and reaching out to others. This was where my big personality was coming in handy.

Later in 2018, our VA paperwork for burn pit exposure was denied. We appealed.

The ongoing stress of the bankruptcy mounted. The average bankruptcy lasts four months, and this one was now nearing a year. I was crying to my lawyer on the phone one day, right around a year after we filed. I was struggling to pay our mortgage. After Gary died, I discovered that we owed more on our house than when we bought it. I told him, "I can't do this anymore. Just tell the Trustees that if they don't close, I'm going to Channel Two, Channel Five, Channel Seven, and Channel Nine, and I'm blowing this up. Because what they're doing is wrong. And I don't care anymore."

Within forty-eight hours, I got a phone call from my lawyer. And he said, "It's done." It was such a relief. We were finally free of that stressful mess. But not really. I knew that for the next several years I'd have to deal with all the repercussions. There was still a short time period to wait, but eventually Gary's funeral was finally paid along with a lot of outstanding bills. I also insisted on making donations in Gary's honor and in respect for those that have helped us.

But we still lost a lot. We had already lost our business, along with all the savings we had sunk into it. We lost investments, and eventually, we just couldn't keep the house Gary and I bought during our engagement and lived in for twenty years. The house where all our family memories took place—the house where he died—had to go.

In 2019, Gary's VA paperwork was denied. I appealed again.

Feeling exhausted, I continued to read and educate myself and talk to survivors. Kaylee and I went to Washington, D.C. and met with our senator. Kaylee gave her the paperwork on burn pits and said, "Look, toxic exposure from burn pits killed my dad. We're not

*Kimberly Hughes*

service connected. I want to go to college." We went to the TAPS headquarters there searching for answers. We started to do everything that we could, using our voices. I called our congressman so frequently that the staff knew who I was by my voice.

I also kept in touch with Rosie. I would check in with her and look over the new items shared online.

Kaylee, who was determined, filled out FAFSA forms and started looking for colleges that would best suit her. Gary had always suggested that we move away from the city, and selling the house helped get Kaylee to the University of Tennessee Chattanooga. It had just what she wanted to study. She also wanted to honor her dad in the ROTC program there, and so we moved to Tennessee. At first, I thought it was a great idea. But trying to find a place to live was a nightmare, not being service connected, with no VA loan, and with a bankruptcy. I had no idea I was in over my head. On top of that, Kaylee was considered an out of state student; so, I immediately got two jobs and did the best I could.

The first thing I did when I could was find the local Veterans Administration Office where I met two veteran service officers (VSOs). The one I worked with the most was Malachias Gaskin. I told him how strange it was not to take a number and wait two hours in line like I did in Chicago. He told me that he would work with me and that I would not have to explain my story ten times to ten other people to get results. We got follow-up paperwork going, and a hearing was set up.

*In 2020, a VA hearing was set.*

I got an email from Rosie about a press conference in D.C. I called her personally and said "I'm in." So, in September of 2020, I packed my folded flag, a set of Gary's dog tags, and his Army jacket. I flew out the day before, and that's when I met Kevin and his wife Theresa. Right there in the hotel lobby, we became instant friends. John Feal and Joe McKay were there, too, and I finally met Rosie and Le Roy in person for the first time. We hugged, and right off the bat, we knew we were going to see this through. That evening, Theresa and I talked about our husbands and why we were there.

The next day, we went to the Capitol Triangle, and the bill, which is now known as the PACT Act, was introduced. The press conference was successful. Just holding the folded flag spoke volumes without my saying a word. It was an honor to represent the survivors for those who had lost so much, for those who couldn't be there, for those caretakers, and for those making funeral arrangements. Jon Stewart, John Feal, and Joe McKay were there. I talked to all of them and told them a little about Gary. They were upset to hear that my family was denied and not service connected. Rosie encouraged me to keep my fight going.

In 2021, three and a half years after Gary and I were first denied, I finally got a hearing.

Once again, I had the task of proving that Gary's cancers were connected to the carcinogens in toxic air due to burn pit exposure. This time, finally, via zoom conference, Gary's service was connected.

But instead of feeling joyful, I thought about all the people I'd met along the way that were just like me and who were still fighting: losing things, filing bankruptcies, etc. So, I didn't stop. I had to continue to fight for others. I didn't want all the amazing people I had met to continue suffering. I shared the information with Rosie, and I continued sharing, networking, and traveling more.

In April 2021, we had another press conference. This time was at the VFW in D.C. I grabbed my hat, dog tags, and folded flag as usual, but this time I was also able to bring my Gold Star flag! We were all reuniting and chatting it up before it began when I suddenly became overwhelmed with emotion, so much that I approached Rosie with tears.

"He should be here! He should be here!" I cried.

My grief was catching up to me. Rosie comforted me with a hug and some uplifting words. I knew the press conference was about to begin, and I wanted to get myself together. Jon Stewart showed up, and Gina, who had her girls with her, spoke on this occasion. I went to talk to them after it was over, and there was a unique connection between us with my Chicago accent and her with her Long Island accent! We were each on our own survivor journey, wanting justice for our husbands and our children. Her girls are amazing, strong, young women.

Through different organizations, I've made connections and found my tribes. I developed many friendships, and sometimes those friendships led to charitable work all over the U.S. I'd talk about how Gary lived and what caused his death. Survivors would share stories. If they had similarities, we would stay connected. These survivors had some of the most incredibly heartbreaking stories. They, too, knew that lives could've been saved. They also lost people who should have lived longer and who shouldn't have suffered. They wanted justice, but some were just so broken and rejected that they felt defeated. I wanted to give them strength.

The Bible says in James 1:27, "Religion that God our Father accepts as pure and faultless is this: to look after orphans and widows in their distress and to keep oneself from being polluted by the world." I know when I work hard to support other widows and other kids left without a parent because of burn pits, I'm doing what God wants me to do.

In March 2022 with all my advocating gear in a backpack, I went to D.C. again for a conference. This is when I met Tim Hauser. I asked him if he was ready to make history, and he nodded yes. We talked afterward. I knew that he knew Kevin and Theresa already; so, I felt like I already knew him. That day we also got to go into the Senate building and listen to the senators discussing the PACT Act. We also got to listen to the Veteran Affairs Committee statements regarding the burn pits.

I got dropped off at the airport to wait for my flight. I would see families going on vacations, young couples kissing, little kids on top of their daddies' necks, older people holding hands, and I would think about Gary. I thought especially about how much I missed holding his hand: such a simple little kind gesture that I miss so much.

Survivors like me who have children are not a single parent. We are an only parent. Those are very different roles. We have to be the present parent and fill the shoes of the other parent in that person's absence. And we will for the rest of our lives. That's just how our lives are.

We had another press conference in May 2022, which meant another trip to D.C. Again. This time it was Memorial Day Rolling to Remember D.C. I grabbed my Army hat, dog tags, folded flag, and my Gold Star Flag, too. I waved it in honor of survivors and those survivors who were not yet service connected. I waved it for those still fighting and for those survivors who should not be forgotten. Burn Pits 360, TAPS, and Jon Stewart were some of the speakers. Kevin, Tim, Gina, and Theresa were there for this one, and having them all there was very special to me.

When the rally was over, I jumped on the back of a bike and went for a ride. Seeing D.C. like that was amazing! The roaring bikes passed by places I recalled visiting years ago when our kids were so young. I remembered showing them monuments and explaining why Daddy had to go away.

Upon my return home, it was Kaylee's twenty-first birthday. Ironically, it was Memorial Day. The PACT

Act that we all worked so hard for was now going to be on the Senate floor for voting! I had set up so many conference calls, had raised awareness in over 20 states for years, and had a rally to "Pass the PACT Act."

I jumped on a flight to D.C. again to support the votes! Another reunion!

When the PACT Act was being voted on for the first time in the Senate Chamber, I sat next to Rosie. We quietly talked about how we had met on Facebook Messenger nearly five years ago. The votes came in, and we were very pleased about the results. Although the bill had to go back to the House of Representatives, we were confident with an 84-14 vote.

Sometimes, afterwards there was some press around. They would ask people questions. I was with Kevin and Tim at the time. Kelly Meyer from News Nation was there. Kevin and Tim told me, "Kim, talk to her. It's your time to talk." And they pushed me in front of Kelly.

I just came right out and said, "This is not about red or blue. This is about red, white, and blue." I was proud that this bipartisan bill was about the veterans and not right or left. I felt relieved that so much hard work was noticed. This bill would go back to the House for a minor change and then back to the Senate, and it would pass.

But that's not what happened.

When it was voted on again in the Senate, the votes had changed. It didn't pass! WHY? I was shocked!

I thought about Gary and how he didn't go to the

Persian Gulf, Iraq, and Afghanistan for any political reason. Why was this turning into a political issue? Our men and women go to war for our freedoms. Period. They don't go to war for just Democrats or just Republicans.

Rosie was still there in D.C., and nobody wanted to leave. They all wanted to stay. Tim Jensen from Grunt Style Foundation called the gathering "Firewatch," which is what the military calls it when you look out after each other.

So, with just a bag and a backpack, my hat, dog tags, and flags, I jumped on a flight back to D.C. to join my friends at the Firewatch on the Capitol stairs. The Uber dropped me off straight from the airport, and I approached the steps, yelling out, "Hey, y'all I'm here! I'm here, and I ain't leavin!" That night I met some new friends and listened to their stories and what brought them there.

The next day on the steps, I met a young student named Eric Kallas who was a first-generation American. His family (we met them, too) were from Brazil. Eric was following the PACT Act, and he offered to hold Gary's picture. I was fascinated how this movement had interested the curiosity of today's youth. He stayed with us a while, and I dubbed him "The Intern." He was such a kind, youthful fellow, learning first-hand how our government works, and I admired that. He helped get food deliveries and passed out water, making sure that others were hydrated, too. He followed the bill closely and knew every senator who came out to talk to us. He was sharp.

I was waving my Gold Star flag. Theresa came for a while, and we stood together on the stairs...side by side again. However, the heat got to her, and she had to leave. Later, I found out she had heatstroke.

The Capitol Police suddenly said we couldn't sit on the stairs, and then we couldn't sleep on the stairs. Then we couldn't be on the stairs. So, then we were on the sidewalk. Then we couldn't be on the sidewalk. We were told to go across the street on the grass. And then we couldn't stay there. We were moved over to another little grassy area, and that was where we stayed and "camped."

Just like a military Firewatch, someone was always there, day and night. So, we would take turns in shifts. But for some, it wasn't that easy to do. I kept an eye on Kevin's and Tim's oxygen machines to make sure the colors were blinking. They would use chargers, but I would worry about them. I checked on the guys like a sister would look out for her brothers.

This was August in Washington, D.C., and it was so hot. Then it rained and became very humid. I had some dry clothes in Ziplock bags, and when mine got wet, I hung them on a tree limb. It was humid, sticky, and smelly. Putting on make-up was not a priority; so, I wasn't looking very pretty.

We were worried about food, but the food kept coming: pizzas, Five Guys, Potbelly, etc. Supporting organizations were sending us some. We kept asking mostly for water and ice because we were going through that like crazy. It was arriving along with other odds and ends, like deodorant and bug spray. We were in for the long haul.

Someone would yell out "Bathroom break!" and a group would walk together about two to three blocks. Along the way, we'd pass by the Belmont-Paul house, the same place where women in the United States gathered and advocated for their rights. I thought about what the suffragettes accomplished by using their voices. I thought about all my surviving friends I've met all over the country, many of whom had already lost their loved ones. I thought about those who wanted to be there with me but we're home watching their loved one die or at a doctor's appointment or receiving an unwanted folded flag at a cemetery. I didn't want any more flags to be draped on top of coffins from toxins that were caused from those burn pits. I was here for them.

At the Firewatch, Jon Stewart, John Feal, and Joe McKay, as well as many others, were voices for those first responders and their families after 9/11. Jon Stewart had that famous speech where he told the politicians to do their job!

Rosie saw the connection with toxic exposure between those first responders and veterans. She reached out to them and asked "Hey, could you help these veterans that were exposed to toxic air?"

And they said, "Yes, absolutely." I mean, they just dropped everything. Jon and John and Joe are all ankle biters. They would not quit. They stayed with us the whole time. And they encouraged us. Always. I let them "do them," and they were amazing. I always say that a good follower lets a leader lead.

We were helping make history happen right there in those days. It almost felt like it was a growing political Woodstock with the number of people who were turning up in D.C. There were a lot of people at the campsite most times. The number might go down a little bit, but then it would pick right back up again.

The Capitol police said that we were a very compassionate, respectful, and cooperative group.

The next day, Eric showed up again, and we welcomed him back. He held Gary's picture as I carried my big Gold Star Flag around. Later that day, we found out that the vote was going to be on the floor. It was confirmed. We were overjoyed! Although I never understood the reason that those senators changed their votes, we were going into the Senate chamber to watch the vote again. Eric got to go, too, and he was there beside me when the re-vote took place. All eyes were on the Senate floor and on Rosie. Kevin, Tim, Gina, and her girls sat nearby.

The feelings in that room were some of the heaviest I have ever known. I will say that the feeling of justice after years of upset, let downs, people not listening, and the memories of those no longer with us were felt throughout the chamber.

That day, the PACT Act passed! 84-14! There were tears. It was so joyous and bittersweet at the same time. We left the Senate building and went directly outside for yet another press conference.

Eric brought me the Gold Star Flag. Gina and I stood in front together.

All the media was in front of us. I leaned over to her and quietly said, "It's an honor to stand beside you today."

She responded, "The pleasure is mine."

I told her, "I share this flag with you now."

We were thinking about our husbands and so many survivors. There was a beautiful blue sky, and the sun was setting.

At the end of Rosie's speech, while she held the phone high with her husband Le Roy watching, everyone started cheering, crying, and applauding all around us, because this fight, which was finally won, was about our veterans, their families, and the survivors.

Jon Stewart said it best when he said, "I'm not sure if I've seen a situation where people who have already given so much had to fight so hard to get so little. And I hope we learned a lesson."

We were all so emotional. Kevin was talking to the press. Tim yelled out "Sister," and I got a bear hug. We knew this historical bill was going to be signed!

Gina and the girls had to get back home to Long Island, N.Y. The drive takes her a while, especially if there is traffic. And before taking me to the airport the next day, Tim, Kevin, and I went to Arlington Cemetery, where we paid our respects at the tomb of the unknown soldier. There, we were all quiet and still, taking in the moment. We each brought our stories there, and with gratitude in our hearts, we only hoped that we helped others—people we don't even know.

This is just one of millions of stories of what those damn burn pits did. Every story is important, and none of them should exist.

It's impressive to see the Changing of the Guard ceremony. You witness firsthand our American soldiers who volunteer to honor us and our country and to defend our freedoms. Fighting this fight was the least that I could have done for them. For Gary.

FAMILY IMPACT TRIBUTE

## *by Justin Hughes*

My dad taught me to be the man I am today. I have always protected my mom and sister as he asked me to. I promised him I would. Now that the PACT Act is passed, I'm considering joining the military, knowing now that our government will not abandon me as they did my dad when he came home sick from burn pits. My dad should still be here. I'm proud of my mom for not giving up, and I will keep moving forward in my Dad's honor.

FAMILY IMPACT TRIBUTE

## by Kaylee Hughes

October 5, 2016 was the day I grew up. Fifteen years old and a sophomore in high school, I was given the news that my dad had stage four stomach and liver cancer. What my parents did not tell me was that he was given six to eight months to live. I had no idea what to think, and my thoughts spiraled.

What could I have done differently in my life? What if he doesn't make it to see my 16th birthday? Will he be there to see me graduate high school? Did I do something to have caused him to get so sick so fast? Could I have been a better daughter?

When I was in first grade, my dad went on his first deployment to Iraq and Kuwait. My brother and I were the only kids in the school who were part of a military family; so, it was hard for us to adjust and relate to others. Though we knew no other life than growing up in a military family, attending that school was the beginning of our new normal. That is to say, I would do things as normal (or what I thought was normal).

For example, my mom was a working mother. She was essentially an "alone mother" of two in the early 2000s with only a little help to rely on other than our school and after-school programs to look after us. I never talked to my dad when he was on deployment because of the distance and minimal contact to communicate other than the monthly phone call we would get.

In fact, I never talked to my dad over the phone. I never understood why, but I hated talking on the phone. To me as a young child, it didn't feel the same as when he was with us. Maybe it was also a defense mechanism that I still carry with me. Cutting things off cold turkey was preferable, and the last memory makes it easier to let go. If I talked to my dad less and he was killed overseas, I would have been at peace with my last real memory of him instead of holding onto a phone call.

I will never forget the night that my mom and dad brought us to the kitchen counter.

"Your dad is going to be deployed again in a few weeks, and he will be gone roughly a year," my mom said, as best I can remember.

They did not give us enough time to prepare. My mom's job at the time was not very understanding of her situation and did not accommodate the amount of stress that was about to happen in our lives for the second time. We were all so defeated and lost at this time, which was the end of the summer, and my brother hadn't even picked a high school to attend.

I went on to be the only student in my 7th grade to have a father in the military. To make matters worse for a 7th grader about to experience puberty, I did not have a present dad for nearly a year.

What if this is the last time I see or hear from him? What would happen if I got the phone call while in school that my dad was killed in action or went missing?

My attachment to my family drifted unintentionally. I felt that if I got too close with any of them, something bad would happen.

*During my dad's second deployment, email was one of our primary modes of communication. We did not have to rely on snail mail taking weeks to talk to one another. Though it was so much easier and better, it still made life so much more difficult than it needed to be. In this screenshot of my email, my dad would email, asking for different things. Because he was not there for Christmas, it was important for him to make the lives of my brother and me a little better.*

Fortunately, this deployment was different. We got to talk to my dad much more than before, and I got over my fear of talking on the phone. This deployment brought up a lot of old concerns. Did he want to talk to me? What if he never comes back?

I felt like I wasn't being a good daughter when I didn't talk to him during his first deployment. I would beat myself up in my head about this and other things that I felt I couldn't control.

Luckily, my dad got back home in nearly one piece. When he came home the second time, he had gotten injured from a bombing he was present for but was ineligible for a Purple Heart. A part of me was also injured when he came back. I felt so guilty—but about what I didn't know. I dwelled on these feelings but never understood them. So, I let them slide. Grateful that my father was back with us, we thought that life would carry on and hopefully be less chaotic. Boy, were we wrong.

My brother drove us to the hospital where my dad was. All I knew was that my mom had packed a bag for the hospital three days prior and told my brother and me that she and Dad were going to the hospital and hopefully would be back soon. I remember the tiny duffel bag filled with my dad's clothes and toiletries needed for several days. My mom knew something that my dad, brother, and I had no idea what. But she knew something was about to happen, and I had a gut feeling that this was going to be a long ride.

My brother and I went into the hospital where we

were met by nurses and doctors who were coming in and out of his room. My brother and I initially were oblivious to what was going on but eventually realized that because our dad was in the hospital for more than just a few hours, something was up. But we never thought that it would be as bad as it was.

The first time I ever saw my dad cry was when I gave him part of my "blankie" to put in his wallet a few days before his second deployment. The second time I saw my dad cry, he said, "I have stage four stomach and liver cancer." I don't remember how I reacted. Time froze. I remember stepping out of the room with my mom and brother while my dad talked to the doctors.

I remember crying to my mom. She cried with me and said, "Daddy wants you both to go on with your lives as if everything is okay." Even in that short conversation, I knew that I was trying to downplay in my head as much as possible the seriousness of our situation.

The next day, my brother and I went back to school. I was in my high school library telling my friends that my dad had cancer before the first bell rang to start the day when I began sobbing uncontrollably in my high school library, unable to move and feeling like I couldn't breathe. That was when it really hit me. It didn't hit me at the hospital or at home that night where I was trying my best to act like life was normal. It was at school. I spent all day in my guidance counselor's room (bless his heart). That was where a battle in my mind started that would persist.

The following months were tough on my fifteen-year-old body. I was dealing with issues no one around me could relate to, and I had no idea what was going to happen next. I spent every day at school wondering if I was going to get called down to the office to have my potentially-widowed mother tell my brother and me the news. This got into my head. I was far too young for this situation.

Everything in me was so pessimistic. I was so mad at everything. Why my dad? Why my family? Why me? Did I do something to deserve this? I do deserve this pain. There is something wrong with me.

As time went on, Dad made it past that six-to-eight-month threshold. He was getting better, but I surely wasn't. I felt bad for wasting this time. But because my dad was getting better, I thought that I had the rest of my life to figure these things out and make them right. Maybe.

When my junior year of high school rolled around, all was good for the most part until Christmas morning of 2017. My dad, having what I believe was a stroke, had to be picked up by the ambulance and taken to the hospital. Thus started his downfall. Shortly before this, he had started to decline. The cancer had spread to his brain; so, he had another brain surgery. After the Christmas incident, he had a second brain surgery. Throughout this entire time, my dad was constantly in and out of chemotherapy and radiation and any other treatments he was offered.

My dad found peace by going to church. To each their

own, but it's something that comforted him and made him feel better. My dad was so skinny, frail, sick, and overall lethargic. I didn't realize this until later in life.

On January 28, 2018 (exactly a month before his passing), my dad had his last outing where we went to my Junior Year Father-Daughter Dance. He did not want to miss it. He talked to some people, made sure that I was happy, and made sure that I didn't wear my heels when I drove! (He couldn't drive, and he was trying to make sure I was safe.) Throughout the time he was sick, he was always looking out for me. Whenever I would complain about not feeling good or about struggling, he would always say, "If I could take away your pain and give it to myself, I would."

I spent almost all of February at home with my dad, who was in hospice. I wasn't going to school, and I didn't know which day was going to be my last with him. He was slipping away right in front of me. I would go to doctors' appointments with my dad and hear him lie to the doctors about feeling better than he actually did (he was always wearing his chemo fanny pack), see him have seizures almost daily in our living room, and watch him forget his words. Brain cancer is no joke.

I'm happy to have those memories and recordings of him, but it's a great reminder that he's at peace now rather than struggling and being so sick. My dad slowly slipped into a coma. Hearing death rattles from your own father at sixteen years old is hard to forget. At a time when I was attending a Catholic high school and feeling the furthest away from religion that I have ever felt, some nights I found myself at my dad's hospice bed in the middle of the night, weeping for someone out there—some God, some higher power—to just take him. I would be content if I had been right next to him when he decided to go.

On February 28, 2018, my dad breathed his last breath and took the road less traveled. He didn't want any of us to see him like that; so, he chose the morning my brother and I were sleeping soundly. My mom was awake and nearby that morning when he was born again into another life.

"Guys, wake up. Your daddy just passed away. Come on; he can still hear us," my mom said as my brother and I jumped awake to the worst morning of our lives. We were at his bedside, talking to him about what a wonderful and loving father and husband he was. Through all the shock from that incident, I did not know where my life would go from there.

Now that my father is dead, what do I do? My teenage years were all leading up to this moment where it was all a "what if." But what now? I essentially had to grow up and learn how to live relying not on two parents, but one. I somehow pulled through, graduated high school, and attended college in Tennessee. Right after my dad's passing, I really thought that was it. I just had to move on.

But that was not the case. I had no idea that my dad tried to get service-connected for his cancer while he was alive. But when my mom had been looking into it and applying, we were denied. I never thought anything about the VA other than, "They're stupid. They're never going to believe us."

But my mom never gave up. Every time we would get a rejection letter, she would send another one. She would contact another doctor my dad saw to get some sort of documentation that stated none of this was his fault, that his cancer did not run in the family, and that it was nothing any of us could predict.

In order to be deployed, you have to be screened to see if you are eligible to be—which my dad clearly was. Even just by looking at how big and fit he was in 2014, you would easily see how healthy he was. For my dad to come back from deployment a year later with stage four stomach, liver, and eventually brain cancer was not something that happened by chance.

I had no idea what any of this meant at the time. I had no idea what being "service-connected" was. I was still trying to wrap my head around the fact that my dad would never walk me down the aisle, be at any of my graduations, see my kids when I decide to have them, or just be a dad to me and my brother. My mom found peace in fighting and meeting other widows who share a similar story.

Once I started getting the whole "dead dad" scene, I started to look into my own way of fighting. I went to the Senate and gave the congresswoman who covered my area of Chicago where I lived at the time documentation and evidence to try to get this ball rolling. As you might think, she thought nothing of it and went on with her life as if she had thrown my paperwork straight into the shredder.

At that time, I then decided that I wanted to go to college and do Army ROTC. I wanted to feel closer to my dad and carry his legacy. Also, his career was something that always fascinated me. I was in ROTC for two years when I went to Fort Knox and had a fall which caused one of my discs to protrude in my lumbar spine. That is a journey of recovery I'm still trying to heal from. But I still went on to fulfill my minor in military science, where I continued to study all things military. However, I was unable to commission and had to find peace in letting that time in my life go.

I have always had to combat my grief since I was damaged at a young age due to my dad's death and other little life hiccups, and sometimes I still fight those battles. So, with my back and my grief, I still feel like I am recovering. Something my dad will never be able to do.

Finding organizations such as T.A.P.S. and Burn Pits 360 made my family feel like we're not so alone in the world. Though everyone comes from different walks of life and ways of living, we are all connected through our shared trauma. We are healing together, and many of those widows feel lost. Some have children, teens, or even babies to look after and care for while trying to live day to day without having to add to it this survivor's guilt and existential questioning. Could I have done better? Could my spouse have suffered less if I had done something different?

I had the honor of going to Los Angeles with T.A.P.S. in July of 2021 in an effort to try and open up, but at that time I was still dealing with things my own way, and I feel like I always will be. But grief has no time-line. Since my dad's passing in 2018, it has not gotten easier. I still feel sad about my dad, wondering things like: Would he be mad I got these tattoos? or Would he be okay with me changing my major after I promised him on his deathbed something else? I wonder something as simple as Would he like the job I have now? Overall, getting myself out there at the right pace can maybe heal this open wound in my heart.

Years before today, I didn't think I'd see myself where I am now. If my dad were still here, I would not have lived the life I have since then. There is a relief know-ing that my dad does not have to sit there in pain, crying about how he doesn't want to die. But there is obviously a big price I had to pay for that clarity.

Nothing will ever replace my father, and nothing will ever truly heal my soul. I will forever grieve and cry about my life milestones that I could only wish my dad was here to see. Ironically, I spent my 21st birth-day (Memorial Day) reserving a shot for my dad at a bar instead of having my dad buy me my first drink or drinking a beverage with me for the first time. He never got to know the people I have met and grown with in college and see how much they've helped me in my grieving process.

There is always the rainbow after the storm. And though it may sprinkle here and there as well, the sky looks a lot better knowing you have some people up there you love. They paint those rainbows to see you smile from above. Not with your chin down looking gloomy, but so you can look up and see that there's beauty in the pain. I know my dad will never be here to give me another hug and to slip me a five-dollar bill when I complain about being hungry, but the little things he's shown me will never be overlooked and will be used on my kids one day. I will show them the love he would have given them, and I will always keep moving forward.

The passing of the PACT Act has opened a window for daughters of these ill veterans to have a chance at living a full life with their fathers and having them walk their children down the aisle someday. That was all I have ever hoped for throughout these years of fighting. I hoped that other daughters never felt this pain and misery so young in their lives, and I will always carry these burdens and this trauma with me for the rest of my life. But not everyone should know what that feels like.

I can't wait to see throughout the years just how much this bill helps those across the United States who are veterans and veteran families. Many people overlook the families of veterans when sometimes they're the ones most affected by the vet for taking care of them and witnessing newly-formed trauma.

America did something right when passing the PACT Act, and now my dad can finally rest in peace.

*Family*

GARY LOVED HIS FAMILY.
AND WE LOVE HIM.

HERE'S A BURN PIT GARY PHOTOGRAPHED ON A DEPLOYMENT.

GARY WAS A MAN'S MAN. HE LOVED SERVING HIS COUNRY & HIS CITY OF CHICAGO.

*Gary*

*Goodbye...*    SAYING "GOODBYE" WAS HARD.
IT STILL IS.

GARY G
HUGHES
MAJ
US ARMY
PERSIAN GULF
AFGHANISTAN
IRAQ
NOV 30 1967
FEB 28 2018
BELOVED HUSBAND
LOVING FATHER

*Moving On* . . . GARY TOLD US TO FIGHT.
SO WE DID. AND WE WON.

*Fighting*   FIGHTING MEANS GIVING IT
ALL YOU'VE GOT!

ACKNOWLEDGMENTS

To my Gary, all the veterans, their families, and the survivors—this was for you and your sacrifices.

Gary and I have been blessed with a son and a daughter for whom I am forever grateful. *Thank you both for your love and patience.* Your father and I are always so very proud of you both.

My Grandma, or as the kids called her, *Busha,* we *thank you* for helping raise us. We miss you.

*Thank you* to all the friends, families, and neighbors who never gave up on us.

*To the following persons, nonprofits, and foundations that worked tirelessly on our behalf:* Rosie and Le Roy Torres, Founders of Burn Pits 360; Jon Stewart of *The Problem with Jon Stewart;* John Feal of the FealGood Foundation; Tim Jensen, CSO of Grunt Style; Bonnie Carroll Founder of Tragedy Assistance Program for Survivors (TAPS) and Candice Wheeler Director of TAPS.

*A special military "thank you" to the following:* ISAF Joint Command Kabul, Afghanistan; International Joint Commission (IJC) Counter-IED; North Atlantic Treaty Organization (NATO); The United States Army, 416th Theater Engineer Command, Darien Illinois; LTC Michael "Goose" Bogmenko Ret. USAR; MSG Steven Galvin; SFC Luke Matheisen; SFC Bryan Beedle. Trace Adkins (American Red Cross); George Strait (Wrangler National Patriot);

USO; Never Alone (in partnership with the Gary
Sinise Foundation); Brantley Gilbert (Wounded
Warrior Project); Janet Manion, Founder of Travis
Manion Foundation; Honor and Remember; Tamera
Sipes, National President of Gold Star Wives; Hope
for the Warriors; Robbie Grayson, Communicatons
Director of Spartan Sword; Boone Cutler, Bestselling
Author of *The Citizen's Guide to Fifth-Generation War-
fare;* Irreverent Warriors; Run to Remember; William
Michael Morgan (Vanderbilt Children's Hospital);
Robert Patrick (Habitat for Humanity and Booze-
fighters); Lorelei Ennis (professional bodybuilder);
David Otunga; Tuesday's Children; Veteran Service
Officers of Tennessee; Malachias Gaskin, Founder
of Warfighter Gardens; First Student Bus Company;
Fallen Heroes; The Patriot Guard; Survivor Outreach
Services (SOS) Fort Campbell; Marni Henderson
(Sunrise Retreats); Folded Flag Foundation; Chil-
dren of the Fallen; Department of Homeland Secu-
rity (National Advisory Council IV; H.E.R.O.E.S.
Care; John Rich (Folds of Honor); Keith Urban
(Fisher House Foundation); Gerri Neylon, Founder
(Christmas without Cancer); Dine and Dial with
Mark Dunlop of Survivor Outreach Services Army
Community Service (ACS); Fort Leonard Wood,
MO; Daryl J. W. Mackin (Author of *A Life Worth Cel-
ebrating* and Founder of A Soldier's Child); Michele
Neff Hernandez (Founder and CEO of Soaring Spir-
its); The Hero's Legacy; Taryn Davis (Founder of
American Widow Project;) Hero Miles (Southwest

Airlines); Williamson & Maury Counties; and the people of Spring Hill, Tennessee; Tennessee Titans; and the Chicago Blackhawks Hockey Team.

*To the following academic institutions:* Dore Elementary School (Chicago); Marist High School (Chicago); Moraine Valley (Palos Hills); University of Tennessee Chattanooga (UTC) Veteran Services; Middle Tennessee State University (MTSU) Charlie and Hazel Daniels Veterans and Family Center.

*Thanks to the following media:* Downriver Girl & Friends, News Nation, Delay Deny Hope you Die (a documentary), No Responders Left Behind (a documentary), AT&T; Taya Kyle (Bestselling Author of *American Wife)*; Ginger Ravella (author of *Hope Found)*; and *The Gulf War Advocate* Podcast.

*Thanks to* Loyola Medical Center, Maywood Illinois (Neurosurgeon Douglas E. Anderson, MD).

*Thanks to those who helped honor Gary:* Steve and Melissa Dunczyk (2013 Ford Mustang GT "Gary Hughes" Showcar); Black Rifle Coffee; GORUCK (Denver, Colorado); Vaune Akers (Blue Help); USAA; Harley Davidson (Rolling to Remember); Home Depot; Lowes; Gibson Gives; IAVA; DAV; Rotary Club; Kiwanis Club; Women's Auxiliary; Garrison (Washtopia); Mission BBQ (Nashville); VFW, Clearing Neighborhood in Chicago, Vince's Pizza Chicago, Cafe 63 Chicago, City of Spring Hill, Moose Lodge.

*Thank you to the people who helped us:* Teresa Kirby; Diana De La Mora; Rene Czerwien; Joe Kalas; Cindy Hildner; Della Stokes; Tim Jacob; Kelly Berger; Ma

Howell; Ivette Velez; Eric Christensen; Ellen McNulty.

*Thank you to the families that helped us:* Eric 'The Intern' Kallas and his family; Cacciatore; Parlin; the several Krizka families; Bilina; Cleary; Quinn; Naccarato; Gontarek; Grah; Mateja; Martin; Cox; McAvoy; Bell; Frank; Holley; Havlicek; Lewis; Matras; Doherty; Wong; Robb; Skowron; Andrews; Pilch; Wambach; Giovannelli; Pavis; Pierri; Hussien; Maldonado; Kostyk; Reyes; Iniguez; Felker; Gehrke.

*Thank you* to all the survivors I've met over the years all over the country.

*Thank you to those in Washington, D.C. who donated during Fire Watch. Many people and organizations provided:* Dunkin Donuts; Potbelly; Five Guys; The Dollar Store; Call your Mother; We the Pizza; Starbucks; Refreshe Spring Water; Nature Valley Granola Bars; Frito-lay; Chic-fil-A; and many more.

*Special honor* to the memory of my godfather, Chicago Police Officer Wayne J. Klacza, who was killed in the line of duty.

*To all those that participated in any way:* your voice was heard and you made a difference!

*Thank you,* veterans, for serving. *Thank you,* veteran families, for your sacrifice. *Thank you,* survivors, for your ultimate sacrifice... and to the unknowns... God-Speed.

God Bless America!

# PART 2
## KEVIN'S STORY
*the way*

# DEDICATION

*I dedicate the following chapters to my
beautiful and supportive wife Theresa;
sons Eric and Jordan; daughters Hayley,
Amber, Autumn, and Anne; my parents
Chet, Marilyn, Josephine Segura, and
Mike Martin; my brothers Ron, Mark,
and Gary; sisters Sherry and Becky;
all my aunts, uncles, nieces and nephews,
cousins, and their significant others;
and finally, our puppy dog Maggie.*

*Always follow your dreams,
and stand up against injustice along the way.
The passage of the PACT Act allows us to
find ANSWERS,
provide HOPE,
and unite us all
in SOLIDARITY.*

# Matching Wits:
# Fighting the VA for
# Covered Treatment

You might wonder why veterans have had to fight so hard for legislation like the PACT Act. After all, they have the VA, don't they? They're all getting free healthcare for life, aren't they? So, what's the problem? Unlike the rest of us civilians, they're getting a pretty sweet deal. Right?

Wrong.

For starters, just like the rest of us civilians, American veterans live in a country where medicine is a for-profit enterprise, earning over a trillion dollars in profits in 2020. Thanks to doctors who opposed the Wagner-Murray-Dingell bill in 1944 by raising the Socialist-Communist specter to frighten politicians, national healthcare in America never had a chance. Looking at those 2020 profits, those doctors certainly made the right move for them.

The Austrian and German troops embedded with Gary Hughes didn't have to go home to fight for treatment. The Italian troops embedded with Joe Cancelino didn't have to petition their governments to pay for their medical care. Healthcare was just part of being a citizen.

Unlike ordinary citizens in every other First World nation around the world, Americans are on their own when it comes to healthcare, despite the fact that the average stay in a hospital costs over $11,000. For the majority of Americans who live paycheck to paycheck, that's a daunting figure.

Now, veterans do have the VA, but it's only free to them on certain conditions. They have to prove that the condition for which they're being treated is connected to their military service. That proof qualifies them as being "service connected." That care is free.

For instance, a veteran shot in battle will have records of the date and time of the battle. They'll have witnesses who saw the wound happen, including a superior officer. The paperwork is all in order. For that condition, the service connection is clear.

The connection gets fuzzier when you consider something like respiratory disease or cancer. These conditions show up sometimes years later, and no one at the time thinks to document the cause, not even the veteran. After all, that servicemember isn't incapacitated at the time. He may cough, sneeze, feel short of breath, or have a headache, but those problems are easily fixable with a lozenge, an antihistamine, or an aspirin.

The job of the US military is to maintain combat readiness to face threats at home and abroad. It does a great job of accomplishing this goal. We all sleep soundly in our beds, largely thanks to this organization and its different branches.

Part of maintaining combat readiness is treating immediate problems and returning Warfighters to active service as soon as possible. Warfighters have to look after their own health, too. Did you know that they can get in trouble for getting sunburned? They're damaging government property. That's a real thing.

Military culture promotes selflessness and service. Those who join it tend to minimize pain and discomfort rather than admitting its severity. They're the kind of people who say, "It's just a flesh wound," and ask to go back into the fight.

The people who choose a military life are not usually hypochondriacs or malingerers. They're not making a big deal of nothing. And they're not carrying around a lot of previous illnesses. They have to be in perfect health to join, and the military checks them again before they deploy to make sure they're in tip-top shape. Chronically ill people never make the cut.

So, when a VA office sees a sudden influx of previously healthy, young, strong, fit Warfighters filling the waiting rooms formerly occupied by veterans of an earlier generation, common sense would tell them that something related to military service was sending them there. Why isn't that the conclusion that VA doctors reach?

There are several reasons, probably more than what will be considered here. One of the biggest ones is the bootstrap mentality. You know – pull yourself up by your own bootstraps. Americans say this phrase proudly. Or they boast of having done so. No one helped them. No one gave them a handout. Their own bootstraps were the only ladder they used.

It's funny, though. Originally, this phrase meant trying to do something impossible or absurd. Sit down on the floor and try to pull on your shoelaces to get up. You can't do it. But we've come to understand what people mean by these words. They're going back to Plymouth Rock and calling on that Puritan work ethic with a dash of Pecos Bill swagger.

Add to that the fact that most of the VA doctors have a military background. They're used to treating immediate problems to get a Warfighter back on his feet and back out to work. That would explain seeing chronic stomach issues like Gary Hughes presented and recommending a Pepcid. That would explain seeing severely damaged lungs like Kevin Hensley's or Tim Hauser's and prescribing an inhaler.

Another motive for treating a lesser problem rather than looking for a deeper cause is being cost effective. No matter who's footing the bill, a pill is less expensive than an MRI. An inhaler costs less than a bronchial scope. And cost is definitely a factor for the VA. It's a government agency, subject to the same limitations and pressures of other government agencies to reduce costs and account for every penny. If a government doctor is going to order a CAT scan, he'd better have a damn good reason.

But these doctors aren't detectives. And they have a huge and ever-increasing caseload. They are not going to investigate whether a symptom is related to service. That's your job, if you're a veteran.

Ill servicemembers and their loved ones are often forced into stressful roles as combination doctors, investigators, and lawyers. Faced with puzzling and troubling symptoms, veterans must enter a kind of internet medical school, learning terms usually reserved for premed students. Then they have to take the information they learn, trace exposures that happened years ago, and find proof to take to the doctors. Then they have to turn into lawyers, arguing the facts they've found and the relationship of the symptoms they're suffering to the service they performed. They have to worry about matching wits with people who are supposed to be taking care of them.

It's a daunting task. And they have to do this for every condition, every appointment.

Some veterans, like Kevin Hensley, seek answers with outside professionals. But those answers won't transfer to the VA system, which forced Kevin to repeat expensive procedures under the eye of VA doctors. He sometimes suffered through the same costly and painful treatments two and three times just to satisfy this complicated system. He carried stacks of notebooks with him to help him litigate his care with his caregivers.

And this is the American way?

You would think that in the land of Edison and Ford and Whitney, we could come up with some better ideas. We're still in the idea business. We managed to produce or attract Bill Gates, Steve Jobs, Elon Musk, and Jeff Bezos, who revolutionized or invented several industries between them in just the last few decades. Healing the sick, especially those who have done this country good, shouldn't be so hard.

Then why is it?

Should we start researching how much pharmaceutical companies contribute to politicians? Our politicians would probably rather we didn't. We might start connecting a few dots ourselves between prior service on the House and Senate floor and the dollars flowing into political war chests. We might start understanding why politicians refuse to cap the cost of life-saving medications for cancer and AIDS patients and diabetics. We might start wondering why political power is so much more important to them than human life.

The future of medicine in this country is still an open question. We place our hopes in the coming generations to think better than we have, to find better ways to solve the problems we leave them. But in the meantime, the PACT Act does one very important thing. It takes those notebooks out of Kevin Hensley's hands. It says to Tim Hauser, after thirty years of denial, "I believe you."

It lets our veterans put aside the need to prove anything. If they were in areas proven to have burn pits, and if they report certain diseases, their care is covered. They don't have to face medical bankruptcy, poverty, homelessness, and loss anymore.

Sometimes decades after coming home, they can fi-

**nally stop fighting for their lives.**

## CHAPTER 1
## *Security*

This portion of our book starts in Pontiac, Michigan in the later part of 1975. My family moved to Davisburg, Michigan, about two months prior to my arrival. We lived there until I enlisted in the U.S. Air Force at 19 years old. I have two older siblings. My brother is 12.5 years older than I am, and my sister is 8.5 years older. Because my brother and sister were much older than I was, they had already left the house when I was still in elementary school.

I played baseball and soccer, in my elementary school days, for a recreation league. There was a group of about four or five kids in my neighborhood that were all the same age who would play football or tennis or hockey or baseball or basketball around the neighborhood. A few of the dads of the neighborhood kids also worked for the automotive industry, like my father did. Growing up, we all had a lot in common; it was a good childhood.

For 28 years, my father worked for one of the "Big Three" automotive companies, General Motors (GM).

The other automotive companies that were part of the Big Three besides GM were Ford and Chrysler. My parents also owned a laundromat in Michigan for about 15 years. They were able offset their income that way because GM would lay people off from time to time. My mother would work at the laundromat while my dad would work at GM. He would come to the laundromat and fix any machines or other things that weren't working. I would tag along with Mom to the laundromat, or I would help my dad at the laundromat.

I went to a nondenominational church in Michigan. My mom and dad still attend church in Tennessee, where they retired. When I was growing up, we went to church every Sunday and had our lunch time with friends or family members after church.

My best friend, who I knew through church, was about two and a half years older than I was; we would go out of town and do stuff on weekends or after school. It seemed like there was a different dynamic there, but little did I know, it suited the rest of what happened to me later in life.

I was very involved with our church's youth group and became the helper in the church with setup and teardown. We'd have parish dinners on Wednesday nights, where the parish could get together, eat, and do a broad spectrum of community activities.

Growing up, I learned about some of my family's history of military service. My dad was in the Navy for seven years. He was in the naval reserves, and he was called up for the Bay of Pigs invasion. But he couldn't go because the Navy doctors found blood clots in his legs. The Navy separated him from the service then because of his medical condition. My brother served three years in the Army as a military police officer, and he was stationed in Germany and in Georgia. One cousin served in the Navy, and another cousin served in the Air Force. I also had an uncle who served in the Marine Corps.

When I was 14 years old, I started working, and I focused more on being able to save for a car.

My parents taught me that if I wanted something, I had to go out and earn it. Even though we weren't in a bad situation, they were setting me up to work hard, do a great job, and take care of a family. Overall, that's what set me up for life down the road.

In high school, I became friends with Theresa (my wife) during French class. We sat next to each other. My French name was Guy, after some tennis player, and she just kept her name, Theresa. We both were seeing other people at that time, but we would flirt back and forth with one another. I used to work in the school store. I got her a little stuffed cow because I knew she used to live on a farm. When we met again 22 years later, she still remembered me getting her the cow. Theresa was a year ahead of me. So French class was her senior year, my junior year. She was gone the next year.

I started working more in my senior year of high school. I was on the work study program, where you take the last two hours of the school day and go to work. That was supposed to be part of your grade. I was more out of sight out of mind than I was anywhere else.

I was a manager for a restaurant called Kenny Rogers Roasters, which is the equivalent of Boston Market. They had three different locations in Michigan. I never knew which location I would go to. I was the fixer. I would go wherever they needed me at that time.

At 18 years old, I was already running the store. I got pretty good at being able to manage the time depending on the crowd flow, just letting people go home to save money and saving products, supplies, that kind of stuff. But I was not getting the support I needed, although I didn't want to lose my chance to have this job.

I had a falling out with my employer my senior year. I was only supposed to work 25 hours a week, and I was already working way over that. Then the owner blacklined my timecard and said he was only going to pay me for 25 hours of work.

I told him, "I've already worked double that this week." I said he could pay me for what I had worked, and then we could work out the 25-hour limit later. He wasn't having it. That's when the argument happened.

I said, "Well, what's right is right, and what's wrong is wrong. So, you need to fix this, or I can't work here anymore."

He said, "This is the way it's going to be."

I thought, "I don't need this stress." Then I said, "Well, I'm not going to be involved in that anymore." So, I walked away. I left.

I had to go back to school and explain that I tried to tell the owner about the rules repeatedly. Unfortunately, he did not want to hear them. I didn't want the employer to get in trouble. I didn't want the school to have a bad name. I was in the middle of this thing.

The school told me there was nothing they could do for me because I quit. I went from having a decent GPA to almost struggling to have a 2.0 GPA because I couldn't find another job to work with me. The school just gave up on me.

I went from working at a janitorial place for my parents' laundromat to working at a place called Buddy's Pizza as a dishwasher and then a pizza maker. After graduation, I worked for a place that was a subcontractor for the Big Three. So, I was working in a warehouse putting pamphlets together, sending out letters for people who inquired about cars, or running pallets on a forklift. I did whatever jobs were necessary. I knew it wasn't permanent because I was leaving for the military.

When I was deciding which branch to join, I called everybody in my family. I called my brother, who was in the Army. I called my uncle in the Marine Corps. I already knew the Navy was out because I went deep sea fishing one time three miles off the Pacific Ocean, and I got sick. I thought, "If deep sea fishing is this bad, I can only imagine what it's going to be like in the Navy."

When I called my cousin in the Air Force, he said, "Once you get past basic training, it's just like an everyday job. You're going to have supervisors you like and supervisors you don't like, and you're going to have situations that aren't necessarily going to be a nine to five job."

I also went and talked to the recruiters. Of course, the Marine Corps and the Army were at the high schools, breaking down doors to get everybody signed up. I thought, "Well, out of the two that aren't here, the Navy and the Air Force, let me go see what the Air Force is about." I went and talked to the recruiter, and took my ASVAB placement test.

I just did it on a whim. I didn't know there was anything you could study. I didn't know there was anything you could do to improve. I just went in there and said, "All right. I'll take it." I'm a horrible test taker. I'm so bad that I could be the instructor for something, look at the test, and think, "Holy crap! What did I do?" It's horrible. But anyhow, I took the ASVAB and qualified for security police at the time. Now it's called security forces.

My cousin told me, "If you go into security police, make sure you go into law enforcement. Don't go into just security, because you'll be counting rivets on an airplane all your life instead of doing real law enforcement."

My recruiter did not lie to me. He said that with the security police, the law enforcement and the security side were going to merge into security forces. They were going to be one. And not even two years after I was in, law enforcement and security merged.

In January 1995, I was on my way to basic training. I flew from Detroit to Minnesota, and I got stuck in Minnesota because obviously it was wintertime. We were snowed in. And I missed a week of basic training. So, when I got there, everybody's hair was cut, and their faces were shaved. Everybody had their uniforms. The other guys called me and one other person in my basic training flight rainbows because we were wearing different clothes when the other guys were wearing their Battle Dress Uniforms (BDUs). So, we were behind.

Of course, we were yelled at constantly because we weren't moving fast enough. We didn't have this. We didn't have that. We just figured it's part of the whole basic training thing where they yell at you a lot and tell you how much you're screwing up. They tear you down, and they build you back up. That's what their job is to do.

I went to church, but I didn't feel like I had a whole lot of free time because I was already a week behind. I was trying to catch up on doing movements, the nuances of making your bed and having your wall locker all squared away, and all that other stuff, while everybody else was doing their own thing. So, I felt like I was always behind, playing catch up with everybody else. Even going into appointments, I would have to go to the double the appointments that everybody else did because I was a week behind where everybody else did it. I always got called out because I had to go see this doctor or this person. I thought, "Is this ever going to end?"

I finally made it through basic training and stayed on Lackland AFB, TX to complete the Security Police Academy. This was a very basic crash course on law enforcement and security procedures and on how to shoot weapons, stuff like that. For the security side, I was an M60 gunner at the time; so, I was learning how to tear apart and put together a pistol, a rifle, and the M60. We also basically set up out in the field and learned how to stay out in the field. It was just like camping with a whole other twist to it.

When I graduated from the Academy, I went to Fort Dix, New Jersey, which is Air Ground Combat Skills Training Level One. We had Army drill instructors and Air Force instructors teaching us, and that was more of a basic training for me than anything else. At Fort Dix, we were doing ground combat skills where we were training in trenches, staying in tents, and going to the sand pit. We put our faces in the sand, and we would be low crawling in the sand. And then they had a huge night firing course. We had to throw grenades and just all kinds of different things.

A lot of people washed out of that because there were obstacle courses, and we were running and doing PT all the time. People's shins and ankles would get messed up from all the continuous rucksack marches and all the other stuff. I had friends there. There was a group of 15 or 20 of us throughout the different cycles. Some would be a couple of weeks ahead of us. And so, we saw these people regularly, but we didn't know if they were going to the next stage. So, I made a few friends with the people that were ahead of us and with the people that were there with us.

Once we all separated when we graduated, we all went our own separate ways. But getting into your new career, your new base, your new people that you're going to be working with, you feel all these different nuances. Then time gets away from you, and the next thing you know, now your friends are the ones that you're working with every day. You're hanging out with them all the time, not only on duty but also off duty as well.

I finally made it through Fort Dix, N.J. and got orders to Moody AFB in Georgia, for my first assignment. At Moody AFB, law enforcement and security were already combined. So, I was already working on the installation entry control gates. A couple of years into it, I was certified on patrol. I was on the flight line where different fighter and cargo aircraft were located.

Dorm life was interesting with two people living together in a small space, sharing a bathroom, and undergoing dorm inspections on a monthly basis. My roommate worked the opposite shift. That was great during work, but it had its challenges during days off. You never truly know somebody till you live with them.

Once I jacked up two flightline workers for not wearing their restricted area badges because they crossed the Red Line. I had them on their knees, just one of me and two of them. They could vouch for one another, if one had their Restricted Area Badge, but neither one did.

"Well," I said to one of them, "Where's your badge?" And the guy said, "Oh, he's got me."

I asked the next guy, "So, where's your badge?" And he said, "Oh, he's got me."

I told them, "Oh, no, neither one of you got the other."

I challenged them and put them on the ground. My flight chief came out there, handcuffed them, searched them, and took them away. Then that part of my job was over. And I went back and kept doing my job. You'd never hear the outcome unless your flight chief briefed you. You'd never hear what went on later.

Of course, it got all over the chow hall because that's the big news. The guys kept saying things like, "Oh, you don't want to mess with that guy. He'll jack you up."

When I certified on patrol, we stopped an employee who was telling his friends which pump at the gas station had a camera that wasn't working properly. They would gas up and drive off. These were just a small portion of the events that would happen throughout my time at Moody AFB.

I had a captain who was a former Army Special Operations officer who transferred over to the Air Force. He was our operations officer. He wanted me on the

44-person team that would go out to the field, where we'd sit in fox holes or do LPOPs, which were "listening posts or observation posts." We would do foot patrols, getting on All-Terrain Vehicles (ATV) or convoys, and we would go out in the field. He wanted newer people that just came out of training to get on this team.

Then in October of 1995, we were in Korea to do an exercise. It was a big exercise that covered the whole peninsula, and several different countries would come. We practiced how to assist the south if anything happened. I was still trying to learn my job, and the next thing I knew, I was in another country.

I came back from Korea, and I continued to learn my job and certify on duty positions. In April of 1996, I deployed to Jordan in support of Operation Southern Watch with a team from Moody AFB, Security Police. This was my first deployment to the Middle East. We were the closest to Iraq after the Gulf War, and we were securing the base in order for our aircraft to control and maintain the no-fly zone. We were watching for illegal transports of oil out of Iraq and some other things as well.

This was before September 11 happened, and we were able to travel off base. I got the privilege of visiting Moses' Tomb in Jordan. I was able to go to the Dead Sea and visit Petra, which was where a portion of Indiana Jones and the Last Crusade filmed.

So, that was a very spiritual and very interesting time, especially going to Moses' Tomb and the religious aspects of that. If you read the Bible, the beginning started between the Tigris and Euphrates River where Iraq is. In addition to the religious aspects over in the Middle East, if you fast forward to me stepping off the plane on Russian soil, this whole evolution of history and religious history and geographical history is all becoming center stage throughout my career.

While we were in Jordan, we would do bazaars on the base, and we would bring vendors on the base for bazaars. Since we were operating the Entry Control Points (ECPs), we would search Third Country Nationals, called TCNs. We would make sure they didn't have any bombs on them or any kind of weapons.

One time we were searching this vehicle. The people there would rig their vehicles in so many ways just to get them to work. So, half the engine was missing in this vehicle. I opened the passenger side door, and then I opened the glove compartment. Inside was a head with eyes just looking at me. The guy was inside the engine compartment, and they were trying to sneak him onto the base.

It was crazy! I thought, "I'm glad the head didn't roll down." But the guy looked at me, and he panicked. I sounded the alarm, and other security policemen detained the vehicle operator and all passengers. We turned them over to the Jordanian military.

By this time, I had a joint exercise in Korea and deployment under my belt. I got more proficient and confident in my abilities and duties after I came back from Jordan and started understanding my role in the squadron. When I came to Moody, I was a slick sleeve, an Airman Basic, and when I left, I was an Airman First Class, an E-3.

I got an assignment to Osan AB, Republic of Korea, in February of 1997. I was going to be stationed there for a year. I dated a few people in Georgia, but after going to Korea and then to Jordan, nothing really seemed to pan out. So, when I went to Korea, I had no commitments. I spent the time in Korea learning the language, and when you're in Korea, you work hard and let loose just as hard.

We'd have exercises where we transferred from peacetime to wartime. We'd be in chem gear (MOPP) on average 12 hours a day. I was a 50-cal gunner. So, I would have to mount a 50-cal on top of a Humvee, and I'd have a driver. We would drive around our sector. This was our practice for if anything happened to South Korea.

When I first started work, I would work the gates, the ECPs, or the flight line. Later on, I got certified to be an alarm monitor. I ran the alarms for one of the priority resource facilities. I controlled entry and access, and I was also running cameras to make sure nobody would tamper with anything in the building. I watched for anybody on the outside, for people doing stuff on the inside, and for any alarms that went off, those that weren't already pre-authorized. I would dispatch the Security Response Teams to the appropriate location. They would have to take care of the situation from there, and we'd have to fill out a report.

I was the equivalent of a desk sergeant for that facility. But I would have to report to the desk sergeant, and then the flight chief and the flight commander would want to know what was going on. These reports would go up to the Commander, and if he had any questions, he found his way to me often. I had so much respect for this officer because instead of getting secondhand information, he would come down and talk to me.

I was nervous at first about what to say and what not to say, and he told me, "Well, I put my pants on the same way you do. I'm just a regular person. You're not going to get in trouble, but we need to find out what's going on." But it was great. He wanted firsthand knowledge of what was going on instead of reading a piece of paper about the whole situation.

As time went on, I was training my replacements. I was showing them places in the building that they never knew existed and different ways to get through the place faster. I pretty much knew that building like the back of my hand from the start. In January 1998, I sewed on Senior Airman E4. My time in Korea had come to an end.

In February 1998, I in-processed to Robins AFB. Two months later, in April 1998, I was on my way to Saudi Arabia. This was my second deployment to the Middle East, and we were near the command center building used during the Gulf War. We were doing perimeter watch and Tower guard and doing patrols.

During this deployment, we found a person who was working on the perimeter wall; he was writing down the distances from where each location was. He was on top of the wall, pretending like he was scraping the concrete on the side of the wall. When we would look away on the tower to watch our areas, he would scribble something down and stash it in his dish-dash. He would continuously do that; so, I sounded the alarm. The Security Response Team arrived, and they contacted the Ministry of Defense (MODA), who took this individual away.

Halfway through the deployment, I was assigned to the armory. In the armory, we issued weapons, assisted new people in sighting their weapons, stored their weapons, and helped those leaving turn in their weapons. I was responsible for weapons inventories and other nuances of the armory duties. As an armorer, I was gaining some more experience with the career field, something different than patrols and tower guards or primary security guards.

I spent a little over four months in Saudi Arabia. I came back in August or September of 1998. I went back to just doing patrol, doing gate duty, and certifying. I'd go out in the field a lot to do training. I became the Senior Radio/Telephone Operator (RTO) and supply person for our 44-person team. In September 1999, I was selected to attend the Ground Combat Skills Non-Commissioned Officer (NCO) course in Texas. My supervisor and other senior NCOs in the squadron saw potential in me to make the rank of Staff Sergeant E5 down the road.

I said, "Well, the sooner, the better." So, I went to San

Antonio for six weeks in the summertime; it was wonderfully hot. I learned how to become a leader on the field, a fireteam leader and a squad leader. I learned to watch out for certain things, to do land navigation, and to conduct other maneuvers. In the Spring of 2000, our 44-person team went to training at Fort Dix, N.J. Along with two other airmen, I attended the RTO and supply training portion, while the others learned field tactics.

## CHAPTER 2

# *Attacks*

While I was at Robins AFB, in 2000, I met another person who was stationed there with the military. In May of 2001, we got married. She had not been in the military that long, and in September they were doing a med board on her to separate her from the military because of asthma. We were in Dallas, Texas, on our way to San Antonio when September 11 happened. We had to get right back to the base.

Because of the attack, they were searching vehicles and checking vehicles. And we had a few gates where civilians and military personnel were trying to get on the base within a two-hour window every morning. It was just a massive onslaught of thousands of vehicles trying to access the installation. Trying to search these vehicles and make sure that there were no explosive devices or contraband coming on to the base was a complete, strategical nightmare.

Back in January of 2001, I attended Airman Leadership School; upon graduation in February of 2001, I was promoted to Staff Sergeant, E5. A couple of months later, because of my deployments and all my other experience, I got selected to be a trainer and go work for the training section. I would have to go out to the gates from four o'clock in the morning until eight o'clock for gate duty. There were two of us. Another NCO and I would rotate morning gate duty. I would do Monday, Wednesday, and Friday, and he would do Tuesday and Thursday. Then the next week he would do Monday, Wednesday, and Friday, and I would do Tuesday and Thursday. We were doing this for about a year.

We would train all the new airmen coming to the base for security police or security forces. We would basically high-five each other. He took half the day, and I would take the other half the day. And then right around the time for my wedding anniversary and our work anniversary, the guy who was doing the searches opposite me committed suicide.

He took his pistol from the armory, went to his house, and shot himself in the head. I got a call from his wife saying that he did it. It was just a crazy time. He worked right across the desk from me. Everything changed, and there was just the craziness of peeling back the onion and finding out why. I went to the funeral.

But I had 35 brand new airmen that had just come to the base, and I had to get them through this time, although they got me through it, too. Had I not focused on them and had they not focused on me, then we probably wouldn't have gotten through the whole ordeal, as bad as it was. And for me, I also shared the anniversary of this work companionship with the anniversary of my marriage. So, it was a rough time.

I did the training thing for a little while longer. My daughter was born in March of 2003. In June 2003, I was tasked to deploy to Pakistan during Operation Enduring Freedom for my third deployment. This was my first one after 9/11.

I left my daughter when she was three months old; she was about eight months old when I returned home. That was kind of perfect because she wouldn't remember me being gone, but it just still sucked because she went through all those firsts without me.

My team left two weeks before I got picked up, and I beat them to the deployment location! The rest of the team was stuck in Afghanistan. I flew out there by myself. I caught a plane that was going directly to Pakistan, and I got dropped off before they even got there.

When I arrived, people asked me, "Where's the rest of your team?"

And I said, "I don't know. They left before I did. This is not good!"

When everyone finally arrived, our squad was attached to an army MP company, MPs from a place in upstate New York. We were attached to Army units often. We secured a base in Pakistan. We were close to where Daniel Pearl was beheaded, the New York Times reporter. We knew there were bad guys there. Going in, we were on constant guard. We were ready;

we didn't know what we were getting ourselves into, especially being in Pakistan. We didn't understand; this wasn't Iraq. What were we doing there? Anyhow, we were guarding some priorities. I can't really go into exactly what we were doing there. We did security.

We secured the place. Nobody even knew what this place was. But we did our jobs. Then Lee Greenwood, the singer, came out to visit. So, we escorted him around the base. The town was right next to our base, and it looked like Q*bert. If you've ever played the game Q*bert, you would know how these buildings were stacked upon each other, stacks upon stacks. And we were worried about somebody getting on top of one of those rooftops and using a rocket against us. We spent about four months there.

Pakistan had a burn pit. But in Pakistan I was more worried about where we were and what we were doing. I didn't really understand the gravity of burning stuff. It was just a big, huge bonfire. I didn't really pay attention too much. But Pakistan was my first exposure to burn pits.

Communication was very lackluster. It was just rough because this was such an austere location, and with the terrain and with the time difference you were lucky to get a call out every other day for 10 or 15 minutes. There were letters, but it was just hard. The military would read your letters, and they would open your boxes. You weren't sure if the packages would get to you, and you had to make sure that nothing would melt in them because you didn't know how long they were going to take to get there. And they would be staged at what we call the hub. The hub was a location we would arrive and then get disbursed to our primary location from there, and then they would send the mail to you.

Our hub was in the former Soviet Republic. Getting off the plane and walking on Russian soil was just a real austere, weird feeling. I mean, I was five years old when the USA versus USSR Olympic hockey win happened. I would never in my life have imagined I would set foot on Russian soil, and there I was, in what used to be Russia!

When I came back from that deployment in late 2003, I got orders to Buckley AFB in Colorado. I moved with my family in the middle of summer 2004. I was stationed there from 2005 until 2010. I was on flight for a little while. I did the law enforcement and security stuff. I was a trainer. Of course, I was a supervisor. So, I'd have 13 or 14 airmen always assigned to me as new people transitioned in and out of that location.

In February of 2006, I deployed to Iraq for my fourth deployment during Operation Iraqi Freedom (OIF). My daughter was born in May, and I didn't get home until after August. She was three and a half, almost four months old by the time I got home. That was hard.

In Iraq, we were attached to the Army as well, as they were rotating in and out of there. We were doing perimeter security. We were doing towers. We were doing patrols. We did a foot patrol through a village that was just outside our location. We made sure that anybody who got injured outside of the base and other Forward Operating Bases (FOBs) was expedited onto the base.

So, we worked mid shift, about twelve to fourteen hours a day. Then we would go work out in the gym and do PT. We did this for six days on and one day off.

We were deployed with a fireteam from Greeley, Active Guard unit. So, we were pretty rank heavy in our squad.

A squad for the Air Force is 13 people. You'd have a squad leader and three fireteams. My job was the Radio Telephone Operator (RTO), and supply NCO for the squad. I would go get the equipment and supplies that the team needed. We worked with a National Guard Squad on the back side of the base. We had no power out there because we didn't want the enemy to see what we were doing. We didn't want them to know where anything was. When mortars came in, we made it difficult for the enemy to target our locations. So, we called that the dark side.

There was a bazaar on base in Iraq, like in Jordan, but every time the bazaar people would leave, we would get mortared like crazy. We knew that they were trying to phone in to tell the enemy where we were and what was going on. The bazaars would happen all over the place in Iraq and Afghanistan. Every time they would leave, it seemed like we would get a barrage of mortars that would come into the base.

I watched it one time from the tower. I watched a

Sunni and Shiite village that were attacking each other. It looked like the Fourth of July. Then they decided to turn their aggression against us, and they started to launch.

I thought, "It was only a matter of time before they started launching mortars at us."

I was fortunate when my daughter was born that the base commander knew I was having a child; he allowed me to be on the phone a little bit longer. I was able to hear what was going on during the birth of my child. My squad leader was in the same boat. We got close because we understood what it was like being away when your child's born. Christmases and birthdays you can get back, or you can try to make up for them. But you can't get back the birth of your child. That still burns with me. I carry that with me still, even to this day.

Iraq was the first exposure to burn pits that I remembered. I started to ask questions about what was being burned. The smoke would come right into our towers, and we weren't able to move. We asked to be moved to another location because, when the wind would pick up, the smoke from whatever they burned would just come right into our faces. We all thought, "Oh, that's probably not good that we're inhaling this, even though we have no idea what they're burning in there."

I got really sick in 2006. Well, peeling back the onion now, that's when I think I got sick. I went to the doctor, who told me I had the Iraqi crud. That's what they basically told everybody it was, but they didn't really tell you what exactly the Iraqi crud was.

But I got so sick that they left me in the tower. I was coughing up black, green, all kinds of different color phlegm. I couldn't keep my temperature down. I was just trying to get through, because it was like anything else. I mean, if you go to the doctor, they're going to give you 800 mg of Motrin and tell you you're fine. Go suck it up. So that's exactly what we were doing. I was just trying to get through these few days of being sick just to get over it. Finally, my fever started to break, but I just felt terrible. The guys were looking out for me, and I knew that if I kept going back to the doctor, they would send me home. I didn't want to be that guy that got sent home too early for whatever reason.

After that deployment, I came back to Colorado in September of 2006. I got a job in training again because that was my niche, I guess. So, I did some training there, and I did a lot of civilian law enforcement training as well, joint training stuff with the base. We went to Colorado State Patrol's driving course, and we did their emergency vehicle operation course with them. As a certified instructor, I trained airmen on speed measurement devices. I became an Intoxilyzer instructor. When you suspect someone of a DUI, you test somebody for field sobriety. You then test them on the Intoxilyzer machine.

We started doing a lot more joint law enforcement training related to active shooters. We were working jointly with our civilian counterparts on the Columbine issue, making sure that DOD schools on base were going to be safe from active shooters. We did close quarter engagements with the local police departments. We also went out in the field and practiced going through buildings doing shoot, move, and communicate drills.

I noticed some health issues remaining. The doctors just kept telling me I had asthma. It was all in my head. But I kept telling them I was having these problems.

It was taking me some time to be able to put things together when I was doing the training. I was trying to come up with ways to help everybody understand the same training concept.

Just because you do it once doesn't mean everybody gets it. They might say they get it, but then when they go out and try to do it themselves, half the people are like, "Oh, we don't understand."

I was just trying to come up with different ways to teach them and to get people to understand. But I just felt like there was a fog, like I was not able to connect with tasks and certainties. I was not the best when I came home. I was having a lot of problems not understanding simple things like where the dishes went.

When you deploy, your life stops; your world stops. But everybody else keeps continuing. Then you're trying to play catch up for that whole entire time that you've been gone. You're doing these minimal tasks, and it's like you're at a new house. You're getting frustrated, and you're not understanding why you're getting frustrated.

And certain things were annoying. One time I was walking down the sidewalk when a car backfired, and I jumped into the ditch. Everybody was looking at me like I was crazy, and I was trying to act like, "No. Nothing to see here. Everything's good." I was dusting myself off in the grass. But that was a reaction. We heard an explosion. What did I do? I jumped on the ground, and I didn't realize this until later. That's what sucks.

Driving around, I was looking under overpasses, and I'd see trash under the overpasses or along the side of the street or a dead animal carcass, and I would try to get over and get away from that as much as possible. That's what the enemy used to blow up convoys. Nobody could really understand what I was doing, and my wife and my kids couldn't understand. And I couldn't explain it to them because it wasn't the time to explain it. There was a lot of disconnect and just not understanding.

I didn't want to go to the doctor because guess what happens? If you go to the doctor and you have Post Traumatic Stress Disorder (PTSD) or something like that, they're going to take your gun away. And guess what I've known since I was 19 years old? I knew to arm up. I knew to go to work. I knew to secure the base. And then you're taking away from me the only thing that I've known since I was 19 years old? I didn't know what was going on. I had no idea, and it significantly hampered my relationships.

It was hard to talk about these kinds of things with

the folks that deployed with you because everybody was sporadic now. Everybody was on a different job. They're on the opposite day shift, or they're on the opposite night shift. So, you don't see these people. It's not like the Army that deploys as a battalion or company together. The Air Force randomly picks people out of the sky that make up the squad. You train together, and then you deploy together. Then they drop you back off like, "Oh, here we go. See you later. Everything's fine."

I mean, you fill out a pre and post deployment survey, but you know that if you do that, you might suffer for it. I had someone in Georgia tell me when I filled out my post deployment assessment survey, that if I turned it in, I would not be in the military six months to a year later. They would separate you.

So, what do you do with that? Your goal is to retire. Your goal is to take care of your family. Your goals are to put a roof overhead and food on the table. My parents taught me that. Telling the truth, you're jeopardizing that way of life and that goal of getting to where my kids will have health care for the rest of their lives. What do you do? How do you figure out what's going on?

I mean, there were times when I came back where I was having difficulties with the two-mile run. Before deployment, I was setting up marathons and half marathons and 5Ks and 10Ks and doing them without problems. When I came back, I started noticing I couldn't even start a run without feeling like I was a fish out of water. And I thought, "What is going on with me? What is happening? I don't get all this stuff that's happening." Of course, if you'd say something, guess what happens? So, do you jeopardize your career? No. You just suck it up, and you try to do the best you can.

In October of 2007, I was promoted to E6, Technical Sergeant. In February of 2008, I went on my fifth deployment to Balad, Iraq, in support of Operation Iraqi Freedom. When I went back to Iraq, I oversaw a squad at this time. We were there from February to July of 2008.

Over there, I started to see how large the burn pits were. And they were sending us out to do bird deprivation, which was shooting the birds so that the planes could take off. And this big, gigantic, enormous burn pit was 10 acres long. Imagine putting eight football fields together, and that was the size of the pit in Balad. You would get out of your hooch and go to the shower, and it looked like it was snowing on top of you with all the soot and the ash that would come on top of you. It was so bad sometimes that you wanted to get back in the shower again because you were going to get drenched with all the ash and stuff like that from the pit. And that ran 24 hours a day seven days a week, just like the other pits at the other locations did as well. And people were getting sick from that.

I had some respiratory issues. I was still having some problems, but I didn't have near what I did the first time. The doctors gave me a Z-Pak or whatever and

sent me on my way. But I also knew not to say anything because yet again I was worrying about jeopardizing my career by being sent back early.

I started to work on the flight, doing law enforcement
and security operations and checking on the ECPs.
Our job as flight chiefs was to go out when the indi-
rect fire mortar round would come in, and we would
help determine where the mortar round came from,
depending on the way the dirt had shifted, the way
the ground was, the size of the ordinance, the size of
the hole.

We called Balad Mortaritaville because there were so
many mortars. On average during a day, you'd have
anywhere between 25 to 50 mortars that would come
around. It was not hard to get to about 300 mortars
in just one month. Imagine triangulating all the time.
You're going out there and trying to find these rock-
ets. Some were blown up, and some were not.

Some of the fins were still going. You could hear
them depending on how close the mortar was. If you
were in proximity, you'd hear whistling sounds, and
you'd know that it was coming up. You knew it was
much closer to you than no noise at all. And it would
blow, of course.

We also ran the biggest hospital in the Area of Responsibility (AOR). When people would get helicopters in, the wounded who were still alive would have a
98% chance of surviving whatever happened to them.
We'd go volunteer at the hospital where we were strap-
ping a lot of people's legs and arms and all kinds of

other stuff because there were just not enough people to be able to do it, depending on what day it was and what had happened outside there.

Downstairs in the basement of the hospital was Saddam's torture chamber. You could see the hooks that were still in the wall. I went down there because, about a month into this deployment, I became the resource protection NCO. I had to ensure that other units' weapons were stored in a proper location so that nobody could gain access to these weapons. Saddam knew that hospitals were safe from the Geneva Convention; we would never attack a hospital. So, they were torturing people underneath the hospital. I was responsible for making sure that the pharmacy was secured so that nobody was getting the drugs out of there.

I was also the plans and programs NCO. I monitored the instructions for all the facilities and all our security areas, our security documents and information, and how we responded to incidents. I took care of how our base defense plan and our Integrated Defense Plan were written so that we could have the best possible security for that area.

I would go out on the perimeter of the base to make sure that the gate or the fence was not tampered with. I would drive right by the pit all the time, and then I would go out and do bird deprivation on my day off. I'd go shoot the birds, and of course, they were all right over the pit because of all the trash. It sounds really stupid, like, "Why the heck would you go do something like that?" But it was part of the mission, and there was a need. It was a requirement. It was something that we had to do.

It was just one of those things that you knew that it was not good, but you just didn't think twice about it. You just did it anyway; you just survived to make it home. You worried about that stuff later after you got home.

I came back in July or August of 2008. And then I became a flight chief. I oversaw about 55 to 60 people on the flight. We were doing protection level one and resource security, which was the highest protection that we could have on the base.

I ran a night shift. We would train my folks, making them think outside the box, and we were doing law enforcement exercises. We trained our guys and gals on how to use speed measurement devices and how to do ECPs, and when the Department of Air Force (DAF) guards came into our realm, we conducted joint exercises with them. I would go over to the fire department and hang out with the fire department because they were on the graveyard shift, too. I was trying to network.

When you worked nights, you tried to find the people who were awake, just to have some kind of commonality. You wanted to find out who was up in case anything happened. You were trying to train a mass of these people to elevate to that next position. I always told them that I would take care of them. "I'll help you up, or I'll help you out." That was the way I looked at it.

I was developing tasks to be kind of like cheat sheets to make sure that they were set up for success. We were on top of the mountain. The flight was receiving accolades from the commander.

We were asked to do a security detail when our protection level required maintenance. We were doing sentry duty out there for protection level one resource. We were just the cream of the crop as far as our standardization evaluations, our success rates, our deployment tempo. We were doing well as a unified team.

The command I was falling under at Buckley was restructuring its junior NCO core. The Air Force called it command leveling of NCOs of E5s and E6s. Basically it meant that if you had been at the base for a certain amount of time, you may get orders to a northern tier base or other remote locations for missile duty. I did a base swap, leaving Buckley AFB Colorado to go back to Robins AFB Georgia. There was an NCO who was swapping with me from Georgia to go to Buckley. We ran into each other, and he couldn't sell his house in Colorado. He wanted to come back to Colorado. They were talking about canceling the program because a lot of the younger airmen, E1 through E4, were having problems paying for it.

We filed the paperwork, and since we were the same rank, the same shred, and the same career field, everything aligned. We were approved for a base swap. So now I was headed back to Robins AFB in Georgia, and my counterpart was on his way back to Colorado to tie up loose ends for his family. It just worked out.

Coming into the latter part of 2009, I finished up the NCO Academy at Peterson Air Force Base in November 2009. All the stuff happening with my health and other things led to my wife (at the time) and I going in different directions and led to inevitable divorce. Right after the NCO Academy, we filed for divorce, and we were already finalized for divorce when my daughters were only six and three years old.

In November 2009, I started getting ready to leave for Georgia. My ex-wife moved to Florida, and between moves and my deployments, it made it extremely difficult for me to see the girls.

In January 2010, I got back to Robins AFB and signed in. In April, I was on my way to the country of Oman and stayed there from April until November. I was assigned as the resource protection NCO and would take a squad out to do base security and resource protection. We built a bare base in Oman, where we secured large cargo transport aircraft and brought home military tactical vehicles and other supplies that supported Operation New Dawn.

When I came back to Georgia and as I was getting prepared to depart for Oman, I met somebody, and we started talking. She got pregnant and miscarried. And then my best friend's mom died the day after that, about two months into my deployment. It was just a whirlwind of bad news. Of course, we couldn't talk that much, and I didn't know what to do. I was running a flight of 150 to 200 people, and I couldn't show any emotion. Then, like I said before, when you deploy, everything stops, but everything keeps going for everybody else back home. We got married in 2011, not realizing what would happen in the future.

Upon returning home from Oman, I became the plans and programs Non-Commissioned Officer in Charge (NCOIC). I oversaw S5, which is the support service for writing policies and procedures and the Integrated Defense Plan, resource protection, doing passes and IDs and other areas on Robins AFB.

August 2011 to February 2012, we deployed to Kuwait. This was my seventh deployment to the Middle East. At one time, there was so much sand blown over top of the base that we had to dig out with shovels and reestablish the whole entire base. And then we found out that the terrorists liked to hang out at this beach area, not even 20 miles away from us. So, we were always on alert.

We were also running back and forth between other locations trying to support our mission. And then also we had to get things back out of the country in different locations. I returned from deployment around February 2012.

When I came back, my relationship had deteriorated, and we separated. During that time, I started working mid shift as a Flight Sergeant. I was in charge of security and law enforcement operations on base. In November of 2012, I was selected for a deployment to Afghanistan that was going to happen in August 2013. In March 2013, I started training for what's called Air

Advisor; our job was to train the Afghans on how to secure their base.

During a training session, I was in full Battle Rattle, which meant I was wearing my gear, including helmet and flak vest and plates. In the middle of that training, my back went out on me significantly. It felt like my spine just snapped in half. It just cracked, and it felt like it was broken. So, I went to the doctor.

The doctor said, "Oh, nothing's wrong with you. You're fine. Here's some Motrin." It was like the military candy: 800 milligrams of Motrin. I had about four or five months to go before my deployment; so I was getting checked out to make sure everything was good to go. Prior to departing for Afghanistan, my wife and I got back together. Then we discovered she was pregnant, and I was leaving for what would be my last deployment.

I left for Afghanistan, my eighth and final deployment to the Middle East, in August of 2013. When I got there, we started doing training sessions with the Afghans. Of course, any training we wanted to do, we had to have meetings because the Afghan Leadership wanted to know what we were training them on and what we were doing.

We were attached to some of our counterparts from Italy. We worked jointly with the Italians, the Canadians, the Brits, and the Hungarians - just the whole gamut of coalition forces. This was the first big coalition mission that I saw firsthand because normally a coalition meant we stayed in our own little groups and didn't see the other coalition forces as much. This was a big eye-opening experience for me.

Not only that, but we were also networking with the pilots, aircrew, and medics, just the way it always should be in the military. We were all armed because of our duties and because in 2012 during an Air Advisor meeting, an Afghan officer that was working for the Taliban came in there and shot nine Air Advisors.

Air Advisor training was at different locations. We wanted to try to prevent what happened in 2012. That is why they wanted all of us to be armed, to understand that type of training, and to know how to get out of that kind of situation.

The Air Force was training the Afghans on how to fly helicopters. Part of our job was to make sure that the instructor/pilots were not in jeopardy if they had their guard down while instructing Afghan pilots. Besides the Guardian Angel program, we were training our Afghan counterparts for entry control duties, for tower duties, and for sentry duties, those kinds of things.

I was only in Afghanistan for about four months, but there was a burn pit, a massive boneyard of planes, tanks, uranium, and exploded vehicles. It was located right next to where our training area was, which was probably not a good idea. It's the same concept as burn pits being right next door to living quarters; it's probably not the best place to be.

They had an incinerator there. It looked like an overgrown paperweight because it just sat next to the pit. I don't know all the facts of this. It was said that General Petraeus and President Obama in 2010 made it mandatory for all these incinerators to come into the AOR, but nobody thought about the operational cost or how to maintain these things properly. And that's kind of why they just sat them next to the burn pits. They cost too much to run.

The Process

CHAPTER 3

## *Infamous*

Right around December, we were near the Herat province of Afghanistan, and a couple of the FOBs were closing. So, some of the air advisors were coming back to base to process back home, or they were trying to decide who was going to stay and who was going to go. The Commanding Officer (CO), our captain, asked us who wanted to go back to the U.S. I got the notification, and I returned home in December of 2013.

I came back from Afghanistan, and in January my wife and I had my third and her second daughter. I had just had surgery; I had some issues. I was housebound, and I couldn't move around well. My wife was dealing with some things, and problems evolved. In February, we separated and then divorced.

Child custody issues became a constant challenge from 2009 until the end of my career. In addition to going through all this stuff, I was getting ready to transfer out of the military. Also, I was going through all these health issues of finding numerous polyps from EDGs. I had over 100 polyps in the lower two thirds of my esophagus. I was the 11th case in the nation, but the number one rarest case in the nation for the number of polyps that were in my esophagus. I was having a hard time breathing. I was having a hard time when completing my PT test.

I sat in the room by myself after going through all this stuff, and once I made that decision to retire, it felt like this mound of weight just lifted completely off my shoulders. It was the right thing to do.

Finally in April of 2014, I clicked the button to retire. An administrator called me and said, "We're not going to let you retire. We're going to med board you."

I said, "What do you mean you're going to med board me? I've got nine months in the military left."

She said, "You fell through the cracks. So, we're going to med board you."

I told her, "Well, your med board takes about 24 to 48 months to complete, and I've only got nine months left in the military. Why can't you let me go ahead and retire?"

She called me back a month later and said, "Well, we've decided to let you go ahead and retire."

I just thought, "Oh, that's so gracious of you."

Then the appointments started piling up for me to retire and out process.

As I got ready to retire, Theresa and I started talking in the summertime, June or July of 2014. We were both going through divorces. We were both going through hard times; we were supporting one another. She came down to Georgia to help me go through my appointments.

In December 2014, I retired from the military. My family came down to Robins AFB for my retirement ceremony, and my sister pinned my retirement pin on me.

After I retired, I initially moved to Tennessee. My retirement pay was significantly reduced, and 65% of my retirement pay went for child support. What I had was substantially lower than the amount I had made on active duty as an E6.

Now mind you, I had all these other obligations; so, everything started to spiral in a downward slope quick, fast, and in a hurry. We tried to sell the house; I tried to short sell it. When it went into foreclosure, the VA bought it back. Now I'm capped on how much money I can use with my VA home loan because of that issue. I tried to make payments and work stuff out with the lenders, and they just weren't having it.

Theresa and I got married in 2015. Things were starting to look up. I started school because I thought the GI bill would help with offsetting some costs while Theresa was working. I got a job, and then I was going to school online. I did that for about eight months in 2015 despite my health problems. I had to take a medical leave of absence, due to medical appointments mounting up. Eventually, around December 2015, I had to quit due to declining health issues.

I got a call from the VA saying that I could sign up for VA life insurance, but it was already 10 months into my eligible time. I didn't know I only had a year to sign up because nobody told me. I signed up for the insurance and put it on direct deposit.

The VA called me five months afterward, which was the 15th month, and said, "You haven't been paying us."

I said, "What do you mean? You've been taking the money out of my direct deposit."

And they said, "Well, something happened, and it just didn't work out. So now you can't get life insurance anymore."

That might have been a blessing in disguise. With all the things that were happening to me, I considered committing suicide. I went from being a leader of 146 people on a flight to not even being able to tell you if I took medication two seconds after I took it. Things were starting to fall apart and spiral down low. I was in a deep depression, and there was more to it than just my health. And so if the VA had picked up my life insurance at the time, I figured I was better off dead than alive without being able to take care of my kids and my family. I couldn't do anything. I didn't know what I was going to do or where I was going to go.

So now because of my treatments and everything like that, obviously that's not even an option. But you've got to understand that in a period of less than a year, I went from being a flight sergeant to losing my cars, losing my home, going through child custody issues, and being prescribed numerous amounts of medications.

I was trying to find some positive light, which was

obviously my wife Theresa and my children. Even though I didn't get to see a lot of my kids, they were a light. And at least her kids started to band together with me and support me as well.

I was trying to pick up whatever I could, but there would just be an onslaught of collections people calling me. I mean, we spent over $30,000 in travel and medical costs, losing vehicles and losing our home. We got to the point where we were just looking at a bill and saying, "Well, do I pay this, or do I put food on the table today?"

It was just demoralizing to me. My dad taught me that to be a man, you must put a roof over your head and your family's head and put food on the table. Guess what I couldn't do?

Theresa and I were trying to find out about my lungs, learning about toxic exposure and the burn pits, and then finding Burn Pit 360. Because of Burn Pits 360, in 2016 we found Dr. Miller at Vanderbilt University in Nashville Tennessee. He had treated soldiers from Fort Campbell; he was not used to treating prior Air Force veterans. Doctor Miller said, "Your lungs are worse than those soldiers that I've diagnosed back in 2003 and 2004."

I was trying to navigate all this medical information. Initially, I was rated at 70% for the VA, and I fought for that. I learned what 38 CFR is, the Combined Federal Regulations and how the VA rates you.

I started researching that, studying that, and finding out what was going on with those rules when they rated me at 10%. I looked at it and saw that I should have been rated at 30%, and then that's where my fight went on. Eventually I got to that 30% because I had the evidence that they said I didn't have.

I separated all my service connection disabilities by my evidence. I spent four hours making stacks of whatever my service connections were, just to make sure I had all the appropriate evidence.

Then every time I would go to an appointment, the doctors would ask, "Well, tell me why you think you have this condition?"

I'd haul out the stack of evidence and said, "Well, here's all my evidence that says I have this condition. So, you tell me why I'm here."

I put the onus back on the doctors and back on the people that were denying the evidence. I finally got the lung biopsy in 2017. You can't prove constrictive bronchiolitis without having a lung biopsy. I went through a battery of tests. I saw Dr. Miller at Vanderbilt eight times in one year. I thought after the lung biopsy, "Well, if it's in my lungs, where the heck else is it in my body?"

This led us in 2018 to CereScan in Littleton, Colorado. They conducted a Single Photon Emission Computed Tomography (SPECT) scan on my brain. We were finally getting answers, and we had the documentation to prove that these illnesses were not in my head or made up. We were giving this data to the VA and turning in all our medical documentation. But all they were telling me at the polytrauma team was,

"We don't know what else to do for you. We gave you a handicap placard. So that's about all we can do for you."

And I thought, "Are you kidding me? You can't validate what you see in front of you? This is validation of everything that I have said all along!"

Then they told me, "We've got this ex-Army Ranger Lieutenant Colonel who's our neurologist. We're going to send you to him because he'll find out if you're making this up or not."

I responded, "I can't wait to see this guy."

That's how they treated me. But I wouldn't go away, and I wouldn't quit. That's why they called me the infamous Kevin Hensley. How many people do you know who are infamous in a positive way?

I went to the neurologist, and I completed all his testing. The polytrauma team with the neurologist did a telehealth call. The guy from the polytrauma team had his arms folded like he still did not believe any of the stuff that was going on.

The neurologist said, "All the tests that you went through, your SPECT scan and everything else, is all represented in what you said you've been dealing with."

The polytrauma guy went from having this stern look on his face to complete concern, like, "Oh, how can we help you?"

They finally gave me 100% temporary disability. I'm on a CPAP, and I had to move from a CPAP to a Bi-PAP. Because of that and because all my ailments were stalemated, they didn't require any return visits.

Then I wondered, "How do I go from 100% temporary to 100% permanent? I want my kids to be able to go to school if something happens to me. I want to make sure my wife is taken care of if anything happens to me." I believed that if I made 100% permanent, they'd be taken care of. That's not the truth either.

So, I went to see a veteran service officer, and I said, "I want to go from 100% temporary to 100% permanent." They put in a claim saying, "The veteran wants to go from 100% temporary to 100% permanent." The VA denied me.

So, then I went back. Now this was months in the making. I went back, and the guy said, "Well, we'll put all your service connection that you want to go to 100% from what your percentage is and see if that'll work because there's no written guidance to go from 100% temporary to 100% permanent. There's no written plan on how to do that."

He put in this next appeal, and I was denied again. They called me and said, "What do you want to do?"

I told him again, "I want to go from 100% temporary disability to 100% permanent and total."

They said, "Why didn't you say that?"

And I said, "I did the first time."

They said, "So, you just want the chapter 35 benefits?"

I said, "No, I want all the benefits that are associated with 100% permanent total if I qualify. If I don't qualify for it, I don't want it." My point is that I never asked for anything I don't have.

They told me, "Well, you're going to have to wait a few months, and then we'll see what happens."

The VA finally gave me my 100% permanent and total, and they backdated to December of 2018. I found out that I must be 100% permanent and total for 10 years to make sure my spouse and my kids are taken care of because my respiratory condition (Constrictive Bronchitis) is not service connected. They still do not recognize it. They told me I have COPD. They told me I have pulmonary fibrosis. They told me I have emphysema, even though I've never smoked a day in my life. They've told me everything I've had except for constrictive bronchiolitis. When I go to the doctor's office or the hospital to get an EDG or a colonoscopy, I have a hard time coming out of anesthesia. Somebody has to watch me when I come out, or I have to do a breathing treatment before I go under. Even though I've given them the medical evidence of my diagnosis, you would be amazed how medical professionals don't understand my conditions.

After my diagnosis of Constrictive Bronchitis, I was put on oxygen, and we purchased an oxygen concentrator that cost us over $3,000. Otherwise, the VA would have given me a little tank with wheels on it, and we'd have to wheel that around. We found this portable oxygen concentrator, and we purchased it. The batteries alone cost a grand, and then I had to get a carrying case. But it was pushing my shoulder down so that I had frozen shoulder, and I had surgery previously on my shoulder. So, I didn't want to put that case on my dominant shoulder all the time.

These medical conditions are constant, with the EOE, the GERD, and the problems with my L5 and S1 and my C3 through C7. I've got what's called rucksack neck, where my neck is completely forward. They're trying to fit me for a brace I have to wear for 20 minutes a day. The doctor said that I would be a good candidate for it.

The condition that I have affects my life daily. The polyps in my sinus cavity and the polyps that are in my esophagus make it hard to breathe and swallow. I also have stricture in my esophagus. I break my food with water and liquids to swallow it because otherwise I would have a hard time getting it down. They've stretched out my esophagus before. They stuck the tube down my throat, and they stretched it out a little bit. I've had about 20 EDGs, the scopes down the esophagus. I've had four colonoscopies because I have other issues with diverticulitis and hemorrhoids and polyps in my colon. I also found out that I had an abundance of food allergies that I wish I would have known when I was younger. I'm allergic to wheat, rye, barley, oats, you name it; so, I can't have pasta. I can't have pizzas; I can't have bread. Those things exacerbate my EOE issues.

In August 2020, I messaged and then called Tim and asked him to join Burn Pits 360, because he kept talking about the Gulf War and how he wasn't getting his benefits. He needed help. I reached out to him and said, "You're another piece of this puzzle that we need. We should be talking about the Gulf War, when folks had the oil fires burning and they had the burn pits there. We need that link to help us bring this home."

He might have thought, "This guy's a crazy. What's going on here?" But look where we are now. He's my brother. I could never imagine my life without him now.

Theresa and I attended a press conference in September 2020 in Washington D.C., and we met all these great people. We met Rosie and Le Roy Torres, the founders of Burn Pits 360, along with so many other advocates and families. We met Kim at this press conference as we were advocating for the "Warfighter Bill." When we met Kim, we had an instant bond. We went to a deli across the street from the hotel. Kim and Theresa hung out and got to know one another, and now she's just like our sister and her kids like our niece and nephew. When we returned to Michigan, Theresa decided to share a Facebook post of our journey and our struggles with my health. That post garnered so much love and support from family and friends that we knew our next course of action was becoming advocates.

## CHAPTER 4

# *Advocate*

In December 2020, I joined with the Veterans of Foreign Wars, Department of Michigan (VFW-MI). We conducted zoom calls with our senators and congressional delegates, advocating for the "Warfighter Bill" that eventually became the PACT Act. It was because of Burn Pits 360 that I became a life member of the VFW, with post #1138 in Monroe, Michigan. The support from the Department and the post was instrumental in passing the PACT Act. I'm so very honored and privileged to be a part of these great organizations, serving veterans and their families.

In January 2021, we attended a toxic exposure panel at the Wyandotte, Michigan VFW, post #1136. We discussed toxic exposure illnesses contracted during our deployments. In March 2021, besides advocating for toxic exposure legislation with the VFW to our Michigan United States senators and congressional delegate, we were invited on a podcast called Downriver Girl and Friends. We discussed toxic exposure and its effects on families and veterans in Michigan.

In April 2021, we went to Washington D.C. and attended a press conference at the VFW Building. This is where Kim, Theresa, and I met Gina. Gina had previously interviewed with Jon Stewart. Gina and the kids are just part of the umbrella of our family with Tim and his family. We've all become so close, during our time advocating for Toxic Exposure legislation. I will tell you this slogan that I truly believe. "We are family by tragedy, advocating for triumph." We went through the ups and downs of the bill changes; there were 12 to 15 bills that legislators wanted to put their own little spin on. The whole entire time that we were doing this, we were doing this for each other.

We all knew presumption was the way to go because of these people who are battling these issues and being ignored. These doctors that you've always been told to trust—they're the professionals and they're the ones that have the answers—when you go to them and get treatment, they're telling you that this is all in your head. Part of the reason is plausible deniability because they don't want to eat the cost. They don't want to treat people and pay for something if they don't have to.

You have to become your own doctor, your own lawyer and advocate. You go through years and years of hearing them say, "This is all in your head." And then as time goes on with the advocacy work, we're finding out that they knew about toxic exposure 30 years ago. They knew about the sarin gas in the Gulf War. They knew that the burn pits would probably cause some kind of environmental problem. We've outlawed this practice since 1979 in our own country.

In August 2021, we conducted a toxic exposure forum. When explaining what a burn pit is to most people, I say, "Imagine taking a backhoe to your backyard, digging a pit, taking all the trash in your trashcan, taking all the stuff that's in your garage, and throwing it into the hole. You need to change your tire? Well, throw the tire in there. What the heck, throw the whole car in there, too. Let's light that pile on fire with diesel fuel or jet fuel. And we'll burn it 24 hours a day, seven days a week. Oh, you've got a family? Aren't you going to let them to live near this pit? Because that sounds like a really good idea. Right?"

Their response is always something like, "Holy cow. We never knew."

I respond, "Well, that's what we lived and worked with and worked around."

They usually ask, "Well, the VA takes care of you for life, right?"

I say, "Yes. If they recognize that you have a problem, and if they say it's service connected."

That's another key, too. Because if they're saying that you don't have something, and you say you do, how is that going to be service connected? If something's not right, and they're not willing to admit it, how do you get them to admit it?

Instead of addressing the problem, they give you this big drug cocktail that we all had. I mean, I was on a numerous amount of pills when I came into the

VA. It was like a full-time job. They just threw crap at me. It was like a wild ass guess; I call it a WAG. They just WAG-ed it. The problem is, when you say that one pill interacts with another one or you have a reaction to one pill, they set you up with a different set of pills. Then you go back again and say, "These pills aren't working." Then they call you a pill popper or pill seeker because you're trying to figure out this whole cocktail that you're taking. You feel like you're in a fog. You're reaching for the refrigerator door, and you can't grasp it because you're just in this fog of Vicodin or Percocet or Fentanyl or whatever drug cocktail you're on.

The medical doctors are allowed to do what's called "off labeling." For example, they gave me blood pressure medication for PTSD because they figured that if my blood pressure were remaining down, my PTSD symptoms wouldn't come up. And I said, "What are you talking about?" All this off-label stuff was just crazy. That wasn't an answer.

It was time for some good news. In September to October 2021, I was fortunate enough to go to NorthStar Hyperbaric and NorthStar Neurology in Tucson, Arizona, through a grant called Healing Arizona Veterans. I received 80 sessions of hyperbaric oxygen treatment for my TBI and my PTSD, but it also helped my lung volumes. The pulmonologist told me before I left that I was depleting more rapidly than the veterans from 2003 and 2004. I hoped that this treatment would let me plateau a little bit or even off. But my lung volumes increased slightly. That wasn't a part of the whole hyperbaric oxygen treatment. That was for my head instead of my lungs. Our family has been very fortunate. We've been very blessed.

For example, after my sinusitis surgery in 2016, the VA said that I didn't have any sinus polyps or masses. Guess what came back in 2021? Another mass appeared in my sinus cavity 13 millimeters large. Had I not received the MRI DTI in Arizona from Doctor Henricks, I would never have known that the mass had returned in my sinus cavity. So how did that come back?

In November 2021, we walked the halls of the Senate in Washington D.C. That day we found out that Wesley Black, who was sick from toxic exposure, was moved into hospice care. He was given three months to live, and he passed away three days later. Between going to Nashville, TN, to see my pulmonologist, attending a toxic exposure panel, and getting the word out on a podcast, the toxic exposure word was getting out. Theresa and I attended a rally in Columbus, OH. This is where Tim, his wife Marcy, Theresa, and I met. After all this time, it was great to finally meet Tim and Marcy in person.

In January 2022, Gruntstyle Foundation invited us out to Las Vegas, NV, for BurBiz event. Gruntstyle awarded us a homé Hyperbaric Oxygen Chamber. This opportunity to receive the chamber has continued to motivate Theresa and me to advocate for veterans with brain wounds. Things started to pick up with our advocacy efforts.

In March 2022, my zoom meetings with senators and congressional delegates started. Pushing toxic exposure was our main focus with the VFWMI. Then came another trip back to Washington D.C. We walked the halls of the Senate, advocating for toxic exposure. One of the senator's offices told us there weren't enough veterans who were sick and dying in his state to support the PACT Act, when there were over 6,800 veterans that had signed up for the VAs Airborne Hazard and Open Air Burn Pit registry at that time in his state. I asked him, "I thought one was enough, but 6,800 is not enough for you to sign on for the PACT Act?"

Then he wanted to know what the cost was. And I answered, "Well, the initial cost assessment, the CBO score, for this bill is roughly $260 billion. We've compromised by taking out a whole lot of these other conditions to facilitate your cost budget analysis. And then you're still going to give us a no? I mean, I don't know what else to do for you. But you can't say that you're America First when you put veterans last, and that's a quote from Jon Stewart. Stewart also said that you can't order a meal and eat the whole thing and then complain about it when the bill comes." We completed March with a rally in Cleveland, OH, and a trip back to Washington D.C. for the Senate Veterans Affairs Committee hearing on the PACT Act.

In April 2022, we conducted peaceful toxic exposure awareness rallies in North Carolina, Kansas, and Kentucky. We dropped off signed letters of support for toxic exposure legislation. We gave speeches and held question and answer sessions. The Veteran Service Organizations and non-profit veteran organizations were coming together to support what would be a huge push towards the summertime.

May 2022 was probably the most monumental month for me. Michigan put up three billboards in the state to support the PACT Act. These billboards went nationwide, even worldwide. People all over the place were talking about our billboards. They were garnering more and more attention. One woman in Michigan lost her husband; his name is Nathan Denryter. He was a Lapeer school teacher, a firefighter, and a master sergeant in the Air Force. He had bile duct cancer, and a screening would have saved his life. But VA neglect killed him at 38 years old. It took his widow two and a half years to get her survivor benefits. The first thing she did was finance one of the three billboards in Michigan. We also participated in Armed Forces Day events to get the word out about toxic exposure. We went door to door with Downriver for Veterans members on two separate occasions collecting signatures to support the PACT Act. Then we dropped them off at our senators' offices in Michigan. On Memorial Day weekend, we went back to Washington D.C. and attended the Rolling to Remember event.

In June 2022, the vote for the PACT Act occurred in the House of Representatives, then moved to the Senate; the Senate made changes and sent it back to the House. There was an issue, and the bill was held up.

In July 2022, we drove out to Washington D.C. for a press conference. Initially we thought we were going to have a celebration or sigh of relief after the Senate vote. During the Senate vote for the PACT Act, as the votes were being tallied, I thought they were going to create a little drama where it was going to be like 60-40 in favor of the PACT Act.

But when they didn't pass it, I went into this deep depression. I mean, I just sank because there were four people in the state of Michigan and their families that I'd asked over the last two years to trust me and believe in me. I told them that I was going to bring this bill home to them, and I felt like I failed them.

I asked them to trust me. They lost their sons. The government killed them. They were refused even to do a screening. Two of them could still be alive today if they had just done something like a blood panel or a proper screening for toxins. I asked these people to trust me, and it took me over two years to garner their trust. I had to call them and apologize to them.

After that, Tim said, "Whatever you need, man, I'm here for you." He had me. It was just ironic knowing that I'd brought him into this. Then the person who brought me back out of that sadness was him.

That afternoon, we went out to the Union Station, and there were about eight of us there that were devising plans on what we needed to do. We were going to come back next week, or we were going to try to rally our folks and get everybody on board. Tim Jensen and Rosie Torres and Amanda Barbosa were there, and they said, "No, we're not leaving. We're going to remain watchful. We're going to go on the steps of the Capitol, and we're going to stay there until the PACT Act gets passed."

Tim and I were looking at each other like, "Well, how are we going to plug in our oxygen? What are we going to do to support this? How are we going to do this? Because we can't stay here."

So, he and I went back to Cleveland, Ohio. It just happened that a guy was doing a rally in front of a senator's office, and we joined him in that rally to pass the PACT Act. Then I went home, back to Michigan, and grabbed my wife and Ann, and I said, "We're going back to Washington D.C. We're going back to participate in the Firewatch." Ann is the founder of Downriver for Veterans, her son is battling illness from toxic exposure. Ann walked the halls of the Senate just to see what it was like because she had been supporting us. We were working together, Downriver for Veterans and Burn Pits 360.

While on Firewatch, people were helping, making sure that our oxygen was plugged in or making sure when we went into a building that we didn't have to think about the logistical nightmare of trying to go to the bathroom or plugging in oxygen or being in the heat. My oxygen concentrator shuts down when it gets too hot. So, I had to go inside. Luckily enough, that first day I was walking the halls of the Senate; so, I didn't need to worry about the oxygen. But when I came out of there and it was still 93 degrees and 100%

humidity in D.C., my oxygen started to shut down.

Well, I had to go find shade. I had to cool it down. I had to change my battery. And so, there were a lot of little nuances that a lot of people didn't see about advocating and speaking out. Where do you sleep? How do you come up with travel money? Where do you find bathrooms? How do you get out of the rain? And we answered those questions by pooling our resources and taking care of each other. We achieved what we did because we helped each other.

When we walked the halls of the Senate, we split up into three teams of eight people going to eight senators' offices and finding out why they voted no on the PACT Act. Had they given the same excuse, I could understand that. But every time I'd talk to somebody in an office, it was always a different excuse.

The PACT Act was not a red or blue issue. This was a red, white, and blue issue. The PACT Act had bipartisan support for legislation. We knocked on the doors. We put boots on the ground, just to hear so many noes and have so many doors slammed in our faces.

I've been up and down the halls of the Senate. But that's just the effect of the advocacy and the networking and the community wrap around as more supporters came. There were initially three people that started on the Firewatch, and there were over 150 towards the end. Thinking back on the interviews and the signs and the heat and the rain, I realized we'd done something historic that hadn't been done in our generation.

We had people that were there from all walks of life. We even had people that were visiting from other countries that were just so impressed with what we were doing that they wanted to hang out and hold signs. We were getting interviewed and blowing the PACT Act up on social media: Twitter and Facebook and Instagram and Snapchat. But we were just out there in the moment, looking out for one another and getting people to share their stories.

When they see the same people repeatedly, people start to tune out a little bit. But when they start hearing the stories from other people and learning about toxic exposure, people started to listen. When you put these stories and news articles and evidence together and you back up what you're saying with facts, things happen.

Finally on August 10, 2022, the biggest piece of legislation in over 44 years and the biggest piece of medical legislation that impacts veterans' health was signed into law. Veterans will be getting the health care and benefits that they've earned and deserve and that they're entitled to receive. Spouses of deceased veterans are finally getting their survivors benefits. They call it DIC, but it's also referred to as survivor benefits.

The people that joined this fight have done something monumental. And some of them have become monumental to me. I think of the relationship I have with Kim, who lost her husband Gary. I had a connection with Chicago because my wife and her family's favorite place to visit is Chicago, Illinois. She loves the architecture, and I do to. Then Kim moved to Nashville. Well, I have family in Tennessee. I go to Nashville for treatment. She met my father.

Now she's met my sister, because my sister was there when we went to the White House. I brought my sister along to experience what this was all about as well. When we went back for the signing, my sister didn't go to the White House with us, but she met a bunch of people and socialized with everybody. So, this has been a huge family affair from the beginning.

I don't know about you, but that gives me hope. Everybody tells me that one person can't make a difference. To them I say: You're wrong. And not only are you wrong, on August 10th when ink was put to paper, you were proven wrong. It takes a village, but it can start with one.

At the end of the day, we passed the bill on Capitol Hill, with my compliments to Schoolhouse Rock. And it's been historic. It's been a ride. This ride has been monumental. This ride has been inspiring. I would have never in my life have dreamed that I would have been allowed even to get a window seat on a ride like this one. There is a reason why I did all this.

If you ask me what the PACT Act means to me, the PACT Act means that as of right now, if I die tomorrow, or if I die in the next seven and a half years, that my family will get their service-connected survivor benefits because of constrictive bronchiolitis, since my terminal disease is now recognized.

I had a huge worry on whether my family was going to be taken care of when I died. That is why we came into this battle. We came into this fight so hard because of the stories of the families that I've heard. Some people died of cancer who wouldn't have died if they would have had a screening; they could have tested early enough for treatment. And I was told when I was 39 years old that I had the lungs of a 91-year-old. Where did that come from? I've never smoked a day in my life. Obviously, that came from the burn pits that they never wanted to acknowledge because of plausible deniability. When we started advocating here in Michigan in 2020, we looked at the burn pit registry, and there were over 2,100 veterans in Michigan. Now it's over 4,600 in Michigan that are signed up for the registry.

If my daughters ever become passionate about anything in their lives, I want them to know how to take action. I want them to have a replica of how we did it when we did it right. So, if they're passionate about any particular issue and they want to advocate for change, I hope and I pray that they realize there is a format, a right and appropriate way to use their voice.

A bill signed into law is proof that we did it right. Absolutely. Now they can do things right with their concerns. We set up that formula and followed the rules. We just kept coming up with ideas and brainstorming together and taking care of one another, and we all came together.

Advocating is how we did something so historic for millions of veterans. Could you imagine if 3 million veterans were standing on the Capitol steps? Holy crap, what that would have been like! But the people in the family that we've made from this fight are with me for the long haul. I couldn't imagine any better people to be with than Tim, Kim, and Gina.

Kim, Tim, and I decided to go visit the tomb of the unknown soldier. It was very symbolic to us, because it represented all those who died from their toxic exposure illnesses, who we never met or never knew. As we watched the changing of the Guard at the tomb, I quietly said, "I hope you all can finally rest in peace."

FAMILY IMPACT TRIBUTE

# *by Theresa Hensley*

Kevin and I became close friends in high school when I was fifteen. Even though we both were dating other people, we used to study together and got along great. We kept in touch here and there after high school over the years and later reconnected through social media. During the time that we were apart, we both married and had children. When my kids started school and I had some free time, I began cleaning houses and babysitting. I eventually decided that I wanted to be my own boss; so, I opened a coffee shop.

My husband at the time started out supporting me with the coffee shop. Over time, however, he was involved less and less until it was completely all on me. It wasn't long before I realized that I was in over my head by being an entrepreneur alone. It was not what I thought it would be. I thought I'd have that continued support. For one thing, my health started to decline rapidly. I had several previous health problems that began when I was a young woman that the stress of business ownership aggravated. One of those problems was endometriosis, which is when the uterus builds up scar tissue outside of it and deposits it onto the organs.

Because there was little research on this condition at the time, I didn't understand the magnitude of it. Though my mom had it as well, she was older when she was diagnosed, and she had a hysterectomy, which helped. My situation was different than hers because I would bleed for months, and I wasn't able to control my bladder function. By the time I was fully diagnosed, I was at Stage 4, which is literally the most advanced. I was having laparoscopic surgeries to address the scarring from my endometriosis. But the scarring spread to my bladder, intestines, lungs, gallbladder, and other internal organs. There was scar tissue EVERYWHERE! The doctors did a number of experiential procedures like burning and cutting out my scar tissue and giving me male hormones and shots (Lupron) to shut off my own hormones. Nothing helped; in fact, it seemed like the treatment made things worse. A lot of my subsequent health problems were because of these earlier procedures.

Because I was young, I didn't know how to stand up for myself. I was taught to comply with doctors' diagnoses and procedures by putting my entire trust in them; so, that's what I did. But surgery after surgery created more scar tissue which required additional surgeries to clean up the new scar tissue. After a while, I realized how insane my situation was. I eventually had a radical hysterectomy. The doctors took everything out and did a biopsy to be sure there weren't any cancer cells. Thankfully, there were not, but this disease put me in a higher category for predisposition.

It's also significant to note that we as women are led to believe that having this procedure will cure endometriosis. It does not. That's the gut-wrenching part! There is no cure for endometriosis. I found this out at my 6-week post-surgical checkup when the doctors had to remove another mass of tissue the size of a golf ball. I was devastated. After all I had gone through, 36 surgeries prior to the hysterectomy and finally making that life altering decision, how was I supposed to feel learning that all the surgery does is slow the disease down?

I was thirty at the time, and that hysterectomy ended up being a tipping point in my life. First, my first marriage was falling apart. Second, I had no help with my children. Third, I was faced with the realization that I might not be able to go back to work. On top of the loss of my female anatomy and my battle with depression, which is a common side effect of losing your main source of estrogen, I now had early full-blown menopause. It was grueling. That caused me to do some serious self-reflection. It was the epitome of the term "life changing."

At this point I told myself that I was going to learn everything I could about my body. I was going to learn what was wrong with me so that I could help myself . So, I went back to school. I began learning about anatomy, function, exercise (which was almost impossible), and changing my diet to an anti-inflammatory one. I got off all the medication that the doctors were giving me to replace my hormones. I started forcing myself to do any exercises I could do. I literally made a complete about-face lifestyle change.

It was through my best friend Kari, who was a massage therapist, that I learned of a therapeutic technique called myofascial release, which naturally gets rid of scar tissue. After having the procedure done on me a few times, I actually started physically getting better. From that point on, I found my passion. I made it my mission to learn everything I could about what worked. I traveled the country, learning these techniques in order to help other women like myself who were being put on hormones or being cut open regularly. I became a sought-after therapist and an educator in the field, and I have been licensed for over eighteen years.

Around the time I divorced, Kevin and I had reconnected after many years. I met up with him for coffee when visiting my daughter in Tennessee while Kevin was visiting his parents in Tennessee as well. We followed up with several more coffee shop visits. We eventually decided that I would move to Tennessee when he retired, and then we would start dating. We did, and we have been inseparable ever since.

Around the time that Kevin and I began dating, I

began to notice that his visits to the doctor oddly re-flected my own experience. Once, I went to see him while he was having an EGD procedure (esophago-gastroduodenoscopy). I already knew that he had asthma. I especially noticed it when he would wheeze when walking any kind of distance. When I asked him about it, he said, "They put me on a desk for the last year [of my military career] because they tried to med board me."

It's true that they did put him on a desk, but I also knew it to be true that he had more than asthma. I would tell him that he shouldn't be that fatigued and wheezing when he wasn't doing anything. I mean, there was absolutely no activity involved that was causing his wheezing, and he wasn't having other al-lergic symptoms. I finally told him that we had to look more in depth at his condition. Something was not right. Thinking of my own health struggles and the fight I had to endure to overcome everything gave me a new purpose to make sure he was heard.

During his EGD, he had to be put under anesthesia. When the doctor was done, he told me that they found tons of little masses in Kevin's esophagus when they only meant to look into his stomach for signs of acid reflux. They were going to send them off to be biop-sied. All of this was new to me; so, I started Googling. We eventually learned that he has Barrett's esophagus, where the esophagus is full of polyps. While the pol-yps aren't cancerous now, they could turn into cancer, because Barrett's esophagus is basically the beginning stages of esophageal cancer. The doctors began cutting and burning out the polyps 20-30 at a time and then doing the biopsies. Kevin had very negative side effects to this approach; so, they slowed it down to every other month. Eventually the doctor learned that the polyps became reactive. Then it was back to the drawing board with what to do for that problem.

When we first started finding out about the extent of Kevin's health problems, he was listening to whatever the doctors were telling him. "It's not cancer; you're fine. It's rare." I wasn't having it; so, after doing some research, I found him a gastroenterologist at Vanderbilt Hospital in Nashville, Tennessee. But because Kevin was retiring from the military and he was under TRICARE, his health care was in the VA. He was put in the VA Choice program because they didn't have a pulmonologist; so, the Vanderbilt doctor worked with them. Of an entire page of problems with Kevin, his nose had a mass that closed off the entire left side of his face. But the VA downplayed it and said it was just polyps. They told him that it wasn't cancerous (even though they never biopsied it) and to take some nose spray, and other things like that. Whenever we challenged the VA, they would downplay the problem. I finally told Kevin that we would find other doctors who would give him proper diagnoses.

Now keep in mind that these diseases that Kevin was being diagnosed with were all rare. They weren't genetic, and they weren't diseases we would consider common. The VA didn't like that. Even though Kevin's issues were technically service connected, we had to fight for that status every inch of the way. The VA didn't make it easy. Even though the procedures were being outsourced by the VA, they stopped paying the Vanderbilt doctor who had been so great to us, and they started sending Kevin to multiple pulmonologists and allergists. Thankfully, at least the respiratory therapist at the VA confirmed that Kevin's respiratory PFT (pulmonary function test) was horrible.

We had a lot going on at the time. We were newly married. Kevin was transitioning out of the military. The VA was downplaying Kevin's health issues, causing us to go outside the VA and pay out of our own pockets to find what was really wrong with him. I was working, and Kevin had gotten a job when he retired. However, the VA wanted their own diagnosis every time we went outside the VA to rationalize their downgrading it. And every time they did a test or procedure on Kevin, he'd end up in the hospital. One month, Kevin had 44 appointments!

After working his job for a couple of months, Kevin had to take a 90-day unpaid leave of absence from HR because he didn't have any more time from FMLA (family and medical leave act). So here we were newly married. I was working and trying to support us, and we didn't have VA support. Things got so tight financially that we literally decided to go back to school to use the rest of Kevin's GI Bill as a way of supporting ourselves. Even then, we spent a lot of money on co-pays.

At the 60-day mark, his boss called him to tell him, "Look, you're either coming back to work now, or I'm gonna let you go."

But Kevin said, "I can't come back to work. I'm supposed to have 30 more days. I still have all these tests to take."

So, his work fired him, which caused a big stink. We ended up calling HR to get that cleared up. But Kevin ended up resigning. After all he had been through, he didn't want to go back to a work environment like that.

All the while, Kevin was getting sicker and sicker. We eventually got a lot of answers with all the things we were doing, but it took a lot of work and a lot of pushing the VA. Every time we pushed back, they pushed back harder. How dare we try to figure out what was really wrong with Kevin? How dare we question their diagnoses? They started calling him "the infamous Kevin Hensley," and that was NOT a term of endearment.

The VA doctors eventually realized that Kevin was really sick, but it took years and a lung biopsy that proved that he has pulmonary fibrosis, Constrictive Bronchiolitis (a terminal lung disease), and scarring of his pulmonary arteries. Another way the doctors initially determined this was by putting him into a group where the members volunteered to be tested.

Because Kevin is a Gulf War veteran, he was being tested for what they called Gulf War Syndrome. There were lots of tests. With the VA being about two and a half hours from our house at the time, that was a lot of back and forth to finally have them determine that, yes, Kevin did have Gulf War Syndrome.

The VA's admission that Kevin has Gulf War Syndrome is one of the reasons that he doesn't have to do any more testing for the burn pit registry, although he did end up getting the biopsy to confirm his pulmonary diagnosis.

Thanks to the passing of the PACT Act into law, Constrictive Bronchiolitis is a covered presumption, but millions of others won't have to bear the burden of proof or the financial cost on their shoulders.

Kevin has lost so much, and he is terminally ill, which is why he has tirelessly given to other veterans by campaigning for their rights. Standing up for himself and others has opened channels for him to meet representatives, senators, and congressmen from the state of Michigan and across the country. They have an incredible respect for him as much as he has for them. The PACT Act means that Kevin no longer has the feelings of failure, hopelessness, or inadequacy. He no longer feels like less of a man because he is sick.

Finding this Burn Pits 360 family and people like Rosie and Le Roy who have taken us under their wings, Tim, Kim, Gina, Joe McKay, and the other advocates has given Kevin back the light in his eyes. He has realized he's not alone in his journey. We are not alone in this fight. We are forever grateful for them.

By honoring the PACT Act, they have given Kevin and veterans like him everything. Most importantly, their voices have been HEARD.

ON ONE PARTICULAR DEPLOYMENT, I
KNEW THAT I WAS SUFFERING FROM
THE FUMES FROM A NEARBY BURN PIT.
I'M SURE THAT WE ALL KNEW IT.
BUT WE DID OUR JOB ANYWAY.

*Militarys Service*

*Theresa*

I OWE MY LIFE TO MY WIFE THERESA.
SHE WORKED ON MY BEHALF WHEN I WAS
AT MY WIT'S END. SHE WOULDN'T LET ME TAKE
IT LYING DOWN. STILL DOESN'T.

THE WORK OF ADVOCACY
IS HARD WORK...

*The Work*

*Together...*

IS HOW WE WON!

OUR DAUGHTER ANNE

ERIC, NIKOLAI (GRANDSON), RACHEL, HAYLEY, AND JORDAN

*My Family*

WE DO THE WORK OF ADVOCACY FOR OTHERS, YES,
BUT ALSO FOR OUR FAMILIES. LEFT TO RIGHT:
HAYLEY, THERESA, AUTUMN, AMBER & KEVIN

LAWRENCE HOUSER JR. U.S. Marine
August 14, 1972-May 22, 2020
Age 47

NATHAN DENRYTER, U.S. Air Force
September 22, 1980 – March 29, 2020
Age 39

TRAVIS OPPERMAN, U.S. Army
March 25, 1988 – June 23, 2019
Age 31

*In Memoriam*

To the families of fallen Michigan Toxic Exposure Veterans

## ACKNOWLEDGEMENTS

I would like to thank all current military personnel (active, guard, and reserves) and their families, as well as all the airmen with whom I had the honor and privilege to serve overseas, stateside, and during deployments. To all veterans and their families. To the Fallen in any category: may we all NEVER forget.

Thank you to Rosie and Le Roy Torres, Founders of Burn Pits 360, and their beautiful family for bringing us all together, for standing up against the injustices of invisible wounds of war, and for fighting on behalf of our nation's veterans and their families.

Special honor and recognition go to the following: my late father-in-law Larry Ray Pounders (United States Navy); my late grandfather Sergio Segura, Sr. (United States Army). To both for their years of sacrifice to our great nation and for allowing me to be a part of their beautiful families.

Special thanks to John Griffith; Ray Lopez; Alvin Bond; James Kruzan; Derek Blumke; Cameron Zibkowski; Brian & Sarah Martin; Kevin & Andy Conklin; Dave Miller; Sarah Anderson; Ben Light; Joe Cobos; Clint Ward; Doug Brinker; Terry Monday, Kimberly Napoleon; Della Steege, and the rest of the VFW family that have supported me on this journey! To Mark Dunlop, MSM of Fort Leonard Wood Survivor Outreach Services (ACS); Michelle Murphy

(LMT) for all of your support, ideas, and encouragement. Thank you to Kevin Burger for being the "other half of the two Kevins" when we started this! And to my dear friend Karla (and Ray) Russell-Thurlow, TAC Auburn Hills, MI and FAC Knoxville Families for your prayers & support.

To the Masters Family (Carole, Bill, Todd, Kim); the Gable Family (Ron, Sue, Sandra, Mark); the Segura Family (Isabel, Jose, Tessy, Lisa, Tony, Ray, Sergio, Rick, Ernie & Phyllis, Renae & Ronnie, Lisa & Jason, Rob & Sandy, Emilio, Antonio, Ryan, and our amazing grandson Nikolai); Mushu; The Hensley Family (Maxine, Frank, Linda, Kim, Ronnie & their extended family); the Ferrier family; the Warwick family; the Skelley Family; the Moran Family; Betty & Shaun Hogan; he Brackett Family; the Puckett Family; Rod & Janice Bullington; the Simkus Family (Mike & Angie, Devyn, David & Lawayne, Joanne & Butch, Joe); the Pounders Family & their extensions; the Nance Family; Ann Rudisill; Mary Combs; Seth Brees; Leon Eggers; Lynette Houser; Kari Keller & Family; Mark & Carrie Opperman; Daniel Meyer; Kim & Tracey Denryter, Erik Pelto; Senator Gary Peters.

Thank you to the senators and congressional delegates who supported the PACT Act. A special thanks to MIchigan Congresswoman Debbie Dingell for all your support; Congresswomen Rashida Tlaib & Elissa Slotkin; Congressman Peter Meijer, John Moolenaar & Jack Bergman; NY Senator Kristen Gillibrand & California Congressman Raul Ruiz for all your hard work, dedication & persistence! To Senators John Tester & Jerry Moran for your support getting this across the finish line!

To all my old brothers & sisters in arms who have reached out or rooted for me throughout this journey and to all our friends, family & colleagues who have been there cheering us on along the way! Thank you for all your support, love, prayers, and encouragement.

Thank you to the family and friends of Nathan Denryter; the family and friends of Travis Opperman; the family and friends of Lawrence Houser; and the family and friends of Robert Wooten.

Thank you to Downriver for Veterans (Wyandotte, MIchigan) and to all Downriver communities. The Veterans of Foreign Wars (VFW), Department of MIchigan. Veterans of Foreign Wars (VFW) Post #1138 City of Monroe, MIchigan. Veterans of Foreign Wars (VFW) Auxiliary members. **Bruce Heinrich-LEADERLimo.com-Kansas City.** Foundation 14 (Milan, MIchigan). Disabled American Veterans (DAV), Chapter 114 (Livonia, MIchigan). American Sportsman for Veterans. Downriver Girl and Friends.

Thank you to CRB Radio 94.7 WCSX, Classic Rock (Big Jim's House); WJR News Talk Radio (Detroit, MIchigan); Fox 2 News (Detroit, MIchigan); Fox 17 (Grand Rapids, MIchigan); WILX 10 (Lansing, MIchigan); and WLUX 6 (Upper MIchigan).

Thank you to MIchigan Veterans Affairs Agency (MVAA); Genesee County-Department of Veterans

Services; Veterans with Constrictive Bronchiolitis (CB); Aaron McCoy of Humana (Cleveland, Ohio); United Autoworkers (UAW) Veterans Conference; American Legion. Reserve Organization of America (ROA); Military Officers Association of America (MOAA); Tragedy Assistance Program for Survivors (TAPs); Warrior Hope Network; Veterans In Pain (VIP); Project Sanctuary (PTSD Retreat); and Debbie Taylor and Roger L. Taylor of Memorial Motorcycle Ride (throughout MIchigan).

Thank you to Doctor Carol Henricks of NorthStar Neurology and NorthStar Hyperbaric (Tucson, AZ); Doctor Robert Miller of Hillsboro Medical Group at Vanderbilt University (Nashville, TN); and Suzi Miller, LPC-MHSP of Knoxville, Tennessee.

Thank you to The Congregational Church of Summerfield, Florida; First Congregational Church of Clarkston, MIchigan; and First Baptist Church of Tellico Village (Loudon, Tennessee).

Thank you to Derek Blumke, who deserves special recognition for his hard work, selflessness, and dedication to veterans.

Thank you to all those who prayed, supported, donated, and helped us along the way to get answers to our medical conditions that other agencies refused to acknowledge.

And a final thanks to the people who called, e-mailed, and/or wrote letters to senators and congressional delegates to help us get the Honoring Our PACT Act of 2022 signed into law. We thank you all so very much.

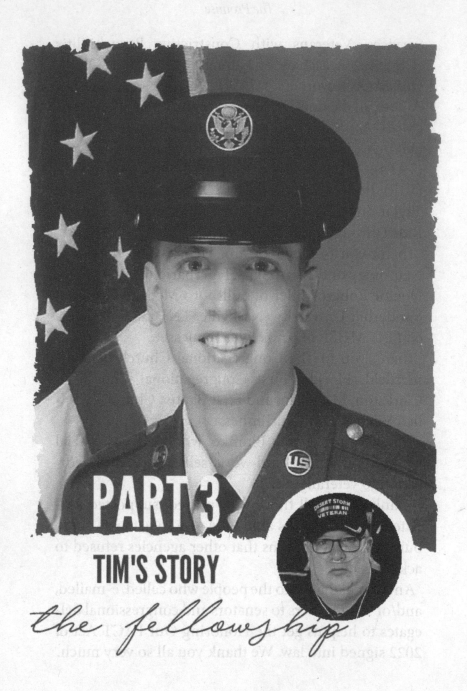

# PART 3
## TIM'S STORY
*the fellowship*

# DEDICATION

*I dedicate the following chapters
to my wife, Marcy, and my son Zakhar.
The sacrifices you have made so that I
could advocate went beyond all my expectations.*

*To my mother, Mae, who is one
of the strongest women I know.*

*To my brothers, Ray, Kevin, and Greg,
and my sister Sue.*

*To my mother-in-law Carolyn,
brother-in-law Doug, his wife Heather,
and their kids: your support
means the world to me.*

*Also, a special dedication
to my brother Dennis,
one of the 22 veterans a day who
take their lives, which Dennis did
on a cold and snowy Christmas Eve.*

INTRODUCTION

# Medical Gaslighting:
## Agent Orange, Opiods & Other Substances That Are Perfectly Safe

The psychological term "gaslighting" comes from the 1944 film, Gaslight. In it, a woman who doesn't know she's married to a murderer starts to believe she's going crazy because the murderer makes her think so. He needs his wife to believe she's crazy so that he can find the jewels he committed murder to possess, which are hidden in their attic. When he's looking for the jewels in the attic, she hears footsteps and sees the lights, powered by natural gas, dimming. But he has an explanation for everything she sees and hears.

American Warfighters have received the same kind of treatment from the Veterans Administration for decades. They experienced symptoms with no other cause than their exposure to toxins in burn pits. They had no family history, no change in lifestyle, and no other poisons in their environments – not to this degree.

They could go to their garages or local hardware stores and see warning labels on paint, paint thinners, and other construction equipment. They could go to their medicine cabinets and read warning labels on medicines. When they lived their daily lives, they could see warning labels everywhere: on cleaners, fuel, pillows and mattresses, and the silica gel packets in pairs of new shoes.

Those labels warned the user of potential hazards to the substances they covered. There were specific ways to use those products and certain ways to dispose of them. Those ways were absolutely not by burning them.

Yet Warfighters reading those labels had uncomfortable memories of doing just that: disposing of construction materials, human waste, body parts, and expired medications by burning them. And they didn't just set the fire and run. They stayed there, stirred the mess, and breathed in all those toxins for months at a time.

When their bodies started responding to toxins in predictable ways, veterans were told there was no connection between breathing poison and getting sick with cancer or respiratory disease. The VA told Kevin that he had asthma and handed him an inhaler. They told Kim's husband Gary that he had acid reflux and gave him some pills. They told Tim they had no idea why his lungs were so damaged and refused to pay for his care. And by the time Gina's husband Joe got to the VA, he didn't have time to discuss treatment. He only had time to ask about benefits for the woman who would soon become his widow.

The VA denied 80 percent of the claims filed by burn pit victims for lack of scientific evidence. Scientific evidence, of course, would have required official records of precisely what was burned, in what amounts, and with which accelerants under observable and repeatable conditions. The whole point of burn pits was to get rid of unwanted material, not to study it. The military and the private contractors it hired were trying to save money, not spend extra to keep more records that would have to be burned.

The Defense Department did pay for responsible waste removal. Some burn pits smoldered away right next to unused environmentally safe incinerators. Warfighters were told different stories about those incinerators. They were too expensive to operate. They were inconvenient or ineffective. Warfighters were mostly meant to leave them alone and light a burn pit.

Who were they to object or to disagree? Good Warfighters followed orders, and these men were good Warfighters. When they were told that the burn pits were perfectly safe, that they didn't need gas masks, they lit the pit. That mindset followed them far past the burn pits to the examination rooms at VA clinics back home.

Any Warfighters who need care will almost certainly end up in an examination room with a government representative who outranks them. VA doctors often passively exercise an imbalance of power because of their rank, their education, and their position as representatives of the United States government. Basic training in every branch of the military teaches Warfighters to obey authority without question, as an instinct. You can't fight wars effectively with people who don't learn that lesson well.

Few civilians understand the extent of that training on the psyche of a person who has served. Civilians can bring independent research to a medical professional, someone they often see as a type of friend. They can question their care and confide their worries and problems, confident that their doctor has their best interests in mind.

A VA doctor cannot behave the same way, and a servicemember cannot see that doctor the same way. Besides the question of authority, there is also the question of ulterior motives. All areas of government face constant pressure to meet budget restrictions. The VA also seems to have an unholy alliance with the pharmaceutical industry, as evidenced by the wide distribution of opioids and benzodiazepines to treat PTSD, depression, anxiety, and sleep issues, despite their widespread side effects – including suicide ideation.

The prospect is grim.

And this is not the first war in which veterans suffered this kind of gaslighting. Vietnam veterans told to spray lush, tropical vegetation with Agent Orange began to suffer the terrible effects of exposure to poisons after they returned home. VA doctors told them that Agent Orange couldn't have hurt them, that it was perfectly safe, and that their debilitating and excruciating health problems were due to some other cause.

With such a track record, how could Gulf War and War on Terror veterans expect any other answer?

What other avenue could they pursue than telling the exact truth repeatedly to representatives of a government that was unwilling to hear them? In those examination rooms, each veteran was alone.

In Gaslight, the wife's situation seems pretty hopeless until she finds a friend. Someone sees the same evidence she does, believes her, and acts with her and on her behalf to stop the lies and the manipulation. Tim Hauser can relate.

Of the four friends in this book, Tim suffered the earliest exposure to toxins in burn pits. The smoke he inhaled during Desert Storm injured his lungs in 1992, ten years before American troops set foot in Iraq and Afghanistan. So, Tim suffered medical gaslighting for the longest time.

The gap between what Tim knew and what the VA told him left him stranded in a life where his lungs wouldn't allow him to work or live as he wanted. He had no help bearing the consequences of that inability. Because the VA would not own up to the dangers of practices the EPA had already deemed unsafe for American citizens, Tim lost work, joy, and independence.

What made the difference? Just like in the movie, Tim found people who believed him. These people saw the same evidence, came to the same conclusions, and offered him hope that he could end the manipulation.

His new friends could see the same things partly because they all had the same brand of common sense.

They all came from the middle class, from families with some kind of religious framework that taught their children right from wrong. They all learned early the value of working hard. They all believed military service was an honor beyond its benefits as a career or a path to financial security. They thought that America was good and worth defending. They expected the government to deal fairly with its citizens and defenders.

When they experienced gaslighting from the government they respected and served, they went to work to correct that gaslighting. And they could only accomplish the kind of broad, sweeping corrections necessary by working together.

The tragedy of lost health and lost lives bonded them beyond friendship into a family. Their children call their other friends aunts and uncles. They pick up each other's phone calls and talk to each other through grief, pain, and bad days. They trust each other.

One reason for that trust is that they've all seen each other fight. Someone can agree with you intellectually, but you gain respect when that person dares to tell an uncomfortable truth to an influential person on your behalf. Each member of this group of friends has won that kind of respect. All have paid travel expenses from their own pockets to speak that truth. Each one knows that the others will show up in a fight.

For people who have lost so much in their lives through no fault of their own, the gift of friendship like that is irreplaceable.

## CHAPTER 1

# *Beginnings*

Growing up, I had four older brothers and a younger sister. We were all born in Newark, New Jersey but raised in Ohio. My dad invented a ball bearing used by auto manufacturers. The company transferred our family to Ohio, where it would be made. We moved when I was three.

My brothers were older than I was. I remember always wanting to hang out with them, but I couldn't because I was too young. Growing up on the shores of Lake Erie was fantastic. I went fishing or boating almost every day.

Lake Erie is one of the Great Lakes, and it's big, especially for a kid. With the sand beach, it seemed just like an ocean. My family spent a lot of time there. Because the beach was on the other side of town, my family would drive, but as I got older, I rode my bike.

I had a happy, active childhood. Of course, I was teased at every school I went to because my mom was the lunch lady. That made it a little bit harder with the other students.

But I had friends, and I joined different activities in

high school. I was on the cross-country team and the track team. I was in art club. I was also the president of the photography club. Those interests stayed with me as I grew. I continue doing art and photography today, intertwining them as therapy for myself.

Toward the end of high school, I had a hard time deciding whether or not I wanted to go to college. I thought about attending the Art Institute of Pittsburgh, but I couldn't afford it.

My parents couldn't afford to pay for college for me, either. My dad told me, "No way are you taking out loans to go to school." This was long before the student loan crisis. Many parents felt their kids should go ahead and take the loans, assuming they would pay off in the end. My dad wasn't like that. Having six kids, you've got to be practical, and he was.

I couldn't even afford the local community college in town. Work was another option. My town was nice, but as far as employment opportunities go, it was limited to restaurant work, and I didn't want to become a cook.

Three of my brothers had joined the Air Force. My brother Ray served in the Air Force until he got injured. He was medically discharged before I went into high school. My brother Dennis and my brother Greg talked to me about the opportunities in the Air Force, such as being able to go to school while you're serving. My brother Dennis was the most significant influence on my joining the Air Force. He served in Desert Storm and Vietnam before retiring.

After talking with my older brothers, I figured the military may be the route for me. I told my dad, "I want to join the Marines." But he and Mom wouldn't have anything to do with that. They had two sons who had already served in Vietnam and had heard horror stories of what happened to people in the Army and the Marines.

My dad said, "You're joining the Air Force if you're going into the military." Because I enlisted when I was 17, they had to sign for me to join. I enlisted before graduation and entered the Air Force a few weeks later, in June of 1982.

Enlisting made me more aware of my surroundings because I had to ensure that I didn't get into trouble or get injured. I learned to care for myself during those last weeks of high school. I knew that there were consequences for my actions.

Five days after graduating high school, I went to boot camp. My family threw a little party to say goodbye. My brothers were already married, had kids, and lived in different places. My sister was still in high school. But the family came together for that party, and off I went.

Boot camp happened that June in Texas. My brother Greg, who had been through boot camp four years before, gave me some tips. With his encouragement, basic training was not hard for me. I was already in good physical condition because track season had just ended five days before.

The hardest parts were the classes, maybe seven classes every day. Much of the information we learned was more than what I did in high school. The Air Force intertwined physical training (PT) and education. In the morning, I would do PT and take basic classes. Then I'd do some more PT. Finally, I'd have some more challenging courses. They made sure nobody was ever overwhelmed.

When I finished boot camp, I started training as a nuclear missile technician in Denver, Colorado. But while I was in school, I found that the training I was getting was a little bit too much for me to handle; so, I asked if I could transfer to a different career. They agreed.

I became a supply troop or a warehouse worker, and that's how I spent the rest of my career. I got all my training on site for that job, not at school. I was transferred to my first real base, where I started my training, in Blytheville, Arkansas, just underneath the boot heel of Missouri, right on the Mississippi River. It was cornfields, Baptist churches, no alcohol, and very, very humid weather. It seemed like every other building was a Baptist church. That was a culture shock for me.

The other airmen and I kept busy. There were lakes; so, we'd go fishing, boating, and swimming. And they had a good sports program on base. On all military bases, they have intramural sports. Squadrons compete against each other all the time.

I was in Arkansas for two years before I was sent to Kadena Air Base in Okinawa, Japan. That was also a culture shock, but I kept very busy. Japan was probably the best place I've ever been to, as far as my military career goes.

I traveled around to learn the history. We had excursions and some adventures with the local Japanese military. We would hunt for artifacts from World War II and recover them so they could be restored. We looked for everything from helmets and guns to airplane and boat parts.

My brother Dennis was stationed there when I was, and we reconnected. Since he was in the military while I was growing up, I didn't see much of him. I was glad we could spend some time together while I was in Japan.

He, his wife, his two kids, and I would go on little adventures, visiting historical art and monuments throughout the island. We also enjoyed going to the beach. The Japanese beaches were beautiful. They had crystal clear water. You could walk on the sand without your feet getting burned. The weather was in the high 70s and low 80s every day.

In between all the fun, I was doing my job in supply. That involved receiving all the new material, making sure it got to the proper warehouses and stored correctly, and sending it out to the squadrons that needed it on time. I helped keep the inventory so that we never ran out of anything. I was out and about a lot. I was doing a lot of manual labor.

I left Okinawa in 1985 and went to George Air Force Base in Southern California, another culture shock. We were in the desert, just on the other side of the mountains from San Bernardino. I didn't like California much because of the earthquakes. Earthquakes are a huge fear of mine.

In 1989, I was supposed to go to the World Series game in San Francisco when a huge earthquake hit. San Francisco is in the northern part of California, while I was in the southern part. I was delayed heading north to the game, and my friends were already in the stadium. I saw the quake on the news, and I knew they would say, "Hey, don't come up. It's a disaster up here." I was at work in a warehouse, and we didn't feel much where we were.

Another earthquake hit years later, right before I separated from the Air Force. That's when we had the earthquake in Big Bear that was 8.0 in Yucca Valley. I was in my dorm room during that quake, asleep when it hit very early in the morning.

We were trained on responding to earthquakes, but that training went out the window when the tremors threw me across the room. I left my dorm room on the third floor and went to the stairs outside; there was no inside stairwell and no elevator. As I was getting ready to take a step down, I noticed that the stairs had pulled away from the building by about three feet. I stepped back and closed the door. I was stuck.

I pulled a mattress from a bed over on top of me in case an aftershock came or in case the ceiling caved in on me. I stayed in my room until the rescue team arrived to get us out of the building.

The crew set up ladders from the third floor to the

ground. These were like firefighting ladders, just great tall things. And we had to climb down them!

I stayed in California from 1985 to 1992, right after the Gulf War. I was deployed to the Gulf to join Desert Storm in May 1991. I was at King Abdulaziz Air Base, Saudi Arabia. This was the first time I was ever around a burn pit.

When I arrived, the Saudi Arabians wanted to reclaim the town we used as an airbase. A building, a new supply depot, and other structures had just been built when I arrived. I was told I would be working the night shift.

The burn pit started out about the size of a football field. By the time it was done, it was the size of six or seven football fields. It was about one hundred yards behind our supply depot, where I worked every day. At first, it was mostly full of construction garbage. Soon, other items were thrown into the burn pit. I noticed that the Marines had put a couple of Humvees in the pit. Our civil engineering squadron dumped paint, paint thinners, and other chemicals.

At that time, I noticed they were bringing dump trucks full of body parts straight from Kuwait. They were trying to clean up Kuwait because their burn pit was full, and they were bringing body parts up to us because we were the closest base. From what I understood, Kuwait's burn pit was already huge, about ten football fields. They also brought dump trucks full of waste up to our base.

When I took the garbage out to the pit, the guys

there doused it down with diesel fuel instead of jet fuel. Then they asked me if I wanted to light it. I said, "Yeah, sure. Why not?" You know, it would give me something to do. They gave me a flare. I lit the flare, and then I threw the flare onto the pile.

Where I was stationed, we didn't have a tent city. The Saudi Arabians built what they called Khobar Towers. These were huge apartment complexes, and the apartments inside were humongous. Palestinian refugees were moved out of the towers so we could be housed there. Several years later, I learned that the building I lived in had been bombed.

From the day I got there, the oil well fires in Iraq were burning. They kept telling us it was fog. But we could tell it wasn't because we were wiping oil off our skin. And you could smell it. Fog usually has no odor. So even before I understood the risks of the burn pits, I was exposed to the oil fires. That smoke was constantly blowing 24 hours a day, seven days a week. At Khobar Towers, on base, everywhere we went, it was hazy and foggy all the time. And it stank.

To be told that it was fog was obvious gaslighting. Looking back on it, I am extremely angry knowing that we were committed to doing our jobs, yet they lied to us. I mean, you expect some lies here and there for security reasons. I'd see specific types of aircraft land that generally were not supposed to be there. Then I'd hear stories like, "Oh, they were just refueling."

At the time, I thought, "I know that's not fog. Why

are they lying to us?" Everybody was saying, "Yeah, this isn't fog." It was only later when I started to get sick that I felt resentment. But while I was there, I concentrated on doing my job.

## CHAPTER 2

# *Lost Soul*

I came back from Saudi Arabia around April 1992. When I returned, I took some time off and went home to visit my parents. After returning to California, I went back to work on the base.

The time came for the annual physical fitness test. Part of the test was a two-and-a-half-mile run. As a former runner, I never had any problem finishing the two and a half miles. I'd always been one of the fastest runners in whatever squadron I was in. The guys in my unit were betting on how fast I would finish.

But this time, I couldn't finish. I failed. It was the first time ever. I lasted about a mile. After a mile, I couldn't breathe. This was a month after I returned and before I separated from the Air Force.

Everybody knew something was wrong by the way my body reacted. Doing my regular job in the warehouse, I got tired easily. I thought it was just exhaustion from long hours of duty over in Desert Storm. But I knew something was wrong when I couldn't finish the run.

In 1994, I started seeing doctors to figure out what

was happening. I filled out the health histories. I had no family history of lung problems. I smoked a little while in the military, but it had never affected my run times before.

At first, the doctors didn't know what was causing my exhaustion and breathing issues. They eventually noticed that the two bottom lobes of my lungs weren't functioning. They decided to scope them to get a biopsy of each of those lobes.

When I woke up from the procedure, the doctors said that my lungs were solid. They were so solid they couldn't get any samples. They said that there was no way smoking cigarettes would cause that kind of damage.

After that procedure, when I was in the doctor's office going over the results, the doctor finally said, "By chance, were you over in the war?"

I told him yes.

He said, "Well, my brother has the same symptoms as you. He was in Kuwait and came back about the same time you did."

I started bringing up pictures I had taken in Saudi Arabia. I could see the smoke and fumes in them. The other airmen and I were breathing in fumes from the oil well fires daily. We also had that burn pit. To figure out why my health had failed so rapidly was just a case of putting two and two together.

That's when I got into the VA system. The very first claim I put in was denied. I started doing more research. I had already built up a lot of medical bills, and that's when I learned that the VA is not free. You must pay them, just like the regular hospital.

Emotionally, I started to become depressed because I couldn't do the things that I loved to do anymore, or at least not in the capacity I used to. Running was no longer an option. My body was starting to break down. I was in physical pain over my entire body and was sick often.

My dad drove me all over the state to different hospitals for tests, just trying to figure out what was happening. Another doctor I saw in the VA said, "We now have the Desert Storm clinic. We need to send you there."

Again, my dad drove me to that clinic. I was there all day getting tests. One doctor said, "All right, we're trying to figure out what's making you guys so sick."

I told him, "I already know. We were breathing in that crap from the oil fires and the burn pits all day long."

He said, "No, we know it wasn't from that. That doesn't make you sick. We're trying to see if you guys were exposed to chemical weapons. But it doesn't look like you were. We have no clue what's making you guys sick."

At that VA Desert Storm clinic, there must have been 100 men and women going through the same testing as I was, and the service members in the waiting room were all saying the same thing. It was oil fires. It was burn pits. One guy there said, "Yeah, we blew up a depot full of sarin gas. It's got to be part of that, too." But the doctor kept saying that none of what we went through was causing this illness.

While my friends and I were advocating for the PACT Act, the news reported that we were exposed to sarin gas, which you know is a deadly nerve toxin. If the combination of diesel fumes, oil smoke, human ashes, toxic chemical fumes, and garbage wasn't enough, we were exposed to sarin gas.

At the time I was being tested, I started to pass out frequently. It was hard for me to find jobs that weren't physical, like working in an auto factory. Without a college degree, these jobs were hard to find. I worked as an unloader at Walmart, where I physically unloaded the delivery trucks every night. That was difficult. I was a landscaper for a while at Cedar Point, which was too physical for me. My health constantly cost me jobs and relationships.

Through this hard time, people would say, "He's just lazy. He doesn't want to work." That wasn't true. I was trying everything I could. It wasn't will; it was ability. And it was hard to lose so much.

I lived with my parents for a while. Because I was so far in debt, the only way to get out of it was to move back in with them. Almost all my debt was medical debt. What wasn't medical debt was living expenses from times when I couldn't work because of my breathing.

I tried to cope. I kept going to the doctors and trying to figure out what was going on with me. My depression was really, really bad. I wasn't the only one. Several years passed, and my brother Dennis retired about the same time I separated. He moved back to Ohio, too. He was fighting demons so dark that he ended up committing suicide. I was fighting what was going on with my depression and trying to keep from doing the same thing he did. It wouldn't be fair to my parents to have two veteran sons who killed themselves.

I worked. I would take a job even though I knew I physically couldn't handle it. I would have to take what I could because I needed the money. I ended up bouncing from job to job for a while. And then, I moved to Akron about 15 years ago, where I got a job as a bill collector. I was sitting behind a desk, and that was working out.

Art was one way I coped. I've always been artistic since I was a little kid. Even before kindergarten, I wasn't doing your typical stick figures. I was drawing and painting more complex stuff. I must have been around ten, perhaps a little younger, when I told my parents I wanted to try photography, too. So, I've been doing photography, painting, and drawing my whole life. I lost doing that while I was in the Air Force.

One day, I was sitting on my computer in my parents' house, and I was just down. I was searching online when something about photography popped up. And I thought, "Wait a minute. I haven't done that in quite a while. I should try doing that again."

That day, I bought a camera and a couple of lenses and started taking pictures. That helped improve my mood quite a bit. Several years later, I thought, "You know, I don't draw or paint anymore." So, I started painting again, which helped put a lot of things in perspective.

As I was painting, I could see images from my nightmares unfolding in front of me on the canvas. That's when I knew. I said to myself, "Yeah, I need to keep doing all this. This is helping me with my depression and my morale."

Much later, I started a YouTube channel to show how I paint. The videos included information about burn pits, PTSD, and veteran suicide. But the focus of my painting was abstractly communicating feelings and experiences.

With my photography, when I take pictures of flowers, the flower is not perfect. There's always a petal missing, or it's crushed a little bit. There's some sort of flaw to that flower. I focus on that as part of the beauty of the flower.

Though my photography used to be natural landscapes, I can't go hiking anymore. I'm now transitioning to macro photography. Macro photography is the extreme close-up shot where you zoom in on the eyes of a fish or the details in a drop of water.

All my paintings are abstract. When I paint, I don't like painting something that looks realistic because I'm already doing that with photography. If I have a nightmare, that dream is going to take over the thought process of my painting. I take the ugliness of that dream, and as I'm putting it on canvas, I'm adding beauty to it because the dream is not perfect. I'm transforming it. Even though the dream was scary and brought me back to a dark place, there's still some beauty to it because I can overcome the pain and difficulty. The art has kept me going and has helped me process my feelings.

Meeting Marcy and her son Zakhar saved my life. I had just gotten out of a relationship and bought a home. And I thought, "I don't know anybody, really." So, I started posting online on a few dating sites, saying, "Hey, I'm just looking for a friend to hang out with."

Marcy responded, and she and I started chatting. Then we moved to texting and calling. Finally, we both said, "How about we just meet?" We were both under the impression that we would just be friends and hang out.

Our first meeting was at Panera Bread in Macedonia, Ohio. We shared a bagel. The first time we met, I came straight out and told her, "Look, I have lung issues. There are times when I can't breathe. I sometimes end up in the hospital, and I've had some other health issues. It's probably associated with that. I also have PTSD, and I have flashbacks and nightmares. If this is something you don't think you can handle, by all means, go ahead and let me know. We can still chat and talk and whatever. But as far as moving on with any other type of relationship, I think you needed to know this first, even though we were just going to be friends."

And she said, "I can handle that."

So that answer alone already had Marcy on a pedestal even before she knew it. I thought, "This is some-body who is special." Even though we thought we would only be friends just hanging out, I already knew it would be more. Several months passed, with us go-ing on dates and hanging out before we both just fell in love with each other.

We were married in September 2020, during the pan-demic's craziness. COVID was rough. I'd be careful about being around people and about where I went. I didn't leave the house much. When I did, Marcy made sure I was well protected. I got vaccinated the first chance I had and got the boosters, too.

Because the VA has me listed as critical, I take a COVID test every time I go into the hospital. The vi-rus is one of the reasons I drive to Washington, D.C., instead of flying. Right after I got the oxygen concen-trator, I flew on an airplane. To me, at that time, it was scary. People took their masks off during the flight. I didn't know who had been vaccinated and who hadn't, and I was worried someone would say they tested neg-ative when they were actually positive.

Getting married during the pandemic, Marcy and I had to think about all that. We almost postponed the wedding because of COVID. But then we thought, "Well, we can do it outside. We'll be fine." We kept it small, and people wore masks. And not one person got sick from our wedding.

I did recently just contract COVID despite the pre-cautions I take. It was terrifying and severe. Marcy drove me to the ER, and the doctor who saw me already knew my history.

He said, "We're going to give you this experimental drug. It seems to work very well and very quickly. We're not going to hospitalize you now. If you do get worse, of course, come in. But right now, your breathing isn't bad enough that I need to hospitalize you."

I got the medication, and Marcy and I came home. For three days, all I did was sleep. Marcy would come in to make sure I was still breathing and bring me fluids and food. I didn't have an appetite. I lost my sense of taste. I had already lost my sense of smell from Desert Storm. I haven't been able to smell for 30 years.

I ended up being hospitalized for several days due to that COVID infection. For three days I was in the COVID ICU. It was very scary. Again, Marcy was not allowed to visit. But I pulled through and finished recovering at home.

Marcy is just great, and not only in emergencies like COVID. She always knows when I'm going into a dark place. She just knows when I'm down, and she's able to lift me up. With PTSD, sometimes my high points get out of control. She's able to keep me grounded.

Practically, she is my caregiver when I have flare-ups. Those are usually bad. I can't breathe. My blood pressure drops to where I almost pass out. I get disoriented. When that happens, I typically end up in the hospital. When I come home, a lot of times, I'm still not back to 100% yet. She takes care of me and makes sure I take my meds.

Sometimes the flare-up isn't bad enough for me to go

to the hospital, but it's bad enough that I'm unable to work. For instance, when I'm doing yard work, she'll say, "Okay, you're overdoing it. You need to take a break and go inside. Lie down for about an hour or two. Don't worry about this outside." She's got to be on the ball 100% of the time.

## CHAPTER 3

# *Full Circle*

While going through all the health and job issues for so many years, I was trying to rally people with me, people who were going to the clinics at the same time I was. I would say, "Hey, we need to let them know that this is definitely from burn pits and oil well fires." But I couldn't get any other veterans to help.

They were going through the same hardships as I was—losing jobs, becoming financially unstable, and going through depression. They just wanted to find out what was wrong with them and fix it. They didn't want to bring up anything controversial about how the government lied to us. They didn't want to buck the system, and I couldn't find any groups at the time who were working on this issue. Social media was new, and I couldn't find anyone organizing there. Speaking out and not being heard was contributing to my depression. For a while, I quit trying to get anyone to listen.

I continued filing claims and continued getting denied by the VA. I finally got my service connection benefits two years ago, twenty-eight years after I separated from the military. When I got that letter from the VA saying that my claim was finally approved, I looked at Marcy and said, "I know my fight's not over. It's time to help everybody else."

What finally turned the tide in my favor was when I received a diagnosis of constrictive bronchiolitis. Those were the magic words.

I was never diagnosed with constrictive bronchiolitis before. I was always diagnosed with something else. I was misdiagnosed a lot. Sometimes it felt like every new doctor I met would give me a different diagnosis.

I could not get a Gulf War Syndrome diagnosis because it's supposed to be a mystery illness where doctors can't even diagnose you with anything. But many veterans and I were diagnosed with lung scarring. Many were developing cancers. We were being diagnosed, which meant we were not eligible for benefits based on Gulf War Syndrome.

Shortly after I got my service connection, I started posting on social media more about being exposed to burn pits and oil well fires. Kevin Hensley messaged me through Facebook and said, "Dude, call me. This will change your life." Then he sent his phone number. He didn't tell me what he wanted to talk about or anything. I didn't know who he was at all.

But my wife, Marcy, said, "What's he going to do, stalk you? Give him a call."

I called, and Kevin told me he was part of an organization called Burn Pits 360. He explained what the organization was all about and told me about the advocacy work they were doing. Then Kevin asked me if I wanted to become a member.

My first response was, "Well, how much will it cost me?"

He said, "Well if you join us in Washington, D.C., all the travel expenses come out of your pocket."

Kevin told me they went to Washington, D.C. a lot to talk to congressmen and senators trying to pass this bill. He told me I'd probably tell my story or give speeches sometimes. I've given more than a few speeches in different settings, that's for sure. He told me, "Be prepared. You might get a phone call at like nine o'clock at night saying that you are needed in D.C. by 8:00 AM the next morning. Would you be able to do that?"

Yes, of course, I'd be able to do that. I'd been wanting to be in this fight for 30 years.

He gave me the numbers of the bills before Congress and told me how I could look them up online. I read through everything and thought, "Man, this is what we needed 30 years ago."

Before our first phone call finished, I told Kevin that yes, most definitely, I wanted in. The next thing I knew, the phone was ringing with calls from other members of Burn Pits 360. They wanted to meet me and hear my story so that they could start putting out some press releases. That was when I discovered I was the only Desert Storm veteran in the group. For 30 years, I couldn't get other Desert Storm vets to talk. Now I had a chance to be their voice and be heard.

Connecting with Burn Pits 360 and having people believe me greatly boosted me. My morale improved. The members embraced me. They are a very welcoming group. One of the individuals who called me was Wesley Black, who said he was looking forward to meeting me.

Unfortunately, the next time they all went to D.C., I could not go because I did not have portable oxygen at the time. The VA only gives you tanks, and you can't fly on an airplane with the tanks. To drive there, I would have to pack 20 to 25 tanks just to be on the safe side and make sure I had enough oxygen. Since I was only given 18 tanks per month and relied on a large, non-portable oxygen concentrator at home, travel was not possible.

My wife and I decided that I would not be able to go until there were other options for me to travel. Unfortunately, that was Wesley Black's last trip to Washington, D.C. He passed away shortly thereafter. I never got to meet him.

I finally got a portable oxygen concentrator about a year ago from Joe McKay, a New York fireman. He worked at Ground Zero on 9/11. I had no idea that he was part of Burn Pits 360 or that he knew what I needed. This concentrator appeared in the mail with a note saying, "Hey, I'm loaning this to you; keep it as long as you need it. I have another one. This way, you can go to Washington D.C. with us. You can travel; you can help us advocate."

The first time I went to Washington D.C. was when

the Senate Veterans Affairs Committee held hearings on the Honoring our PACT Act that had just passed in the House. The Senate had just passed a different version that was not as comprehensive. We visited several senators' offices explaining why we needed to pass the Honoring our PACT Act, not the one they had just passed.

That was also the trip where I met John Feal and Jon Stewart for the first time. I had been on several conference calls with them, but I never got to talk to them until then. We all went into the hearing together.

The committee interviewed the Secretary of the VA, McDonough, who was sitting at a table. All the senators came in and found their places for the hearing. I was sitting two rows behind the VA Secretary. I was also sitting next to a few other members of Burn Pits 360 who were from Ohio. They already knew Senator Sherrod Brown. He came up to say hello to them, introduced himself to me, and asked me to tell him my story.

I told him the short version of my story, and he asked, "How long did it take you to get any benefits?"

I said, "It took me 25 years."

And he said, "Holy cow! That's just not right."

The hearing started, and Senator Brown went to his seat. During Senator Brown's time to talk, he turned to the VA Secretary and said, "Mr. Secretary, I'd like you to turn around and meet Tim Hauser, a constituent of mine who was in Desert Storm. It took him 25 years to get his service connection for his toxic exposure from burn pits."

Secretary McDonough turned around, saw me, and turned right back around to face Sherrod Brown. My wife was watching the hearing live on TV on C-Span, and she texted me at the same time. She could only see from my shoulders down; she couldn't see my face. But she texted me that I must have had my bitch face on because he turned around so quickly. That was pretty much right. I felt a lot of anger.

Afterward, the organizers let me say a few words at the press conference. That was meaningful. It was also therapeutic meeting the senators, explaining why this bill would have helped me 30 years ago, and convincing them why it's needed today.

For once, I was being heard—not just heard but listened to. That helped my morale tremendously. Even when the Senate didn't pass the bill the second time they voted on it, getting my story out to the public was a huge source of healing for me. It was like redemption.

For so long, the VA told me that my illness was all in my head. I was just lazy, or I was disgruntled. It was meaningful to me that media from other countries asked, "Can you tell us exactly what you went through so that our readers and viewers will know why this bill is important?" To be able to do that and know my voice was important was highly therapeutic.

During his confirmation hearing in 2021, the current VA secretary said, "I will work tirelessly to build and restore the VA's trust as the premier agency for ensuring the wellbeing of America's veterans. After all, there is no more sacred obligation or noble undertaking than to uphold our promises to our veterans, whether they came home decades ago, or days ago."

I felt like he was talking through his teeth at the time because later he told us that there was no scientific proof that burn pits were making us sick. By then, my trust in the VA was already gone. Even before he made that statement, veterans were at the point of needing action, not words, to regain any trust.

He was probably the most qualified VA Secretary in recent history. But it was the VA's mode of operation to withhold service connection because when you get your service connection, you also get compensation. They didn't want to give out that money.

That's what it boils down to, because even a VA Secretary will tell you that smoking cigarettes will kill you. We have all watched Breaking Bad, right? All the chemicals that go into making meth were in these burn pits. The paint thinners, the antihistamines, the acetone, the expired cold medicines that the hospital threw in—all those chemicals were in those burn pits. Walt and Jesse wore gas masks the entire time they were messing with that concoction. We were not. So, the VA had scientific proof. They just didn't want to pay us.

As my speaking engagements increased, I started bringing up other beneficial points about the bill that weren't being talked about, like finances. I had been strapped. I filed for bankruptcy twice. Veterans continued to be weighed down with medical debt, trying to get the health care they needed.

The VA charged them for care. Private health insurers have dropped veterans because they paid out too much for the huge medical needs of sick and dying veterans. These veterans have to make a decision. "Do I pay the rent? Or do I buy my prescriptions?" They lose their homes if they want to live and choose their medications. Another benefit of this bill is helping to keep veterans from becoming homeless because they won't have to choose between prescriptions and their house payments. Their prescriptions will be covered.

Suppose they decide to pay the rent instead of buying the medicine. In that case, they may start to rely on alcohol and illegal drugs, which are cheaper than prescription drugs. They may end up becoming addicts. This bill will help stop that from happening, too, by paying for the health care veterans have earned and deserve.

Finally, this bill is giving veterans hope. It gives them dignity. They won't be driven to hopelessness and desperation. I believe this bill is going to help reduce veteran suicide.

After the Senate voted our bill down the second time, Jon Stewart gave a moving speech. You can hear me yelling about veteran suicide during that speech. Later that day, we were in the Senate offices together, and he said, "Hey, you're from Ohio, right?"

I told him that yes, I was. And he said, "Portman's office is just down the hall. Let's go down there and raise some hell."

Rob Portman is my state senator from Ohio and has been since 2011. I had heard what Senator Portman said to the Burn Pits 360 advocates when I could not be there. He said that there weren't enough Ohioans sick from burn pits for him to care about the issue. So, I told Jon Stewart, "Yeah, let's go!" And off we went.

As we walked, I started apologizing to him for yelling during his speech. But he said, "No, no problem. It was fantastic. They needed to hear that."

After we spoke to Senator Portman's office and videos got out of that interaction, he changed his stance on the bill. His statements have changed. But I believe that he still would have voted no if I hadn't spoken out.

Passing the PACT Act will make a difference not just for all veterans but also for me personally. I continue to be diagnosed with new illnesses now considered secondary due to complications from my burn pit exposure and lung diseases. I'll also be able to apply and get healthcare covered for those illnesses.

The way things worked with the VA before the PACT Act, if I were hospitalized in the VA system, my insurance was billed, and I would also be billed for what insurance didn't cover. Now, my healthcare is covered by the VA. I'll be able to apply for secondary diseases to be included in my service connection. I've recently been diagnosed with pulmonary hypertension, which will now be considered a service-connected illness.

Passing the PACT Act is not the end of the work for

me. There is still a lot to do. I did a TV interview on Zoom with a TV station in Cleveland, and they asked me what was next for me. Without even thinking, I said, "I need to find all the homeless veterans affected by this bill and see if we can't get claims filed for them so that they can get their compensation."

I talked to Rosie Torres, one of the founders of Burn Pits 360, about what I told the TV station, and she said, "You're right. How do we get that information out?" I thought about what I could do and decided to start doing a podcast, going live at least once a week. On The Gulf War Advocate, I have guests who talk about issues relating to veterans and their families, such as the PACT Act, food banks, veteran service organizations and nonprofits, and helping homeless veterans file their claims.

People listening to the podcast can chat and ask questions as we broadcast. I am encouraged to have guests lined up to share about the PACT Act and other issues.

Some documentation has come out about veterans exposed to sarin gas during combat who were not awarded Purple Hearts. They deserve Purple Hearts. So, I'm going to be fighting for that now, too.

Preventing veteran suicide has always been important to me. I believe a bill will be presented to address that. Hopefully, I can advocate and work on that bill to get veterans the care they need and prevent veteran suicides.

I have my work cut out for me. Winning the PACT Act, seeing that promise kept, isn't the end of advocacy. It is the beginning.

I'm glad that my stepson has been able to see this win. When I first met him, he was seven. We could play outside together: kick the ball around, play basketball, or catch a football. I can't do that anymore. I didn't need oxygen when I first met him. Now he's twelve, and I need oxygen. I use a walker now when I leave the house because my blood pressure can drop at any time. Because of me, he learned what "terminal" means as a medical term.

He's supported me in being an advocate. He would say things like, "Hey, Dad – let me hear the speech you're going to say tomorrow. Hey, can I go with you to D.C. this time? You need my help to get around. You've got to make sure somebody's looking after you."

Not only has he personally supported me, but his Boy Scout troop got involved, too. I presented them with a flag that flew over the Capitol that my congressman, Dave Joyce, was able to get for me to present to the troop on his behalf. My stepson is a real encouragement. Shortly after I met him, we became best friends. He was the best man when I married his mom.

He's very curious. He asks a lot of questions. When he was a little older, I shared with him how and why I got sick. We watched documentaries on it together. He's watched The Problem with Jon Stewart. The first episode had Rosie and Le Roy Torres, Will and Wesley Black, and Isaiah James. Zakhar is exceptionally well educated on burn pits.

When I first met him, Zakhar told me he wanted to be

a medic in the military when he grew up. He's one of the best war historians I've ever met. You can't watch a war movie with the kid and not have him point out everything that's wrong. "In that era, they would not be wearing that type of badge on their uniform," or "That helmet was from World War I, not World War II." He used to go out in the backyard and play war games by himself.

He doesn't do that anymore like he used to. He and Marcy just went to Conneaut here in Ohio, where they have this big D-Day reenactment. They go every year. And Marcy said Zakhar was excited to be there, but this year he was asking different questions than he usually asks.

He wasn't asking about the type of weapon or type of bomb used. He asked, "Did they have burn pits in World War II?" It has opened his eyes quite a bit, I think.

*All chapter titles in Tim's story come*
*from the names of art pieces he created.*
*You can find them on his YouTube channel*
*Tim Hauser Art: @timhauserart6572*

## *by Marcy Gansler*

When Tim and I first met, I knew he had lung and stomach problems. It was before his diagnosis, and I assumed that it was asthma or something like it. It wasn't anything that I thought would be life-threatening or a big deal.

We connected online through a dating app. He never made me feel pressured. He was such a gentleman. We talked about life and our dogs, and we texted for a long time before we met in person. Finally, I said, "Let's meet tonight."

The first time we met, he was so polite. We met at Panera Bread. As I pulled in, he was getting out of the car with flowers in his hand. Our eyes met, and I knew it was him. We ended up staying at Panera for over three hours talking. We really hit it off. We agreed to meet again, and the rest is history. Tim is such a genuine, humble person who amazes me every day. My son

231

absolutely loves and adores him.

We started dating in April 2018, and Tim moved in with us in August 2018. At the time, I wasn't keen on getting married again, but I told everybody that I'd never been more sure of a person. He was the real thing; he was exactly who he said he was. Early on, we talked about not keeping secrets from each other. We're older; so, if we have issues, we just talk about them. We don't really fight at all.

Tim had tried to apply for benefits through the VA for years, even before I met him. They would never acknowledge that Tim may have gotten sick from his time of service. He would get a letter from the VA, denying him benefits, and he would be crushed.

In 2019, the doctors put Tim on steroids and tried all sorts of treatments. He'd been to lots of doctor appointments by that time and was constantly having tests done. Right before COVID hit in January 2020, Tim went to a particular doctor's appointment. Afterward, he called me and said, "I want to come to see you." I didn't work far from the hospital in downtown Cleveland. So, he came down, and we went to lunch.

"The doctors figured out what's going on," he said. "And it's terminal." They had diagnosed him with constrictive bronchiolitis, which meant that a part of his lungs had hardened and was basically dead. It was progressing, and the doctors told him that his only chance would be to have a lung transplant. The problem, however, was that he wasn't yet at the stage to be put on the lung transplant list. We both cried.

"I'm here for whatever this is going to be. I'm here for you," I told Tim. He seemed to relax when I said that. I think he thought I might have said, "I don't know if I can handle this," because I have a little kid. But that never crossed my mind. I immediately responded with, "We're in this together. We're going to get through it. It'll be whatever it will be, but we'll be together."

Then COVID hit, and a lot of the things he needed—like a lung biopsy—got pushed back. We had to be so careful during COVID. I was so afraid he was going to get sick. I started working remotely as soon as COVID surfaced because I thought, "I can't expose my husband, who has terminal lung disease, to COVID." My office shut down two weeks after I stopped going in.

From the time we started dating until now, Tim has been hospitalized for pneumonia seven times. It is always rough on him. During COVID, he got pneumonia again, which was very concerning. Thankfully, he didn't get COVID during that time. He has probably had more COVID tests than anyone I know from his frequent hospital visits.

We were super careful about limiting exposure. Tim barely went anywhere. I wore gloves and a mask when I went out, disinfected all the groceries, and washed all the fruits and vegetables. My son was home attending virtual school. We were hermits like everybody else to limit the chance of exposure.

Tim asked me to marry him in late March 2020 (I changed my mind about marriage because he is the best!), and we were married (in masks) at a small out-door wedding in September 2020. It was one of the happiest days of my life.

Tim finally had the lung biopsy in November 2020. He almost didn't do it because he had already received a diagnosis, and it was a very invasive procedure. But the doctors would be able to get tissue samples for a transplant, and tests on the tissue would help other people because the diagnosis was relatively new. So, he decided to do it.

Unfortunately, it was a rough surgery, and he ended up in the ICU for several days. It was terrifying be-cause they could not get his oxygen up, and his blood pressure would crash. Because it was during the time of COVID, I couldn't go see him in the ICU.

In typical Tim fashion, he pulled through, and the biopsy gave the doctors some answers. It was a long recovery for Tim, and his condition has worsened, which is what happens with this illness. People don't always realize the terminal nature of his medical con-dition. There is no cure.

Tim has been on steroids for a long time because they helped with his breathing, but he ended up in the hos-pital because the steroids almost killed him. The doc-tors took him off all the steroids he was taking. They only give them to him sometimes when he's in the hospital. While it has been a long road, I tell people, "He's not going to get better until there's a lung trans-plant in our future. It's going to continue to progress."

Sometimes Tim goes to the doctor but doesn't get answers. They try to relieve his symptoms but can't treat the condition because so much is unknown. His only chance is the lung transplant, but he hasn't progressed to the point that doctors feel he is ready for the transplant. It's frustrating and heartbreaking to see him suffer.

A lot of veterans with toxic exposure have many of the same issues. They have serious lung issues, polyps throughout their sinuses and throats, and they get cancers. Tim has a lesion in his brain, and doctors haven't quite figured out what it is. Suppose you're exposed to toxins, breathing them in for 24 hours. In that case, you will have a higher risk of cancers and other serious diseases. Tim was exposed for a year every single day. He was at that military base, breathing the toxic fumes from burn pits and nearby oil well fires.

When I first met him, he was energetic. He liked to work in his garden and take hikes. He's unable to do the things he enjoyed the way he used to. Unfortunately, with the steroids, he put on a lot of weight, making everything a little more challenging. He gets winded very easily now. Initially, he was never winded unless he was really exerting himself.

Unfortunately, he got COVID in August 2022 and has since had trouble going up and down the stairs or bringing something in from the car. He's winded doing what used to be simple tasks. His energy levels are lower, and he sleeps more. When he was in the hospital for COVID, the doctors told him his lung capacity was 50%. It's unclear if that will ever increase.

Tim had to quit his job even though he was working from home. He was doing customer service on the phone and had to go on medical leave because he could not talk all day. It was just too much, and he couldn't catch his breath. That means I am the only one working in our household.

He has been on and off oxygen. He was on it for a few months, but the doctors felt he didn't need it and took him off. And then things got worse, and they put him back on. Now he's on oxygen permanently. If we go out, we must make sure that we are back before he runs out of oxygen.

Joe McKay, one of the 9/11 first responders, loaned Tim his portable oxygen concentrator. That was life-changing for Tim because he had more freedom to go out or take trips. Before, we wondered, "How could we even go out of town for a weekend?" The oxygen tanks he had only lasted so long. Oxygen is something we have to think about every time Tim goes anywhere. Even the portable oxygen concentrator has limited battery life. Either we have to make sure he's near a plug, or we have to get an oxygen canister from home. We are so grateful that Joe was able to loan Tim the portable oxygen concentrator and that Burn Pits 360 was able to get him his own portable oxygen concentrator. It has given Tim much more freedom.

When I first met Tim, he wasn't taking many medications. Now he takes many. I try to help him keep them organized.

Tim loved to go hiking and take pictures, but he can

no longer go by himself because he was at risk of losing oxygen and passing out. The doctor told him he had to take someone with him if he was going hiking. Tim can't just say, "I feel good today. I want to go fishing."

With chores and projects around the house, it's challenging to keep up with everything without his help. We have two dogs and a son, and I have a full-time job where I sometimes travel. He does the best he can, but there are things that he can't do anymore. He still wants to be the man he was when he could physically do whatever he wanted; so, he does too much sometimes. And when he overexerts himself, he's back in the hospital.

The advocacy work is so important for Tim. He has had a lot of different jobs, and he has not always felt like he could find his place in the world or in life. But with the advocacy work with Burn Pits 360, he has completely come alive. This work has given him meaning, passion, and a way to make a difference.

In the beginning, when Tim strongly felt that his health problems stemmed from his service during the Gulf War, he tried to uncover what was happening. He ended up connecting with veterans on social media who were sick. He would hear some of them say, "They told us that the burn pits were safe, too." He saw that there was a real problem with all the similar things they each were experiencing separately. For one thing, nobody was getting the benefits they applied for. Secondly, they had to prove that the illnesses were connected to their service. And in the middle of all of this, the most convincing proof was the veterans themselves getting sick and dying.

Tim passionately felt this injustice on behalf of every sick veteran. He felt like he'd found his community among the people going through the same things. For so long, he had felt like it was just him. He became a sounding board for a lot of veterans.

Tim started calling legislators daily, asking, "What are we doing about this? And are you even aware of what's going on?" Eventually, Kevin Hensley saw that Tim was all over social media and contacting people. Kevin connected with him on social media and said, "Give me a call. This will change your life." When Tim connected with Burn Pits 360, it certainly did change his life because he finally had a group to advocate with him. It wasn't just him alone anymore, trying to get the word out about all these veterans.

A lot of the work was very frustrating. There were a lot of tears, especially when a bill didn't pass or when politics would get involved. It was an emotional roller coaster. The advocacy travel to D.C. was hard on him, but he felt he needed to be there to represent Gulf War veterans. Sometimes, he would return from D.C. and need to go to the hospital again. But I knew how much it meant to him.

On the one hand, we're all celebrating the PACT Act. But a lot of these veterans still have terminal diagnoses. Although this will make getting care easier for them, the fight for their lives is still going on. And unfortunately, it's too late for some. But their loved ones might be able to get survivor benefits.

The word is getting out, and we hope that people will go get care. The VA has been overwhelmed in the past; so, funding will go to hiring more people to process claims (which is part of the issue, too). Caregivers will have more education and training on how to help veterans. The VA can be scary; so, it was amazing that this small group of people overhauled the VA system in ways that have never been done before.

Tim received his 100% benefits in 2020. He could have said, "Well, I got mine, you guys. Good luck with you." But Tim felt so passionate about these issues that he wanted to help his brothers and sisters in the military get their benefits. And that's just who he is. He cares about other people. He shakes the hands of veterans at the store and says, "Thank you for your service."

Because of COVID, we had a minimal wedding at a park. There was a pond there, but I couldn't see it from where I was standing. We were just getting started when Tim told the pastor, "Hold on a second." Then he yelled across the pond, "Sir? Are you okay?" I couldn't see him, but an older man on the other side of the water was fishing and had fallen and rolled down the hill. The man got up and called out that he was okay. During her sermon, the pastor said, "What just happened shows who this man is and who these two people are."

Tim always offers to help. He took pictures at our

church for free for anyone who wanted to get their family pictures done. He shares himself easily. He's very gregarious and friendly, but he also pays attention when people are hurting and tries to help. He tries to be a beacon of light, even for a moment. He makes friends easily, and he talks to people all the time, everywhere we go. His dad was his hero, and Tim is so much like his dad.

Tim taught me that we're not alone. We're all in this together. We can help each other, and we can look out for each other. That's who Tim is. Advocating for fellow veterans has helped him fulfill that place in him that always knew this was who he needed to be.

# A Family Affair

MY CONTRIBUTIONS WERE NOT POSSIBLE
WITHOUT THE LOVE AND SUPPORT OF MY FAMILY.

SENATOR
JON TESTER

PETE BUTTIGIEG
(SECRETARY OF TRANSPORTATION)

CONGRESSMAN
TAKANO

PRESIDENT BIDEN
(SALUTING)

*Thank You,*
*Mr. President,*

DISTINGUISHED SENATORS, CONGRESSMEN,
AND OTHER OFFICIALS WHO MADE THE RIGHT
DECISION ON BEHALF OF VETERANS
AND OUR FAMILIES!

The "Others"

AND THANK YOU TO THE COUNTLESS OTHERS WHO USED THEIR PERSONAL AND PROFESSIONAL INFLUENCE SO THAT OUR VOICES COULD BE HEARD!

*As an American...*

I WAS HONORED TO DO MY PART.

"22"

"INTO THE FIRE"

"WOUNDED"

*Tim Hauser Art*"

ABOVE ARE THREE PIECES FROM MY COLLECTION
OF ABSTRACT PAINTINGS ON THE VETERAN EXPERIENCE.

@timhauserart6572

# 988

## SUICIDE &
## CRISIS LINE

ACKNOWLEDGEMENTS

I would like to thank Rosie and Le Roy Torres, co-founders of Burn Pits 360 and all the advocates at Burn Pits 360.

I would also like to thank the following persons and groups: Senator Sherrod Brown and his staff; Congressman Dave Joyce and his staff; Twinsburg, Ohio VFW Post 4929; Twinsburg Boy Scout Troop 223; Matt Eck and the Cleveland Cavaliers; the entire town of Twinsburg, Ohio; Senator Kirsten Gillibrand and her staff; Red Roof Inn of Alexandria, Virginia; Senator Tester; Senator Moran; John Feal; Jon Stewart and his staff; and President Joe Biden.

I would like to acknowledge the following for all their support: United Church of Christ; WKYC; WJW; WEWS; WOIO; Sue Frankart; Jodie DeCaro Palmer; President Joe Biden; VP Kamala Harris; and all the people and restaurants that kept us in water and food during the Firewatch.

Each one of these individuals and groups worked tirelessly to get the PACT Act into law. I appreciate each and every one of them for their dedication and loyalty to this new law.

# PART 4

## GINA'S STORY

*the message*

## DEDICATION

*To my husband Joe—*

Forever loved, forever missed. I could never adequately put into words everything you meant to us. The void that you have left in our lives is felt daily, but remembering and speaking of you brings us comfort. You were a larger-than-life personality who brought laughter, adventure, kindness, comfort, protection, and so much more to our lives. You are simply irreplaceable. You always looked after others, and you served your country and community with pride and distinction. We carried that service on in honor of you.

Although we realized too late to help you, we've helped to ensure others receive the care and benefits they earned. We did that in honor of you, and we'll continue to do what is right to help those affected.

Thank you for watching over us as we continue on our life journey with you tucked safely in our hearts.

*My kids, Ava and Isabelle—*

I could not be prouder of you both. You are strong, funny, kind human beings despite all you have been through. Life hasn't always been kind to you, yet you persevere, you push forward, and you adapt. Keep being you, and continue to shine brightly...the sky is the limit for you both. Thank you for supporting the jour-

249

ney to get the PACT Act into law. Thank you for keeping me going and being my constant. You will forever mean more to me than anything in the world, and I will always be here for you.

*To my mother, my first cheerleader—*
If not for you, I would not be half of the person I am today. For everything you taught me, for everything you showed me, for everything you did, and simply because you loved me, I'll always love and miss you, Mom.

*To my siblings, siblings-in-law, and my nieces—*
Thank you for your love and support always. Through the good and the bad you have been there for us. For two and a half years you supported us while Joe battled for his life. We are forever grateful for that, and we will never forget.

*To Joe's family—*
Please take comfort in knowing and always remembering that Joe loved you and he always will. He wanted me to make sure that you all knew that.

*To everyone who helped and supported us along the way—*
We sincerely thank and appreciate you.

INTRODUCTION

# Meaning, Strength & Purpose:
## The Rise of the Survivors

No one wants to see how the consequences and politics of war affect everyday life. We all know it exists, but most of us do not ever feel its impact or see the pain and destruction it leaves in its wake. The same thing happens when we look at a flag or a monument. We don't want any disgust or criticism clouding our patriotism.

If we think too hard about such things, we might become disillusioned and disappointed—even despairing—about the potential of our country to do anything good for its own merit. If we acknowledge behind the scenes all the conjecture and pettiness of politicians and the ways our government treats our veterans, well, we might be disheartened by what we find.

In fact, for any legislation to pass through the House of Representatives with its wildly disparate membership, a Senate just as monochromatic as it is geriatric, and a president who might come from either end of a polarized electorate—for that to happen is nothing short of a miracle. Any legislation meeting the criteria must be either so inoffensive that opposing it would be shameful or pointless, or so encumbered with special favors and obligations that the necessary number of lawmakers has ulterior motives.

The reality is, though, that politicians have to get elected. Period. They have to respond to the people who send them to the nation's capital, once every two years for representatives and once every six years for senators. Representatives have a whole lot more to lose if they make the folks back home unhappy, while senators can weather some temporary protest. That makes them less likely to be swayed, which could be good or bad, depending on the legislation in front of them.

What sways a politician reliably is a grassroots demand from a group of people with nationwide influence and the ear of the media. If an action group can present a clear moral choice, keep the pressure going from all areas of the country, and use the media to raise the temperature, that group can get something done. So, the solution for shady backroom deals is a loud voice telling the truth in the clear daylight. A told secret loses its power.

When Kimberly Hughes was losing everything, including her husband's pension and life insurance, to bankruptcy lawyers, she invoked the media to stop the harassment. The lawyers didn't want to be seen leaving a soldier's widow penniless. It didn't look good for them.

Jon Stewart accomplished something similar with the First Responders Bill, urging reluctant lawmakers,

"Do your job!" He made visible the plight of firefighters, paramedics, police officers, and others who stood in the smoke and ash of the Trade Center towers and saved people's lives. The toxins from the burning pits of rubble damaged their lungs and caused cancers and other illnesses, which showed up years after the attacks. Stewart held Congress to account to support those heroes. Leaving them to suffer medical bankruptcy and die didn't look good for people who had to go back home on reelection campaigns.

And that's what finally swayed the balance for the PACT Act, too. Rosie and Le Roy Torres took care of the first part of the equation, the national grassroots campaign, by starting Burn Pits 360 to advocate not only for Le Roy, who is a burn pit survivor, but for all veterans and survivors. They wisely saw the connection between the materials in the 9/11 rubble and burn pits: jet fuel, construction materials, plastics, and human remains. They then used the scientific research to combat the claims of the VA that burn pits could not be scientifically proven to cause any illness.

Military veterans and their spouses across the country recognized the truth of Rosie and Le Roy's research and subscribed to their registry. They formed the core of the national presence and pressure that could make politicians listen. Teaming up with Jon Stewart and other 9/11 first responder advocates like John Feal and Joe McKay, they called press conferences and arranged meetings between veterans, surviving spouses, survivors, and their political representatives.

Gina Cancelino, a military spouse whose husband died from burn-pit-caused cancer, spoke several times at such press conferences. Jake Tapper from CNN interviewed her and one of her daughters alongside Jon Stewart after one of those press conferences. The story of losing her brave Marine and NYPD officer husband moved hearts, especially with her two equally brave daughters beside her.

The PACT Act was on its fourteenth version in the summer of 2022, having shuffled around Congress for eighteen months. It looked like it was about to be passed when a cadre of senators changed their votes at the last minute, claiming that one party was trying to add egregious spending to the bill.

However, that really wasn't the truth. The wording in question was from the word mandatory to the word discretionary. That wording change was necessary to fit the reality of emerging medical science and the expanding knowledge of how the original problem was continuing to impact veterans.

Without that wording change, every time doctors linked a new disease to the original cause of burn pits, people suffering with that disease would have to start the whole process over again. And they would have to do it without the national support and media attention of the first wave. It's hard to rally people once, let alone repeatedly over decades.

The process was going to wear down future survivors and future veteran patients unless the people making the law now put a stop to it. And that's exactly what they did. The provisions in the bill to add new medical conditions, the discretionary spending, removed the need for veterans to submit to scrutiny regarding the source of their illness. It was not a ploy to increase spending; it was a measure to protect our veterans.

Another important aspect of the PACT Act is that it also cares for the surviving spouses and children of Warfighters lost to toxic exposure. Because of decisions made in government halls, decisions like who wins paramilitary contracts, people like Gina Cancelino can't hold their husbands. Children like Ava and Isabelle Cancelino are growing up without fathers. Servicemembers lost to toxic exposure didn't die from enemy fire; they died from a sinister kind of friendly fire—"friendly" poisoning that their commanding officers required them to inhale.

Joe Cancelino should still be alive. A healthy, middle-aged man who survived enemy fire should be attending high school graduations and elementary-school plays. We the people are responsible for his absence, and we the people need to make this loss right with those who suffer it.

## CHAPTER 1

### *How Joe and I Met*

J oe and I were both born and raised in Long Island, NY. Like many, we had our struggles we endured while growing up and early in our lives before we met, but that's not where this book starts. I'll save that for another time. This book starts when Joe and I met, what we went through as a couple, what we lost, and what the kids and I gained after we lost him.

Joe's Marine Corps reserve unit, 2nd Battalion, 25th Marines, Garden City, N.Y., was activated just four months after the September 11th attacks. They were sent stateside to Camp Lejeune, N.C. This wasn't the first time Joe had been activated with his unit. He'd been stateside in California for Desert Storm and had served a three-month deployment to Cuba during his time with the unit, but this one would be different. This time he would bring something home that would ultimately be the enemy that took his life. I had a friend who was deployed to N.C. with Joe. I'd call my friend to see how he was, and I'd end up talking to Joe more than I did to my friend. Our relationship continued by phone until July 4, 2002 when Joe was home on leave for the weekend. In the evening, he called and asked me what I was doing. Fortunately for me, I was home with no plans; so, we decided to meet in person. He came to my house, and we went out for drinks. The rest, as they say, is history.

We made spontaneous plans the entire weekend, starting with breakfast and then going to a local waterpark called Splish Splash. On our way out to the waterpark, we stopped at nearby outlets for towels and bathing suits, and then we spent the entire day at the waterpark. Day soon turned to night; so, naturally we just continued on to dinner. Unfortunately, the next day the weekend came to an end, and Joe returned to North Carolina. But from that moment on, our relationship began to grow.

We spoke daily while apart, and one day shortly after his return, Joe told me, "I'm going away to St. Thomas with my sisters for a week. When I come back, the unit has to go to California for training. I won't be able to see you again until September, unless you want to meet me in St. Thomas. This is the flight my sisters are on. Maybe you can meet them, if you want, and you won't have to fly alone."

I was so excited that the idea had even entered his mind. It felt so nice to know that even though he was away, he was trying to figure out ways to spend time with me. I would realize over time that this was something he would always be good at doing.

I didn't have to think long before I told him I'd love to go, booked a seat on his sisters' flight, and went to the airport. I met them for the first time at the airport before we flew to St. Thomas together. We met Joe at the hotel and spent our trip sightseeing, relaxing on the beach, going to dinner, and snorkeling. Joe used to tell the funniest story about that snorkeling excursion.

Unlike Joe, I hadn't snorkeled all that much prior to that trip; so, I let him lead the way during the excursion. At one point, he started guiding me away from where we were looking. He seemed to be moving with purpose but not in an alarming way.

When we were back at the boat, he asked me "Did you see that barracuda?"

I answered, "Barracuda? What barracuda?"

That was how he protected people-he'd do it without you even knowing that there had ever been a threat or a concern. Every time he told that story, the barracuda grew in size, and the story became funnier. That was typical of him. He had an incredible way of telling stories and making people laugh. I might have some great pictures from that trip, but they pale in comparison to the incredible memories.

After that trip, he headed back to North Carolina and then to California for training. Despite the distance, Joe was always very good at keeping in touch, letting me know he was thinking about me; whether through phone calls or emails, he was always reaching out. My birthday is in October, usually falling around Columbus Day weekend, not a holiday that would generally grant a Marine leave. In one of our calls, he told me, "Yeah, I'm not going to be able to make it home for your birthday." I told him it was okay; of course I understood. What he was doing was more important than a birthday.

The night of my birthday, my doorbell rang, and to my surprise it was him. He had driven twelve hours in the pouring rain with one of his friends to surprise me for my birthday. That was just one of the ways he showed me I was already a priority to him.

He did all of the things you hope someone does when you're in a relationship. Though he was in North Carolina and I was in New York, we were growing closer, falling in love, and learning what mattered. He told me with words and showed me with his actions that he was a caring, kind, and considerate man-he was all of those things and more.

During his time in North Carolina, Joe received a call from the NYPD, informing him that they had reached his name on the testing list. They wanted him to come in for more qualification testing to see if he'd be accepted into the academy. This had been a lifelong dream of his. He advised them that he was on active duty with the military and unable to attend the required testing. That meant they would put his application aside, and he could call when he was no longer active and be reinstated into the process.

In December 2002, the Marines deactivated Joe's unit. Although they were sent home for the holidays, they knew they would be reactivated before long. Knowing our time together was limited, Joe and I enjoyed the holidays together, took a few ski trips to Vermont, and continued to build memories and our relationship.

In February 2003, we started to receive word that the new orders for the unit would soon be coming down, and that's when we started to prepare. It was clear that although Operation Enduring Freedom was still continuing in Afghanistan, the U.S. was most likely heading into Iraq as well. The unit had heard that their deployment would be to one of those two locations. The call came down locally, and the process began stateside. Physicals, medical assessments, vaccinations, and required shots were administered, and wills and powers of attorney were generated for everyone deploying. Joe named me as his power of attorney, asking me to handle any matters that may arise during his deployment. He asked me to facilitate payment of his bills in his absence. He entrusted his stateside life to me, and that's when reality truly set in.

The unit started to prepare gear, reporting daily to their local base. While they were preparing, Joe asked me if I would be interested in volunteering for a family readiness program called the "Key Wives." This group of extraordinary people would serve as family contacts and as conduits between the battalion and families during deployment. I was honored to be thought of for such a role and immediately agreed to participate. Once all of these matters were addressed, it was only a matter of time until they left.

The call came toward the end of February 2003; the unit would be leaving the following week. They deployed the first week in March 2003 to Iraq. Where exactly in Iraq, they were not able to share with us, but at least we knew it was Iraq.

During the first few weeks of his deployment, I did not hear from Joe. The families were made aware by the battalion that the unit arrived safely in Iraq, but that was the extent of what we knew. Being involved with the family readiness group at this point meant not only did I receive updates but I gained a family of women who were in the same situation I was, except that in several cases they had children to care for as well. We spoke to one another frequently, spent time together, and relied on each other for support. I still speak to most of them today, and I'm grateful for those families, as was Joe. We would let each other know when we'd spoken to our Marine to make sure everyone knew they were okay. We would be happy for each other when the opportunity arose for one of us to speak to our Marine, though we also knew it was disappointing to whomever we were speaking since that person didn't receive a call. But that's part of the beauty of belonging to a group like this: we get it. It's much like the friendships the kids and I now have with Kim, Kevin, and Tim.

After a few weeks, letters started arriving via snail mail from Joe, and then there would be the occasional phone call and eventually emails once they had settled into their location. The unit had a satellite phone, but Joe would let the younger troops use it first to call their parents and let them know that they were okay. He was a staff sergeant during his deployment, and he would tell me, "I know you're getting information from the battalion and from the other wives. It's my responsibility as a leader to make sure that the younger guys call their parents." Joe would call his family, too, although while he was away, I would provide them with information as well, per Joe's request.

I still have every letter and every email between us during his deployment. While writing this book, I found two dusty, dirty, Ziploc bags containing all of the cards and letters I had written to Joe. His messages to me were mostly letting me know he and his unit were okay; then they'd move to him asking what was going on back at home, as well as talking about a vacation we were going to plan when he returned. There was one time we received information about a gastrointestinal parasite that was running through the unit. No one could figure out what caused it or where it came from. They ate MREs and drank bottled water; they could not determine the source of this illness. Through my advocacy work, I have come to learn that this happened to many veterans during and after their deployments. The cause has now been tied back to their exposure to burn pits and all they had been inhaling.

I would send Joe boxes of Italian dried sausages, pepperoni, and hard cheeses. I would get jars of olives and peppers and things like that, and I would bubble wrap them really well and ship them out to them so that the guys could have some good food. Joe told me he would open the boxes, and they would all gather on

Sundays for a nice meal.

I would often stay late at work waiting for Joe's call, since I knew around the time he usually called due to the time difference. Working in Manhattan and living on Long Island meant that my commute home included subways and trains, which took me underground where I'd lose cell service. There were several times when I'd come out of the subway or out of that Long Island Rail Road tunnel, and I'd have a missed call from Joe. It was nice to hear his voice in the message and know he was okay, but it was upsetting knowing I missed an opportunity to talk to him.

Once I made it home, I was in charge of Joe's apartment, which included his collection of indoor house plants. Joe had a green thumb. I, however, do not. The running joke in my house is that Joe went to Iraq and left me in charge of 11 plants. When he came back, there were two. I even brought my mother to the apartment so she could see them and let me know what I was doing wrong. It did not help! Joe never let me be in charge of plants again. When we have plants now or plant our garden like he used to, I'm certain he's helping me from the heavens because some have quite literally come back from the dead!

When Joe was in Iraq in 2003, his contract with the Marines expired, which brought him to 17 years of service. So, while he was there he re-enlisted for the remaining three years to bring him to twenty years of service, eventually allowing him a military pension.

Once the unit had been given an estimated return

date, I worked on booking our trip. We had decided we wanted to go to Aruba for ten days. Joe came back in August of 2003, and after about a week or two home, we headed to Aruba for ten days.

A few days before our trip to Aruba, there was a massive blackout in N.Y.C., where I was working. Everything went dark. You can imagine how, after 9/11, something like that is extremely scary. The first thing that comes to mind is some sort of terrorist attack again. After a bit of chaos trying to determine what was happening, our office learned that it was a power grid blackout. Once we knew it was safe, we needed to figure out a way home since nothing was running. All street lights were out, which created an extreme traffic condition. A group of us walked over the Brooklyn Bridge to our coworkers apartment.

I kept in contact with Joe as we tried to figure out how I could get home. After some options didn't work out, he said, "I'm coming to get you." I knew he was concerned about my safety, given that the entire city was without power. Since there was no power, there were no traffic lights, and you could not get gas. Thankfully, as a Marine always is, he was prepared. His car had gas, and he was able to navigate the streets even without traffic lights. I was glad when he arrived in Brooklyn to take me back home to Long Island.

He was Mister Take Charge. "If there's a problem, then let's figure out a solution." That's why he was always successful in the Marines and the NYPD.

.We had such an amazing vacation in Aruba, and

while it was still a bit surreal for Joe and he was still adjusting to being home, we enjoyed our trip. The Marines kept him on active duty at the battalion head-quarters on Long Island upon his return so that he could do inventory and accept all of the equipment that was returning after the unit. He was also promot-ed to Gunnery Sergeant, the last rank he had wanted to achieve.

We got engaged on Christmas morning of 2003. Then he came off of active duty in January 2004. After that, he was deciding what career path he wanted to take; so, I encouraged him to pursue his dream and contact the NYPD to have his name resubmitted for the de-partment.

Joe was above the hiring age limit at that point, be-cause there is a cap on how old you can be: 35. How-ever, because he had been called before that age and had to defer the opportunity because he was on active duty, he remained eligible. Once his name was rein-stated, the process began with the required testing, physicals, evaluations, and paperwork to allow him to be accepted into the police academy.

During the year Joe was waiting to hear from the NYPD, we got married. We paid for it ourselves, and we were being cost effective. We found this little place that we really loved; it was called The Thatched Cot-tage. It was nice inside, and it had a gazebo outside on a little creek. We got married on a Sunday, saving money so we could instead put it toward things that were important to us. And I do mean us, because he was involved in everything.

Joe came to all of the showcases and was involved in all of the decisions that were made for our wedding. Clearly with his green thumb, it made the most sense that he took the lead on the flowers! As for attire for him and his friends, he wanted to be in a tux, but he wanted his Marine friends in their dress blues. We did not have a wedding party; we had a maid of honor, a best man, and flower girls. Joe's best man was in his dress blues. We invited all family members with their children; we wanted everyone to be involved. We extended our cocktail hour, since the outdoor space was so nice.

A month or two before our wedding, Joe had his annual two-week deployment for his reserve service. That year it ended up being a deployment to Japan. Joe even had a day during that deployment where he was able to climb Mt. Fuji, which he thoroughly enjoyed. Thankfully, most of the wedding details were done.

The day of our wedding, we woke up to rain; sometimes that just happens. By the time the church started, the skies had cleared, and the sun was beaming. When the photographer came to my house to take pictures, she wanted me to go on my mother's lawn. Clearly, I was concerned about doing that since I did not want to get my dress dirty before the wedding. The photographer took the white sleeve of her shirt and wiped it across the lawn to see if it was wet. It was completely dry! We ended up with a beautiful day that everyone enjoyed.

On our honeymoon, we thought we should go back to Aruba, but since that had been our post-deployment trip at the same time the year before, we decided to research the rest of the ABC islands: Aruba, Belize, and Curacao, since they are off of the hurricane belt. We ended up choosing Curacao. Although we enjoyed ourselves, we wished we had chosen Aruba again; we almost moved mid honeymoon!

CHAPTER 2

## CHAPTER 2
# *What We Went Through As a Couple*

In January of 2005, Joe received the call from the NYPD, and he started the police academy. He became a police officer in July of 2005. NYPD academy classes are large, due to the size of the police force. Therefore, they break the candidates up into groups called companies. Each company is given a company sergeant who serves in a leadership role and leads the group through daily PT drills. Joe was named company sergeant.

All the physical drills did not present a challenge for Joe, given his career as a Marine, his activity in the reserves, and his recent deployment. As everyone knows, drill instructors try to intimidate and distract cadets while they are in training. It's a means to prepare them. But our families were loud, and Joe had served nineteen years in the Marines. So, he'd tell me, "These drill instructors were yelling at us, and I thought, 'That's nothing.'"

The Police Academy was a great experience for Joe; he truly enjoyed it and excelled at it. He would go to the library to study, study on the train ride into the city, and take notes with his index cards. Along with the physical aspect of the academy, there were written tests along with memorization and understanding of the law.

He graduated from the academy in July of 2005, approximately one week after my sister's wedding, which he could not attend due to the academy. But we understood that. My sister and brother-in-law were nothing but proud and happy for Joe. My mom and I attended the graduation ceremony along with Joe's mother, sisters, and nephew.

After the completion of the police academy, Joe was given his precinct assignment. It was then that he decided for his final year of his Marine Corps career he would enter the IRR (Individual Ready Reserve). This allowed him to establish himself and enhance his NYPD career.

Once his NYPD career started, Joe had truly found the job he was born to do. He was successful and extremely happy. He loved everything about going to work, which included finding ways to help and counsel people he came into contact with. His efforts did not go unnoticed, as Joe was awarded Cop of the Month honors four times and Cop of the Year once.

Aside from Joe enjoying his career, the summer to the end of 2005 was extremely busy for both of us. We purchased and moved into our first home. We decided that we needed to add another family member to our new home; so, we adopted a puppy, a black Labrador mix who would keep me company when Joe was working. We named him Maximum, after a character in a book we both loved. We always called him Max for short.

He was the most amazing dog you could ever ask for. Part of the reason was because of his temperament; the other part was that Joe was really good at training him. Joe trained him so well that Max would sit on our front lawn by himself just watching people walk by. He would walk himself to our neighbors' houses on each side of us and then walk himself back home to continue his people watching. He was also a great protective watchdog. He was our first baby. We bought a house that was closer to my mother and where I grew up, since my mother had retired. We figured that my mom could help us with kids if we decided to have them. This also meant that Joe was closer to any precincts he may be assigned to during his career, making the commute tolerable.

Our house needed so much work; it was insane. Thankfully, Joe could do a lot of it. For instance, we priced out the windows and found how much the company wanted to charge. Joe was like, "Oh, hell no. We'll buy the windows and I'll put them in one at a time." And he put in all the windows, even our bay window. Joe worked very hard to make our house a home. I'm thankful that we have that now that he is gone.

Given Joe's busy schedule, we decided that we had to hire a company to handle putting siding on our house. Joe's dad was retired by this point; so, he'd drive the 45 minutes to our house to watch the installation project. It was nice for Joe to have him there to bond over this experience.

Joe was working, building his career, and accepting any overtime presented to him in order to make more money. Shortly after his graduation from the academy, I had been advised that I needed to relocate to Boston for my job or I would be laid off. Since Joe had just attained his dream job, we had just purchased a new home, and our families were on Long Island, a move was not an option for us. I decided it was in the best interest of our family to accept a severance package. My next thought moved to what jobs would enable me to work around Joe's ever-changing schedule.

I determined it was in the best interest of our family for me to obtain my real estate license and begin a career as a realtor. I started working at the real estate office where I worked as a receptionist from the end of high school through college. This career change allowed me some flexibility with my schedule; however, most people don't realize that buyers and sellers want their realtor available around their schedules, meaning when they aren't working. That means a lot of nights and weekends spent showing houses to buyers and presenting market analysis materials to sellers to list their homes, as well as days during the week doing research and scheduling for those appointments.

In March of 2006, we found out we were having our first child; we were due in November. Joe and I were excited about this new chapter of our lives. Everyone was thrilled when we told them the news. Things were all falling into place, until June 2006 when Joe received a devastating call from his sister, telling him that his father had passed away from a massive heart attack. This was a shock to the family and was hard to process during what was supposed to be a happy time. Everyone tried to do the best they could during this challenging time.

Joe was his usual helpful self during my pregnancy. He made sure I had anything I needed or wanted and ensured that the baby's room was set up before she was born. We found out we were having a girl before she was born, but we decided to keep that to ourselves. It was at this time that Joe's contract with the Marine Corps expired. Since he was in the IRR, there wasn't much fanfare around his retirement. I don't even think we received any paperwork for his retirement. But since we had so many other things going on, we just let that go. He always said he'd handle it later on.

Our oldest daughter was born at the end of November in 2006. The day prior to her due date, my water broke at about 12:30 am. I called my mother to let her know, and Joe called his mom. Shortly after I arrived, my mom arrived with my sisters Alexis and Daurene, as did my mother-in-law and my sister-in-law Suzanne. The hospital accommodated me with a room large enough for all of us to stay in.

At this point it became a waiting game, with a lot of people there to watch. The nurses would come in and out of the party, checking on me. When things felt bad,

I'd hold up a finger just to say, "Just silence yourself for a second." Then I'd put it down to signal, "Okay, that passed. Now you can continue."

After a few frequent episodes of that, the nurse checked on me and said, "Are you feeling what I'm seeing?" Since it was my first child, I was just waiting until someone told me it was time. That's when she said, "It's time now. We're going to take you to the delivery room."

Finally, after twenty-six hours in the hospital, our first daughter Ava was born via c-section. I had a picture of the doctor, my mother, my sister Daurene, my mother-in-law, and my sister-in-law Suzanne next to Ava in the bassinet right after she was born and cleaned up. I wish I had printed that. In 2019 I found out that our external hard drive became corrupt, and I lost that picture as well as many others. While I was in the hospital, all of my siblings and nieces came through to see the newest baby girl. My mom and Joe came every day.

We settled in nicely to being a family of four (we always considered Max a family member). Ava was a good baby, and Max, like Joe and I, adored her. He was protective, gentle, and patient.

Joe wanted more than one child, and in November 2007, we found out we were having a second child. Unfortunately, in December of 2007 at our monthly check-up, we found out that the baby did not have a heartbeat and that a DNC was necessary. After some time passed, we continued to try to grow our family, but it was not to be.

At this time, we made the decision to seek additional medical testing. We went to a fertility doctor to see if there were any potential conditions hindering our progress. Joe and I had different feelings on this. I felt that since I had one healthy, happy child, if that was all I was meant to have then so be it, but I went anyway. We came to find that Joe's sperm motility rate was low, meaning his sperm did not travel at the rate of speed as most. This was potentially the reason for our inability to conceive another child. I, however, did not wish to pursue the next steps of drugs and in vitro.

During my advocacy, I was made aware of potential fertility issues among toxin-exposed veterans, just another red flag I wish I had been made aware of. This was another reason we would have had to seek out early toxin screening. Perhaps this would have found his cancer early enough, but we were not aware.

We continued our life journey as a family of four, and if we were meant to add a fifth, then it would happen on its own. Life was pretty routine for us. Joe worked as much as he could to support our family, and I worked when I could fit it in between his schedule. Since my mother was close and retired, she would watch Ava when both Joe and I were working. It also meant that Ava, Max, and I spent a lot of time with her when Joe was working and I was off. Max always accompanied us to her house when we went there.

My mom was an exceptional woman. I have four sisters and one brother. She raised the six of us on her own, as my father left when I was very young. She reinvented herself, reestablished herself in the workplace, and worked hard to keep everything together. Her house was always a meeting place for all of us, especially on Sundays. She often made gravy, pasta, and meatballs for us all to enjoy. She was a good cook; she never used a recipe, though. Everything just cooked on 375 degrees until it looked done; that's still one of my favorite cooking instructions. We enjoyed our time with my family.

Since Joe's mom and sister lived about 45 minutes east of us, we'd visit them on his days off, and of course Max would come with us. We would also try to go there when his other sister was in from out of town. That usually meant our niece and nephews would also be there. His mom and sister always made dinner and dessert for us. I remember this one time we went there Joe admired this elephant statue his mom had; it ended up coming home with us! I still have it in our living room; it makes me laugh every time I see it.

Joe and I always loved going on adventures to new places before Ava was born; so, we continued our travels with her. It started with places like Sesame Place and Dutch Wonderland. My mom even came on some of the trips, even though she didn't like roller coaster rides. If she wasn't on a trip with us, she and my sister Denise would watch Max for us at her house. If she came, my sister Denise would watch him. Since he was our first child, it was important that someone we trusted and someone who loved him watched him.

We would go to Disney on Ice, local interactive Disney events, and local plays. I'd always offer a ticket to my mom, since she helped us so much with babysitting Ava. In 2008 and 2010, we made our first trips to Disney, and of course my mom accompanied us. She enjoyed watching Ava experience these events, and she even went on some of the more low-key rides, too! My sister Christine and brother-in-law Greg met us there both times (they live in Colorado).

Life was treating us kindly; things were progressing nicely. Joe was deciding how he wanted his career with the NYPD to progress. He knew he wanted to move up in the ranks; he was a natural born leader. He would ask me, "What do you think I should do?"

I used to tell him, "You are part of a very small percentage of people in the world who love their jobs. There's not a lot of people in this world that get to say they love their jobs. So, I can't tell you what you should do. You have to decide what you want to do, because you have to remain happy with what you're doing." Joe worked so much to provide for us that I wanted nothing but for him to continue to enjoy what he was doing.

He had two avenues he could pursue for promotion in order to earn more money: detective or sergeant. Detective promotions are meritorious, while sergeant promotions are done based on a test. Once you pass this test, you are put on a waitlist based on your score. As they need sergeants, they call officers from that list for a set amount of years; when that test expires, if you have not been called, you need to retest to remain eligible. Joe decided he was going to take the test for sergeant; so back to studying he went.

It also meant he needed to have a bachelor's degree, which he did not have at the time. In order to fit it all in, Joe took online college courses. He was also able to receive college credit for his police academy coursework, as well as his MCIs- Marine Corps Institute classes he had taken over his twenty-year career. This enabled him to have the required amount of credits for his degree.

In January of 2012, he got promoted to sergeant. The promotion ceremony was during the week, which meant many of our family members were working and could not attend. I went with Ava and my mother. Joe's mother met us there with his sister Robin and our nephew Philip. It was both a proud and exciting moment for him, surrounded by people he loved, especially our daughter Ava.

Being promoted in the NYPD means your precinct assignment must change. Joe was given a Transit Sergeant position in a precinct about an hour and fifteen minutes farther than his previous precinct. He went from having a commute of about fifteen to twenty minutes to a commute of an hour and half to two hours. As he was adjusting to his new position, he began to realize that the activity level was quite a bit different then he was used to. It was too quiet for him and not exactly what he was looking for; so, he put in for a transfer out of the Transit district.

In December of 2012, life took a tragic turn for us, again. While visiting my sister Christine and brother-in-law Greg in Colorado, my mother had a stroke. My sister realized what was going on immediately and provided her with the help she needed quickly. However, everything that could go wrong did go wrong.

Ava was six; though she was in first grade, she was home sick with a double ear infection when this happened. Actually, right before her stroke, my mom had called for the second time that day to check on her. She also called to tell me she was going out to purchase the Christmas gift we had decided to buy my sister together. I'm forever grateful for that last conversation.

We found out after her stroke that Mom had afib – atrial fibrillation - which is an irregular heartbeat. Although she received medical care immediately in Vail, the clot in her brain was not breaking up. The medical team made the decision to transfer her to a hospital called Swedish Medical, one of the top stroke facilities in the country. It was there that they tried to break up the clot manually, but it kept going back together. Most likely the clot was calcified, and it had been in her body a very long time.

Once we knew how bad things were with my mom, we knew we had to get to Colorado. Since Ava had the ear infection, she couldn't fly, and I have a sister who does not fly. But we needed to get everyone there.

Joe told his job what had happened, and they said, "Go, take care of your family."

They were really good to us. We rented a car, and Joe drove the 28 hours to Colorado himself.

By the time we arrived, my mom had had a secondary clot in her leg, which a vascular surgeon was able to address, but the brain clot was still doing its damage. By the time the brain clot had infarcted, it damaged two thirds of the left hemisphere of her brain, rendering her brain dead. We took Mom off life support December 19, 2012, one week before her 74th birthday. We stayed with her until the very end, as we knew she'd do the same for us.

While we were with my mom, Joe took Ava and my nieces. He made sure to get up early that morning and quietly make his way to the hospital to say his goodbyes to my mother; this way he could stay back later to watch all of the kids. This was just Joe being Joe; no one had to ask him.

I wish I had more years with her. I wish our family had more years with her. She always gave so much to us and still had so much left to give. She was the glue that held it all together. My only relief comes from the fact that she did not suffer; she did not spend years losing her independence and having to live a life she didn't want. Losing my mother was extremely difficult. She was my first cheerleader, the person I turned to when I needed guidance and when I needed someone to listen. Devastated by her loss, I used my love of my gym, CKO Kickboxing, as a means of coping and therapy.

Seven months later, we received quite a surprise, or

perhaps a gift from my mother, when I found out I was pregnant. Joe and I were happy, yet shocked about this news.

When I told Joe, he said, "Wait a minute. I'm in my 40s. Is this really happening?"

Much like when I was pregnant with Ava, Joe was helpful and supportive. After the first twelve weeks, we told Ava she would be becoming a big sister. She was in second grade and thrilled that she was getting a sister. We had found out we were having another girl.

During my pregnancy, Joe found out that his request for transfer had been approved and he would be transferred out of Transit into a precinct in Queens again. This made him very happy. Given our new situation, he also decided to apply for an overtime position as a counterterrorism sergeant in addition to his full-time precinct sergeant position. The counterterrorism unit was composed of people who covered big events where the NYPD wanted to deploy more officers for security reasons. His military background, coupled with his success within the department, made him an ideal candidate for this position. His application was processed, and he was given the additional job. He was very proud that he had been chosen. Things were getting back to normal at work for him, and he was back to really enjoying his job.

I was still selling real estate while pregnant, but since Joe had both positions and my mother had passed away, it became more difficult to do. I did take on one sale, and that was when we decided to sell my mother's house. I'd say that was my most difficult sale.

In 2013, we made another trip to Disney, this time in December when it was decorated for Christmas. I had always wanted to see it decorated that way. As is tradition, my sister Christine and brother-in-law Greg met us there. Since I was pregnant, I could not go on any rides, and it was our first trip to Disney without my mother. It was a bittersweet time for me, but we enjoyed it. My sister Alexis and nieces Jacqueline and Hailey decided to join us on this trip as well, as they were going through a difficult time in addition to losing my mother.

Our daughter arrived in April 2014. She, unlike her sister, decided to arrive a week before my scheduled c-section. Our plan was for my sister Daurene to meet us at the hospital whenever necessary since she lived the closest and her kids were the oldest. My brother-in-law Steven could be home with her girls. We arrived at the hospital around six in the morning. Since my sister had been there when I was in labor with Ava, she remembered how I internalized my contractions. She was laughing at how I did the same finger pointing gesture this time around as well.

While Joe and I were in the hospital that day, she took Ava to the mall to Build-A-Bear to do some shopping. We decided that our newest daughter should be named after my mom; her name is Isabelle. She only took about three hours and forty-five minutes of labor to be born. Since she was born so early in the morning and I was in my own room by mid-morning, my whole family came to visit in shifts throughout the day. Everyone was excited about having a new baby in the family, this joyous bright spot during a time of sadness.

Later in the evening, my sister Daurene came back with Ava, who was carrying her newest Build-A-Bear! Ava had a good day as well, but was very excited to see her new sister! The hospital was great; they never rushed people out. Joe and Ava were even allowed to stay overnight if they wanted. Since we had Max at home, they left in the night time, after I was settled and Isabelle went to sleep.

The next day, Joe took Ava to school. That was usually my job, but they did well together. Ava was so excited to tell her teacher and class all about her new sister. After school, Joe picked her up and headed to my mother's house, as the engineer's inspection with the potential buyers was taking place. Thankfully, my friend Tom went in my absence as well; he was a mentor and great help to me during my real estate career. I have a few very good friends from that office, friends who have always been there for me. Yes, I mean you, Jill and Sue, but I digress.

Once the inspection was done, Joe and Ava headed to the hospital for a visit. Ava loved the pizza and Jell-O from the cafeteria; so, every visit included a stop there! After a few days, Isabelle and I were able to go home. Ava picked out Isabelle's outfit she would come home in. Joe dropped Ava at school and came to the hospital to pick Isabelle and me up. Ava came home from school and found us all home. Of course, Max jumped into big brother mode again and knew immediately that his job now included protecting Isabelle. We were one big happy family.

A few weeks later, Ava was making her communion. My sister Christine and brother-in-law Greg came in from Colorado to celebrate with us. They were extremely helpful with setting up her party at the house, ensuring that it was exactly what she wanted. She was so excited that all of her aunts, uncles, and cousins were there. Everyone had a great time. It's challenging having special occasions when you've lost a loved one. There is always a void that cannot be filled, and my mother certainly left a large one.

We closed on the sale of my mother's house in July 2014, and life as a family of five started to settle in nicely. That summer we took a trip with all of my siblings, siblings in law, and nieces to Hershey Park; it was a lot of fun. We actually ended up making that an annual trip with my sister Alexis and her girls, my nieces Jacqueline and Hailey. They had had some obstacles to overcome in their lives; so, we always tried to support them. We also added an annual end of the school year trip to Splish Splash, the local water park where Joe and I had gone the first weekend we met.

In September of 2015 or 2016, I decided it was time to give up my real estate license, which was costing more money to keep than it was bringing in. Since Joe was working so much, it was not feasible for me to continue. We agreed that I would go back to work when Isabelle was in kindergarten.

In February 2016, we took our first trip to Disney as a family of five. Of course, my sister Christine and brother-in-law Greg met us there. We had a wonderful trip. Isabelle was almost two, and Ava was nine. Isabelle was so outgoing; she went up to every character she saw and took pictures. We decided during this trip that we would add in a visit to Universal Studios. Ava and Joe went on every ride she could go on in Universal and in Disney. Isabelle and I joined them on the ones she could go on. While in Universal, Christine and Greg would stay with Isabelle so that Joe, Ava, and I could ride some of the rides together. We really enjoyed it.

In the summer of 2016, we took a trip to Colorado to visit Christine and Greg. We went with Alexis, Jacqueline, and Hailey. We stayed for two weeks, while Joe stayed for one week due to his work schedule. While we were there, we visited an amusement park called Glenwood Springs; it was built into a mountain. Joe and Ava went on some extreme rides there. They went on a large swing that swung them out over the edge of a mountain and regular swings that spun over the edge of the mountain. I couldn't even watch them on these rides. I made my niece videotape them on the large swing for Ava because I couldn't. They went on that twice. Isabelle went on a roller coaster she was big enough to go on. Ava convinced me to go on a mountain coaster that went down the mountain. I was hitting the brake the entire time! It was probably a ride better suited for her and Joe. Life was back to normal, as my heart had started to heal from my mother's passing and we were enjoying our new family.

CHAPTER 3

## What We Lost

Shortly after our return from Colorado, Joe started experiencing some pain and swelling in one of his testicles. His first thought was that it was from his pants or work belt weight and a few extra pounds he had put on during the past few months. He purchased some new pants and gave it a few days to see if it got better, which it did. This is the time I wish we had known the cancers that were being seen in our toxin-exposed veterans. I wish we knew that we had hit yet another red flag, much like the high blood pressure and fertility red flags we had missed due to lack of knowledge distribution. There are so many missed opportunities to find illnesses early, due to lack of information being provided to our veterans.

Joe had been a sergeant for almost five years; therefore, he was eligible to take the lieutenant's test that was being given in the summer of 2017. This was the next step he wanted to take in his NYPD career. It was time once again for him to hit the books.

Shortly after Christmas, the swelling and pain in Joe's testicle returned. This time he knew something

286

was wrong. On January 17, 2017, Joe went to a urologist who diagnosed him with testicular cancer after a physical examination and sonogram of the testicle. Further testing was necessary to see how advanced the cancer was. Joe was sent for CT scans to check the natural paths the disease takes when it spreads. Upon review of those tests, it was discovered that Joe's cancer had already spread to his pelvis, abdomen, and lungs.

The first step in combating this disease was an orchiectomy, which is the removal of the diseased testicle. Joe had his orchiectomy on February 3, 2017. It was an outpatient procedure, and after some time in recovery, Joe went home.

I began researching the best facility for treatment of his cancer; my priority was providing Joe with the best care to maximize his rate of survival. We had excellent medical insurance with the police department, and since no one had advised us of cancers or illnesses related to Joe's exposure to burn pits and toxins while serving overseas, we had no reason to seek care or assistance from the VA.

Joe went to work and told them what was happening. His intention was to work around his treatments and appointments as much as possible. Since he enjoyed going to work, this seemed like an option for him. His commanding officers and friends at work told him he should concentrate on healing himself. It was then that he decided to go out on medical leave. This was a big decision for him, considering he had just received an award at work for never calling in sick over a five-year span of time. I can probably count on my fingers the amount of times he called in sick in the twelve years prior to his cancer diagnosis. He simply did not believe in doing that; he'd power through anything so as not to leave his precinct short.

As our primary care physician had been a friend of mine since I was 14 years old, I contacted her for her opinion and support. We sent all the images and tests to her as well. We both researched and found that there were two excellent facilities for the treatment of this disease. One was Memorial Sloan Kettering Cancer Center right in New York City, and the other was Indiana University, where Lance Armstrong was treated by the gentleman who created the standard of care for testicular cancer. Since both facilities were top rated and one of the doctors at Sloan Kettering was working on new avenues of treatment, we decided to go to Memorial Sloan Kettering in New York City.

Our first appointment there was in February 2017. They reviewed the scans Joe received and requested an additional brain MRI. They reran the pathology from his orchiectomy at their facility. Testicular cancer is something they refer to as a mixed gem cell cancer. This means there is usually more than one type of pathology within the tumor. Joe had some embryonal cancer, but his pathology report stated clearly that the majority of his cancer was choriocarcinoma, which is the most rare and aggressive form of testicular cancer. Given the advanced progression of Joe's disease and his pathology, he was in the most advanced stage of testicular cancer, stage 3C.

Joe also had thyroid cancer. I believed that this was found during his treatment for testicular cancer. However, in speaking with our primary care doctor while working on my VA disability paperwork, she made me aware that it was there from the beginning. She had noticed it on one of his scans, but in discussions with his oncologists, it was more critical to address the rare, aggressive testicular cancer. The thyroid cancer was a sarcoma isolated in the thyroid and deemed less critical at that time. Also, while treating the body for the testicular cancer, we could potentially destroy the thyroid cancer; worst case scenario, we'd remove the thyroid.

The oncologists tried to remain optimistic while also letting us know the severity of the situation. They explained the treatment options available and the next steps. Memorial Sloan Kettering Cancer Center is a treatment hospital as well as a research facility. They offered Joe the option to take part in a chemotherapy trial they were performing. This trial was putting the standard of care treatment against the second line of treatment to see if one outperformed the other. It was a randomized trial in which the computer picked who was assigned to each group.

Joe and I discussed his participation and decided it was an option he should pursue. We were both of the mindset that no matter which treatment he was assigned, it would benefit him. We were hoping for the second line of treatment, given the advanced stage of his disease. We had believed that skipping the first step may help us attack the disease faster. Of course. he ended up being assigned the standard of care, known as BEP. The treatment started in March of 2017.

This treatment meant a week of daily chemotherapy infusions administered in the New York City facility, followed by three weeks off. Each cycle was considered one round, and Joe would be receiving four rounds. I would take Joe to his first few treatments. Thankfully, my siblings would take turns taking off work in order to watch Isabelle and keep Ava company. Ava was in fifth grade, and Isabelle was in pre-school. Sometimes, Joe would take the train and then the subway to get there; this way no one had to stay with the kids. He did this a few times, until one day when he received a call from his CO from work. He was calling to see how Joe was doing. Joe told him he was on the train and he'd call him back since reception wasn't good.

When Joe walked in the door that day, he was on the phone. I heard him saying, "Yes sir", "Okay sir", "Thank you very much." Very curious as to what this call was about, I asked him as soon as he hung up. He said, "He told me that he did not want me taking the trains into treatment. The precinct is there to support me, and when I have appointments, I should call them to have someone transport me to and from."

Joe was humbled by the support his fellow officers were giving him. He never liked to bother people, but he did take them up on that offer sometimes. They would also take him to his monthly or bi-monthly required appointments with the NYPD medical division. Since he was out on long term sick leave, they wanted to physically see him, as well as be kept informed of the oncologist's reports. They treated him very well.

On the days that I went with Joe, my family rotated through our house, and whoever could get off work came to help. My brother-in-law and sister would fly in from Colorado, stay a couple of weeks at a time, and help while my sister worked from home. When I would go to all the doctor's appointments and some of the treatments, one of my siblings would come. We would fill it all however needed. One sibling would take the first part of the day, and another would relieve them. Or a niece would come to watch Isabelle and keep Ava company after school. I've come to find out Isabelle relied on Ava a great deal as well while I was away. I should have realized that then.

Joe was feeling okay. He'd have his moments right after treatment where he wouldn't feel that great, but as was his personality, he'd power through it. He did end up with one long term side effect from the treatment, neuropathy in his hands and feet. They would feel numb or as if they had pins and needles in them. His oncologist gave him some medication to try to see if it could be reversed.

Here is a little background on what they look for to determine efficacy of the treatments. Obviously, they utilize scans to view existing tumors; they also take blood to monitor two tumor markers which elevate in testicular cancer patients. Those markers are alpha-fetoprotein (AFP, also called alphas) and human chorionic gonadotrophin (HCG, also called beta). If those numbers go down, it is a positive sign.

The embryonal cancer would elevate the alphas, while the choriocarcinoma would elevate the betas. After the first round of treatment, the alpha level went back to normal range and stayed normal for the entire two and a half years of treatment. The betas went down more slowly, but they did go back to normal after the first round. We also noticed via scans that the existing tumors were shrinking. We were getting excited! However, since the tumors were still visible and the beta markers were slowly starting to elevate again, Joe needed to proceed quickly to the next phase of treatment.

The next step in treatment for someone at such an advanced stage of this disease was a surgery called a retroperitoneal lymph node dissection, RPLND for short. This is a very invasive procedure where they cut you open from your chest to your pelvis and manually remove tumor-affected lymph nodes in the pelvis and abdomen.

In July of 2017, Joe had his RPLND surgery. My sister Christine and brother-in-law Greg came into town and met me at the hospital the day of the surgery. My mother in law and sisters in law Suzanne and Robin all came to the hospital as well. My other siblings and nieces spent the day with the girls. The surgery took all day. The doctor met with us after the surgery to tell us that he had removed 49 lymph nodes and found that some were another aggressive pathology called teratoma.

We were thankful that Joe's alpha and beta markers had stayed normal, allowing the doctors to perform the surgery. He stayed in the hospital for a week, not allowing the kids, his family, or his friends to visit. He didn't want people to see him that way. I was the only one he wanted to come visit. His sister Robin and Dominick ended up coming as well, but Joe was glad to see them anyway. My sister Daurene came with me just to keep me company during one of my visits that week. At that point, I wasn't comfortable driving to the city alone, and parking was difficult, so the precinct sent officers to transport me the entire week. I always went home to the kids at night. Of course, my family stayed with the kids when I was at the hospital. Joe's precinct took care of our transportation the day he was coming home.

That surgery took quite a bit out of Joe. He spent most of the summer healing from that, as we discussed the next treatment steps with his oncologist and our primary care doctor. His beta markers started rising again shortly after his surgery. During his recovery, they decided to proceed with a brain MRI, since that was another location this disease progressed to and they wanted to see if anything else was contributing to his rising markers.

They found a tumor on the bottom left hemisphere of Joe's brain. They said, "We're not sure if something this size would be producing the large elevation of your beta markers, but let's address it first with focal radiation." The radiation started in August and was completed by September. They advised us that it would take a few months before we would know if it worked. The tumor would swell, but as long as it didn't grow, it was a positive sign. We needed to proceed with systemic treatment as his beta marker numbers kept rising and the lung tumors were still present.

The next treatment regimen was more chemotherapy, called TIP. Again, Joe entered a randomized trial which was comparing the next two lines of treatment against one another. Again, we received the standard-of-care next line of treatment. This treatment meant a week-long stay in the hospital for chemo infusions, followed by two weeks off. This would continue for three cycles.

As was the norm for us now, my family made their schedules around when we needed help with the kids, especially since Joe would be in the hospital for a week every round. We never had to ask them; they just did it and ensured that we had coverage whenever we needed it. We were so thankful for that. Joe used to talk about the party he wanted to throw for everyone after he was better, because of all of the help they provided us.

Given the level Joe's beta markers were at, his oncologist wanted to take a precautionary step prior to TIP starting in case he had to proceed to the next line of treatment. That treatment would mean high dose chemotherapy, followed by a stem cell transplant with Joe's own cells in order to rebuild his immune system. The high dose chemotherapy would completely wipe out his immune system. They harvested his stem cells via a leukapheresis catheter prior to the TIP treatment. They kept the catheter in after the stem cell extraction in order to administer the TIP treatment. It meant fewer times they would have to try to find his veins to administer this round of treatments, and for that, Joe was thankful. They always had a hard time finding his veins for treatments and blood draws.

The TIP treatment was a bit more taxing on Joe than the first round of BEP, but again, he powered through it. He tried to continue doing as much around the house as he could when he felt well enough. Some days he just needed to rest, and those days it was nice that Isabelle was only in pre-school because she'd sit with him on the couch and watch TV with him. They'd play games, and he'd just enjoy sitting with her. He'd be home when Ava came home from school, and I know he was thankful he had that time with her as well. We would go to the movies if there was something out, and he'd come to events at the preschool or middle school if he was up to it. He was cherishing his time with his girls; they were what he was most proud of in his life.

During Joe's treatment weeks, I usually went in to see him every other day, so as not to leave the girls so much, per Joe's request. He always took a laptop and our external hard drive with him so he could look at our pictures, and he always FaceTimed with the girls. I'm a big hockey fan, and I love the New York Islanders. We'd watch games while I was there, and then I'd listen to them on the car ride home. Joe would always call me about the game when I got home. It was a nice distraction. We'd often talk about getting season tickets when he got better, because he knew I truly enjoyed it.

As the holidays were approaching, we received a wonderful surprise from Joe's police precinct. They had collected money from everyone to give to us as a Christmas gift; we were so grateful for this surprise. Even though we had great medical coverage, we still had utilized several thousand dollars paying our co-pays, and we were accruing more debt with every treatment. This extra money was very helpful.

Joe's last round of TIP ended on Christmas Eve. I drove into the city by myself to pick him up. Meanwhile, back at our house my whole family was preparing and arriving for our annual Christmas celebration. Ever since my mother died, Joe and I had been hosting Christmas Eve at our house, and after discussing it with Joe, we decided to keep it that way for this year.

Even though Joe wasn't feeling that well, he was glad everyone was at our house and that the kids were enjoying Christmas Eve. I tried to let the kids sleep in the next day so that Joe could get some rest, but since it was Christmas morning, it was challenging. He always enjoyed waking up Christmas morning to watch the kids open their gifts, and this year was no different. He toughed it out this year with his cup of espresso and a smile.

After we opened our presents, I told him to go back to bed and rest; we were having his family over on Christmas Day. The kids and I made sure the house was set up; my family had helped reset the table before they left on Christmas Eve. Thankfully, Joe's family had done all of the cooking and was bringing everything we needed for dinner. He enjoyed having them there even though he wasn't feeling his best.

Joe spent the next two weeks recuperating from the latest treatment. He had to go for bloodwork and scans to see how his tumors had responded to this round. Unfortunately, his beta markers were not lowering the way they needed to, and he was not in normal range. The scans showed that while his lung tumors had shrunk some, they were still visible. These two results ensured that he had to proceed to the next round of treatment: high dose chemotherapy with a stem cell transplant. This would be three rounds of treatment that included a few days in the hospital. It also included daily trips to the city the days following the treatment in order to support his immune system recovery as needed. There was a specific area of the hospital that handled such cases. It meant blood transfusions, rehydration, platelet transfusion, and support with other supplements he became deficient in. It also meant a lot of trips to New York City and a lot of support needed at home.

Joe made it through round one okay; it was rough,

but better than we expected. We continued to make the daily trips to N.Y.C. until his immune system had returned to a normal range. They realized during that treatment that his catheter was not working as efficiently as it should. It was determined at that time that they would need to remove the existing one and insert a new one. This meant another out-patient hospital surgery to put the new one in.

After the second round of treatment while at one of our daily visits, I noticed Joe's face was red and one side was swelling. They noticed he was dehydrated; so, down to the emergency room we went. After their initial examination, it was determined that he had a fever, and more testing was needed to figure out the root cause. Since his immune system was so depleted, he was extremely susceptible to infection. Review of his facial x-ray and the rest of the tests performed showed that he had an infection underneath a capped tooth. Round two of treatment would need to be delayed as they extracted the tooth and cleared the infection with antibiotics. His beta markers continued to rise.

Once they felt he had recovered enough, he moved on to his third and final round of high-dose chemotherapy. This round would be the worst by far. After the infusion, the daily visits started. It was the beginning of April, and Isabelle's birthday was that week. Joe asked if he could have the day off from his daily appointment in order to celebrate her birthday. After consulting with his oncologist, they allowed it. They decided to give him extra fluids so he would be okay missing the one day. We celebrated Isabelle's birthday with cake at home, but Joe was not feeling very well.

The next morning was a Saturday, and Joe was supposed to arrive at his appointment mid-morning. Given what he was going through and our travel time, they gave us some leeway on this. I tried to wake him up for the appointment, but he kept saying he didn't want to go. He was very lethargic and was too tired to get up. The hospital called to remind me that Joe absolutely had to be there before their section closed. I finally got him up and got him to the car. He was tired and moving slowly. I was concerned heading into that appointment because he was clearly not well.

As soon as we arrived, they took one look at him, put him in a hospital bed, and wheeled him down to the emergency room to be admitted. He was running a high fever, starting to hallucinate, and rapidly declining. They started administering fluids, tests, and blood draws; something was not right. Thankfully, my family ran over to be with Isabelle and Ava; so, I stayed with Joe until they got him settled.

He was feeling really bad, and he didn't really want me to go. But then he would say, "No, you've got to get home for the kids." Unfortunately, they didn't have any beds available; so, he stayed in the emergency room. Thankfully, there it means a private room with a good amount of staff.

When I returned the following day, Joe had been moved to ICU in an isolated room where visitors were limited and required to wear masks, gowns, and gloves to enter. These items had to remain on during the entire visit. Joe was not any better than when I left him the night before; in fact, he was worse. His fever would drop for a short while but come right back after the medication started to wear off. The infectious disease doctors there couldn't figure out what the infection was or where it was coming from. They were working along with his oncologist to determine what was happening and how it could be treated. That wasn't the only complication, either.

Joe's body was rejecting the high dose chemo, which is really poison, right? I mean, it is there to kill the cancer cells and possibly cure you, but it can't discern good from bad. It attacks everything. Therefore, his body started expelling it and rejecting it uncontrollably, and it was deeply upsetting to him. He was a very proud person who always took care of himself, but he couldn't control this reaction. The nurses had to help him get to the bathroom. When I wasn't there, they had a nurse stationed outside his door in case he needed any help, because he would try to get up himself. He would call me or text me and say, "Bring me extra clothes." We were just throwing his stuff out. Then while administering some medication, one of the nurses forgot to open the catheter line, which made it burst. Everything was happening all at once.

Finally, the infectious disease doctors determined that Joe had a staph infection, which they believed was caused by the catheter. Thankfully, the antibiotics they had started to give him seemed to be keeping the fever at bay, and the hallucinations seemed to be coming to an end. The uncontrollable rejection of the chemotherapy had subsided; things were starting to progress in the right direction.

The doctors advised us that Joe would need to come home on 24-hour IV antibiotics, but since his catheter had to be removed, they needed to insert a PICC line to administer the antibiotics. When I arrived at the hospital, Joe told me that the nurse's first attempt was not successful; so, she had to switch arms. It had been uncomfortable, and he was annoyed and frustrated, rightfully so. He had been through so much already. As we were talking, I was thankful Joe was coherent now. I noticed that the arm where the PICC line had failed was red and swollen. I paged the nurse for her opinion. She agreed and set up a CT scan of his arm to access the problem.

The CT scan showed Joe had a blood clot in his arm. This meant Joe was going home with another medication, oral blood thinners. A few days after this discovery, Joe was finally released from the hospital. He had spent fourteen days there, and because of my family, I was able to be there every day. I'd come home at night to be with the kids, but my days were spent with Joe. While he was in the hospital, I didn't let on to anyone how bad he really was.

When I took Joe home, he had gotten very skinny. This treatment had worn him down, and he needed time to recuperate. They showed me how to change the antibiotics and sent us home with the bags of medication and supplies. Joe had to wear the infusion machine 24 hours a day, and I had to change it once a day. He was a very independent man who was not used to relying on people for help. He was usually the one providing the help.

After all of these treatments and doctor's appointments, he'd come to rely on me for a lot. I was happy to provide whatever assistance I could for him. He would thank me all of the time for helping him and staying with him. He'd tell me he was glad I was there. I would remind him that that's what you do when you love someone. You help them through whatever they need you to; you don't abandon them, especially not when times get tough. My job was to listen to what the doctors said, understand it, research it, and make sure we were doing everything we could to cure him. He'd often tell me I should become a nurse or a doctor; I would laugh at that. I did not want to become either of those things; I just wanted to make sure Joe was receiving the care he needed to grow old with us.

Thankfully, Joe's oncologist gave him two weeks off from appointments. His first appointment back was to the infectious disease doctor. Once he gave him the all clear, it was back to the oncologist. At his first appointment back, the oncologist said, "You were in a dark place," which just reminded me how bad he had really been.

After all of that, we had hoped we would get some good news, but Joe's beta markers were never in normal range and were continuing to rise. His CT scan of his lungs and PET scan of his body showed miniscule lung tumors and no new tumors. This meant that the lung surgery to remove any residual tumors was not an option due to their size. The only remaining tumor was the one they had done radiation on in his brain. It had grown slightly, but they could not determine if that was just residual swelling from the radiation or actual growth. His oncologist believed, due to the beta marker levels, that the cancer was in his blood and had just not yet presented itself. The decision was made to watch the tumor and see if any new tumors presented themselves, while giving Joe more time to heal. It would be the first time in sixteen months that he would have a break.

Joe worked hard to gain his strength back. As he started feeling better, he started doing more. We put the pool up in the backyard so that he could go swimming with the kids. We took our annual trip to Splish Splash, but this time even more people came. As was tradition, my nieces Jacqueline and Hailey came, but so did my sister Christine, brother-in-law Greg, my sister Alexis, my sister Denise, my sister Daurene, and my nieces, Katie, Jennie, and Julia.

We took our annual trip to Hershey Park with my sister Alexis and nieces Jacqueline and Hailey. We also took our family trip to Rocking Horse Ranch, something we started doing after my mom passed away. Everyone came on that trip, my brother Michael, sister in law Kathy, sisters Denise and Alexis, sister Daurene, brother-in-law Steven, and my nieces Katie, Jennie, Julia, Jacqueline, and Hailey. My niece's boyfriend Luke came, too. It was a great trip; Joe was healed enough to enjoy himself, even though the neuropathy hadn't gone away in his hands and feet.

This was also when we decided to make a trip to the VA to discuss his military pension, his retirement, and if his cancer was related to his exposure to contaminated water while in Camp LeJeune.

First, we were told that Joe was only entitled to his pension once he hit sixty, and if he passed away before that, the kids and I were entitled to nothing. Joe was in disbelief; he said, "Wait a minute-I served twenty years, and they get nothing. How can that be? That's awful."

Next, the VA representative tried to tell Joe that he didn't see in his system that Joe had completed his twenty years. He had no idea what an MCI was and advised him to call the Marine Corps to square that away.

Lastly, he tried to tell us that Joe's cancer was not on the contaminated water list and that Joe wasn't there long enough anyway. I had researched this issue because something in my mind kept telling me his cancer was caused by some exposure. He knew Joe did a tour in Iraq, but he never mentioned burn pit exposure or toxin exposure and the illnesses being seen from it.

I would come to find out through my advocacy work that there were memos that were disseminated through the VA letting them know that they should be on the lookout for these rare cancers and illnesses from the toxins our veterans were exposed to. And the VA representative didn't say anything.

He told Joe he could go across the hall to make sure he was in the medical system. We did that to clarify that he was in the VA medical system, which he was, but we did not seek care there. There was no reason for him to change care when he had the NYPD medical coverage; plus, we were just told that his cancer wasn't related to his service. We both were disappointed when we left there. Joe felt very deflated and disappointed that after twenty years of agreeing to put his life on the line for his country, they would dismiss him as they did. I made the decision after that appointment to keep researching, as I was convinced something out of the ordinary caused this rare, aggressive cancer.

Soon enough it came time for our next steps in treatment. Joe had been given all of the known treatments for testicular cancer, yet his beta markers would not decline. They tried one round of brain radiation during the summer, but we weren't seeing the changes we needed to see.

Doctors don't take performing brain surgery lightly. I discussed this with them since it was the only location with a visible tumor. Joe's oncologist told us that the markers they were seeing were most likely not just from the brain tumor. The tumor was not large enough to be producing those numbers. He was convinced that the cancer was in Joe's blood and had just not yet presented itself. I persisted, as I did not see the harm in removing the brain tumor since it was in a more outer area of the brain.

We scheduled an appointment with the neurologist to discuss our options. She advised us that she could not definitively say whether the tumor was or wasn't dead. She advised us of the risks and allowed us to decide. Joe and I discussed it with our primary care doctor and decided to proceed with the brain resection. We deduced that the benefits outweighed the risks. They believed that the only possible long-term issue that may occur would be an issue with peripheral vision on one side; on the off chance that that occurred, we'd deal with that later. If this kept him alive, it was worth it.

They scheduled his brain resection for September. I was there, along with his mother and sisters. The doctor informed us after surgery that it went well, and we were thankful. We were able to see Joe in recovery, and once we realized he was okay, we left because they had no room for him to be moved into. I went back to see him the next two days. Since they still had no rooms available to transfer him to, they had kept him in recovery. Given this situation and how well he was doing, they decided it was okay for him to go home. They drew blood to check his markers before we left.

His oncologist called to see how he was doing and to ask us if we had seen the bloodwork results on the patient portal (they utilize an app which shows all appointments and test results). Joe's beta markers had dropped by seventy-five percent. We were all so cautiously optimistic. Could this have been the smoking gun? Could this surgery be the treatment that put him into remission?

My Peggy Positive personality was jumping for joy. I always used to tell Joe, "The brain's really powerful. You have to think positive."

Joe was probably a little more real than I was. He would mention things that he wished for and things that he wanted for the kids. He used to say to me, "You have to listen to me; these are things I want if something happens to me. These are things I want you to do for the kids if something happens to me."

I'm glad he did that. I wish I was a bit more realistic at some points, like he was. Our kids meant the most to him, and he would always say to me, "Gina, if it were just you and I, I could take it on the chin. It's just what happens. But my kids don't deserve this."

As we waited for Joe to heal and to see how his body reacted, medical co-pays kept mounting. Our medical insurance paid a great deal, but the copays added up. Between those, Joe losing out on his overtime, and my not working, by the end of the two and a half years of treatments, we were about $60,000 in debt. I was trying to pay them what I could, because the hospital was willing to work with us, but it was becoming too much.

The hospital had a program that provided us travel money for gas and tolls. I finally said to his oncologist that the co-pays were becoming a financial burden. He advised me to contact the financial department I worked with to have them do a financial analysis to see if we qualified for any assistance. It's funny what you forget when you have so much to handle. It can truly be a blessing at times; you tend to filter out the things that really don't matter. My sister reminded me of this, when I was writing this part.

When I made the initial call for the analysis, the woman who handled our travel money said to me, "Don't you think you've already gotten enough?" As I write this now, all I can think is, based on what my husband gave for his country, "No, ma'am, no I don't." She provided me the contact information for the person in charge of the analysis. Ironically, after their review, they decided that we qualified to have our copays forgiven; so, even they felt we deserved assistance. We were grateful they took this financial burden off us.

Unfortunately, our optimism began to fade as Joe's beta markers started to rise again, and rise quickly. The lung tumors started to present and grow again as well. At this point, there were no known treatment options left to cure his disease. His oncologist advised us of an immunotherapy trial he qualified for, and of course Joe agreed to sign up for it. He was willing to try anything to stay here with us. This would be three rounds of treatment. If it was helping, it could be continued; if no improvement was shown after three rounds, it would be stopped because it was not going to work. Joe started that in October 2018.

While all of this was going on, the nagging in my brain continued. I thought, "This isn't right, there is some underlying factor that caused his cancer. Joe's out of the age range for testicular cancer. This is the rarest form of testicular cancer you can get, and there is no familial link."

This particular cancer is known as a young man's disease. The age range for testicular cancer is 13 to about 35; in some cases you'll see the range go to 45. Joe was 50 when he was diagnosed. Something inside of me kept saying, "Something's wrong. This is not bad luck. Something caused this."

Since the VA had rejected my initial thought regarding the contaminated water in Camp Lejeune, I went back to researching. That is when I discovered Burn Pits 360 and Rosie and Le Roy Torres, and I was sure I had found the underlying factor. They had an abundant amount of helpful information on their site. After reading this information, I found that Joe's cancer was listed on their site as one of the top ten cancers being discovered amongst our exposed veterans.

Joe never talked much about his deployment. People would ask him about it, and he'd say, "We went there, did our jobs, and thankfully everyone came home." Then he'd start to talk about the packages I would send him and how they'd all eat the food I sent together on Sundays.

So, I asked Joe if he was around burn pits during his deployment to Iraq. And he said, "Yeah, I was."

I told him, "There's a VA registry for burn pits. I think this is what caused your cancer. We should add your name to that registry."

He made a few attempts to do so, but he could not remember his logins. He sent a request to have his passwords reset, and we went back to worrying about his care. You have to remember the point we were at in his treatment and how much he had gone through. He was not concentrating on this matter as much as he was on his treatment and possible outcomes.

We had decided to book a trip to Disney for the beginning of December; of course, Christine and Greg met us there. All of the walking was a lot for Joe, but as usual, he powered through. We packed in as much fun as possible; character breakfasts that we usually did once, we did twice. We even added another with Isabelle's favorite characters mid trip! Everyone had a great time, even though we all knew where Joe was in his treatment. All of us, including Ava (Isabelle was too young) knew this might be our last trip together. No one said a word about it; we simply tried to enjoy the time together.

Upon our return, we found out that the immunotherapy was not working and they were stopping the treatments. We asked, "Well, now what do we do?"

And the oncologist said, "There is nothing else. There's just palliative care now. We can give you some chemotherapy and try to prolong your life and see how that works."

Joe started those chemo infusions at the end of December. The chemo infusions weren't really working; so, they were stopped. We switched to chemo pills, and they seemed to be working a little bit. They were keeping the numbers level, even dropping them a little bit. I kept doing research and asking his oncologist about any other treatments. At this point, I expanded my search to other countries as well.

In addition to this, Max's health started to decline. He had had some hind leg issues in the past that were surgically corrected, but his hind legs started to fail him again. After several trips to the vet and some treatments, it was discovered that he had something called degenerative myelopathy. This is a spinal disorder that causes paralysis which starts at the tail and works its way up to the brain. There is no known cure or treatment for this disease. We would have to see how he progressed over the next few months.

Since Joe was in palliative care, his oncologist's office told us of a program that the hospital had, much like the Make a Wish foundation. He told us to call and have them set up something we'd like to do as a family. The financial department handled this as well; it was the same woman I mentioned before. We told her we'd like to go back to Disney. She started planning a Disney trip for 10 days. Joe finally caved; he agreed he would use a scooter to make it easier on him. They were planning all sorts of magical extras for us, and we were so excited.

Shortly after Isabelle's birthday in April, we made the extremely difficult decision to put Max to sleep. His condition was getting worse, and he was no longer able to walk much on his own. Even standing was difficult. Our hearts were completely broken on April

10th when we had to say good-bye to him. Joe and I stayed with him, while Ava and Isabelle said good-bye and waited together in the waiting room. Joe stood where Max could see him, and I held him until he took his last breath. I can only imagine what Joe was feeling and thinking, given his situation.

As the trip to Disney was being finalized, Joe started having trouble breathing. I immediately called his oncologist to see what we needed to do. He told me he didn't want Joe getting on an airplane. If he had a clot, it could be really bad. He scheduled some scans at their Long Island facility.

We dropped Joe off at the facility since we had some appointments scheduled. Joe was okay doing these tests on his own, and we didn't expect the results immediately. I was always there when he was given results.

However, he FaceTimed me when the doctor came in to tell him she was going over the results. I felt horrible not being there with him, but I'm sure that's nothing compared to how he felt there alone. We found out that the cancer had now spread to his liver and spleen and that his lung tumors had grown. It was devastating. His oncologist followed up shortly after with his own phone call.

The oncologist told me, "Listen to me. Given where it's progressed, this can get bad very quickly. Joe could be fine one day, and then the next day, he could be coughing up blood and progressively get worse. I want to prepare you, because this could change really quickly. I need you to know where we are." Joe decided we had to cancel the Disney trip because he wasn't well enough.

Shortly after this news, we discovered a lump growing out of Joe's back. Since we weren't sure what it was, I contacted our primary care physician. She came over to take a look and test it. She found that it was a cancerous metastasis. These types of metastases are usually associated with terminal, end stage cancer progression.

We were preparing for the inevitable when we discovered a trial for a new medication. I reached out to his oncologist at Memorial Sloan Kettering, who said, "We're not doing that trial right now. Philadelphia is, but Penn Medicine might not have anything open." He provided me with the contact information for the oncologist running the study, and he put a call in to him for us as well.

When I called the oncologist at Penn, he said, "Once we get through this last phase of the first round of testing, we can open round two where we will add more patients."

I asked him to please keep us in mind. We received a call from him at the end of May advising us to go down to Penn Medicine to sign consent forms for phase two of the trial. We went down to Philadelphia on June 4th and signed consent forms for Joe to participate in the trial.

The trial was a monoclonal study targeting a protein called Claudin-6 that they found in people with testicular cancer. It's a protein that is typically only found in infants. Since doctors were finding it in testicular cancer patients, they thought it may work to target it. We would try anything to save Joe, and since this was the only treatment available, we were going to try it.

Isabelle graduated from preschool on June 12th, and thankfully we were home for that. We were all so happy. Ava took the day off from school so she could be there, too, and my sister Christine and brother-in-law Greg came as well. They had come into town to stay with the kids when we were going to Philadelphia. Joe was exceptionally happy. Joe's health had declined, making many things difficult for him to do. He did whatever he could manage to do, but he needed to take rests in between. He kept waving and smiling at Isabelle during the ceremony; he was so proud.

The week of the 17th of June was Joe's first round of treatments in Philadelphia. Because it was a trial, there were parameters that you needed to remain in to stay in the trial, as well as testing requirements since it was a new therapy. Joe would receive a dose the day of treatment, and then there was blood work taken to monitor him at 24 hours, 48 hours, and 72 hours. This meant a four to five day stay in Philadelphia.

This was finals week at school for Ava, who was now finishing seventh grade. Our kids had never been away from both of us overnight. They'd been away from Dad because he had to be away for the police department, but they had never been away from me overnight. And here I was leaving to go to Philadelphia at the worst time for her. We had told her that this was a last ditch effort, a hail Mary pass, to save Joe, but even if we hadn't, she was old enough to see for her own eyes he wasn't well. She understood, but I know it was hard on her.

Ava had two really bad teachers that year. They would tell me to my face that they would help her, but they would not. I had met with all of her teachers, the principals, and her guidance counselor in October and told them what was going on, and I would meet with them periodically or email them updates to keep them informed. I sent them all an email letting them know what was happening with Joe and that "I will be away in Philadelphia during finals."

While I was away with Joe, I happened to check my email. I received an email from Ava's English teacher telling me about an essay that they had to do in school that counted for 20% of their grade. They weren't allowed to bring it home. Ava hadn't handed hers in. Her English teacher not only had time in class to assist her, she had her for the last period of the day, which our school calls self-help. Each student has this class; it allows them to do homework, see other teachers, and take care of any issues they need to. The English teacher had that whole twenty-five minute time period to help Ava as well. She chose not to. Instead, she asked me to make sure that Ava completed it that night and brought it into the final.

I immediately called my sister Christine (who is highly intelligent and a very good writer) who was

315

with the kids, and asked her to help Ava with the essay. That teacher gave my daughter a 65 on the essay, which is the lowest passing grade.I was furious, but it wasn't something I could handle at the moment; it would have to wait.

When we returned from Philadelphia, Ava had finished finals, and school was over. Joe wasn't doing well; there were obvious signs of his body starting to shut down due to the cancer taking over.

We made a command decision, as Joe would say, to do a full family trip to Hershey Park. My entire family, my nieces, my sisters, my brother, my sister-in-law and brothers-in-law, and my niece's now fiance - everybody would come with us, and we would schedule that trip for the end of June. From there, the kids would go home with one of my sisters, while Joe and I split off and went to the next round of therapy in Philadelphia.

Joe was on a scooter the whole trip, because he was not well enough to walk around. I know he wished he could go on rides with the kids, but he enjoyed watching them having fun. We had breakfast and dinner together, and he scootered his way through the arcade to watch the kids play. He always played arcade games with them. He was really good at the claw games and taught the kids to play. Even though Joe couldn't go on any of the rides at Hershey, he told my sister that it was the best trip he ever went on.

We went from there straight to Philadelphia, but Joe wasn't well enough to receive the treatment. His red blood cell count was low, and he needed blood. The doctors knew how far along he was; so, they agreed to allow him to stay in the trial even though his blood cell count was out of trial parameters. They did this because they knew his condition was from the disease, not the effects of the medication. Cancer was going to kill him, not this medication.

They told us to go home. Our primary care doctor set it up so Joe could receive blood at a local hospital on Long Island the next day, which was July 3rd. They allowed us the day off for the Fourth of July; we were to return to Philadelphia for the treatment on July 5th. Joe always loved the Fourth of July, and it was our dating anniversary. I'm glad we were able to spend that day home.

By the time we got down to Philadelphia on the fifth, Joe needed a wheelchair to get into the building. And he was having a really hard time breathing; he needed oxygen. He was given the treatment, but he was not well the entire time we were there. I worked with our primary care doctor while we were there to ensure he had oxygen at our home when we arrived back there that day. This round did not require an extended stay. We headed back home the same day. Thankfully, our doctor was able to get us the oxygen Joe needed, and it was there when we arrived home.

That next day, July 6th, was my niece Katie's 21st birthday party. She turned 21 on the 5th. Joe said to me, "I don't want to go. I'm not feeling well enough, but I don't want to be by myself. Stay with me." So, I stayed with him. Ava stayed home as well; she understood what was happening. Isabelle went with my sisters because she was only five, and she didn't quite get how bad Joe was. He was trying to sleep that night, and he actually said to me at one point, "I don't want to go to sleep, because I'm afraid I'm not going to wake up. Please keep talking to me." I did my best to stay awake and talk with him, but I fell asleep at some point.

The next day, that Sunday, he woke up and said to me, "I think it's time to call hospice."

I told him, "Okay." I called our primary care doctor, who arranged for his in-home hospice care and made herself his hospice doctor. She came over to see him.

My poor friend. She was looking at Joe, and he said, "Can you fix me?"

And she told him, "No, I'm sorry."

He said, "Okay, go away. You're dismissed."

But she knew him so well. She knew what he meant; she wasn't offended. She was more upset because all she ever wanted was to be able to save him.

Now, I think people have a little bit of a skewed perception of how in-home hospice care is structured, because even I didn't know. Nurses come maybe once a day, for maybe an hour, and they leave you with medication. They say, "Call us if there's any problem." Some stay the hour; some stay 20 minutes. They just have to come and check up on the patient. And that's it.

Joe's pretty stubborn. We got the bed; we got all of the medical equipment to take care of him, but he refused to go in the bed. He sat on the couch, and then when he got uncomfortable, he'd ask me to help him move to another spot. He continued to try to do as much for himself as he could. Isabelle didn't want to leave us. She just kept staying there, falling asleep on the couch with us. Ava didn't come out much from her room. Though she'd come out sometimes, she knew what was happening, and she did not want to see her Dad that way.

I contacted the NYPD to let them know Joe was in hospice care. They were extremely helpful and supportive. The SBA (Sergeants Union) went into action to support us as well. We were so grateful for their support and assistance. Joe was able to rest knowing they were taking care of the girls and me.

His family came to visit for a few days. I know Joe was torn about that because he didn't want anyone to see him this way, especially his mother. He never wanted her to have to go through that. As he kept declining, it became too much to withstand.

My siblings and nieces came over to see Joe, knowing that they were saying their final good-byes. My sisters tried to occupy the girls and took them to a local carnival that they would go to annually. Isabelle really didn't understand what was happening, and it was too hard to explain to her at five years old. The kids always made sure to say good-bye to Joe before they left.

As Joe's illness progressed, he became less and less conscious and able to communicate. The last day he spoke, we sat on the couch together, and he said some last words to me. By that time, he had several outward metastases on his back, and I hated seeing him this way. That was the last time he spoke.

For a full day, all he did was make noise. The NYPD commissioner of employee relations at the time, Bob Ganley, came to the house to discuss Joe's pension, benefits, compensation, and other matters. I wished Joe was conscious, but I had a feeling he heard that conversation and knew they were taking care of us. Bob was so helpful throughout everything, as he continues to be to this day.

I sent Isabelle to my sister Alexis's house for a sleepover, thinking it was the best thing for her, because Daddy didn't want her to see him that way. I sometimes wonder if that was the right decision, but at the time it seemed right. She slept there for two nights.

The following day, Joe stopped making noise and was unconscious. The hospice nurse came for a daily visit, and she, my sister Christine, and I moved Joe into the bed. He looked like he was peacefully sleeping. She told me, "If there's anybody that wants to say goodbye, they should come by." I didn't call Isabelle back home because I didn't think that she would understand it. It was a very difficult choice to make.

That night she called, and I put the phone to Joe's ear. I told her to talk to Daddy, and she did. My sister Daurene, brother-in-law Steven, and niece Jennie came by in the nighttime. My niece wanted to say one more good-bye to her uncle. While they were there, I fell asleep on the couch. I was exhausted because I wasn't sleeping. Ava woke me up around 12 o'clock. She said, "They said goodbye; they just left," and went back to her room.

I might have said it out loud or in my head: "I'm going to do the dishes, and then I'm going to come lay with you." I could see Joe over this little ledge that's in my kitchen. On the other side of that was my den, and that's where the bed was. He was right there.

All of a sudden, I heard Joe make a noise; I immediately went over to him. Next, he let out a long sigh, and that was the last breath he took. I felt his chest for a heartbeat and felt for breath by his nose; he was gone. I leaned down, gave him a kiss, and told him I loved him. That was 12:49 am July 17th, 2019, the first of three times in less than twenty-four hours that my heart would break. I went into Ava's room to break the news to her, and it broke my heart again to have to tell her.

I called my sister Christine; she and my brother-in-law Greg said they would come over. I decided to let Isabelle sleep; sometimes I wish I had told them to wake her and bring her, too; other times I know it was the best idea to let her remain sleeping at my sister's house. My sister Christine called my brother Michael, and he said he was heading to our house as well.

Then I called our primary care hospice doctor and called the hospice facility. The hospice nurse arrived, completed their paperwork, and took away the medications they had given us so that they could be disposed of properly. Our doctor arrived with her assistant and confirmed Joe's passing and time of death for her paperwork. We called the funeral home, and they came to pick him up. My doctor and her assistant stayed.

She said, "When they take him out, go inside. I've seen this a million times; you don't want to see it. I'll make sure he's fine."

The next morning, Ava and I went to pick up Isabelle, and I had to break the news to her that Daddy was gone. She said, "I never got to say goodbye to Daddy." I tried to explain to her that she did over the phone. I told her that the last day she was home and said goodbye to him was the last day he spoke. I told her he wouldn't have answered her back if she were here because he was asleep. I also let her know he didn't want her to see him that way. This was the third time my heart would break.

Once I distributed the news of Joe's passing, one of his Marines who served in Iraq under him posted a story about him. This story perfectly summed up how Joe made people feel, people that trusted him to take care of them. It was a story that Joe never shared with me, because he was humble and he probably never gave it a second thought. The story went like this.

While they were packing gear to deploy to Iraq, the radios were not working, not one. This Marine said to Joe, "Staff Sergeant, we're all going to die, aren't we?" Joe replied, "No, we're going to be fine." That Marine told me, "And for some reason, I believed him, and he was right. We all came home." He just had that way of making people feel safe.

The NYPD did a beautiful job with Joe's funeral detail; he received a sendoff from them that would have made him so proud. So many NYPD friends and military friends attended his wake. The police department provided me and the girls with a folded flag at the funeral home. The day of the funeral, the NYPD closed off the street in front of the church and lined it with personnel. The entire right side of the church was filled with officers and commanders Joe worked with and for. They provided bagpipes, a trumpeter, and a helicopter flyover at the church.

Some of his military friends came to the church as well. The NYPD coordinated with local police departments to block off the roads to Calverton National Cemetery so that our drive there would be faster. They provided us with vans to transport us throughout the wake and funeral days. The Marine Corps provided a gun salute and trumpeter and presented the girls and me with a folded flag at the cemetery. They were all well-deserved honors.

As life moved on that summer, the girls and I decided to adopt pets. We adopted a cat, which Ava wanted, so she picked him out and a puppy. They breathed some life back into us, and I often wonder if we saved them or if they saved us. Either way, I guess we were both saved by one another.

October brought us another loss. I received a message from my niece Carissa on October 5th, that my mother-in-law unexpectedly passed away. It was so hard to have to tell the girls that news as well. Now they were without a father and grandparents. As usual they amazed me through the wake and funeral. They are both so strong.

CHAPTER 4

*What the Kids and I Gained*

As 2019 came to a close and we'd gone through the first holiday season without Joe, I decided I needed to do more research regarding his Marine Corps pension. I had been given a VA pamphlet at the cemetery, since Calverton is a military cemetery. I reviewed the numbers on the back and decided to give them a call in January of 2020.

I was advised that the information we received from the VA representative we spoke with in 2018 wasn't entirely accurate. There were forms I could complete to see if the girls and I qualified for any benefits; she was going to send me those in the mail. I had one year to complete them. I also asked the VA representative I was speaking with about adding Joe to their burn pits registry; the response saddened me. I was told that you cannot posthumously add someone to their registry. What that said to me was once someone dies, they no longer matter, and that angered me.

While I awaited the VA paperwork, I went back to the Burn Pits 360 website to review their materials and added Joe to the registry they had started compiling; they allow you to add veterans posthumously. At least I'd have him on that. I reached out to Rosie Torres, co-founder of Burn Pits 360, to ask her what documents from their website would be helpful when submitting my claim. She was kind enough to assist me with that request. We spoke for a short while.

After that, I started compiling the Burn Pits 360 documents and Joe's medical documents. I started reaching out to his fellow Marines to see if they could provide any information or pictures for me from their deployment. Through my discussions with these Marines, I came to find out that their tents were across from a burn pit and burning human waste barrels. I was even sent a picture which showed how close their tents were to the burn pit and the waste area and another photo of Marines stirring the burning waste barrels. I was informed by another Marine that the burn pit in the picture wasn't the only one in the area; when they would travel back and forth to other Marines in the units' positions, they would pass many other burn pits. He also told me that the smell from the human waste would get so bad that they'd coat it with lye in order to reduce the smell. When the smell became too much, they doused it with jet fuel and lit it on fire. This was their environment for six months, something Joe never mentioned.

Thankfully, he was okay at the time of his deployment. But I found out from his Marine friends that he and other Marines would wake up choking in the middle of the night, requiring water to make it stop.

Their airways were closing up on them in the smoke while they slept so that they couldn't breathe. That's what they felt. They all just hoped and prayed that nothing would happen to them.

This deployment was the only time Joe was exposed, because he retired in 2006. The unit went back two or three more times, but he was already out. That just tells you how bad these burn pits were, that a short exposure could cause such an aggressive cancer.

The VA paperwork arrived, and I reviewed it. I was getting ready to put everything together when COVID hit. The kids went remote for school, like everyone else, and the paperwork got moved to the back burner.

In January of 2021, I realized that I had to finish and submit the DIC form for disability compensation, as my one-year time limit was running out. I reached out to Rosie again to confirm what I had was accurate. We had a great conversation, and I began to learn from her how big of an issue burn pit and toxin exposure really was. I submitted all of the paperwork to the VA.

I received my first letter back from the VA in February 2021. It said, "Since your husband was not receiving service-connected disability, you need to provide medical evidence that his illness and death were directly related to his service." And they needed a copy of the death certificate.

I had sent them a stack of paper, and I swear, the death certificate was in the stack. I sent everything that Rosie advised me to send from the Burn Pits 360 website, one of which was a list of all the chemicals they were exposed to, every lab test, his blood work, the resections, and every pathology report highlighted with the aggressive type of cancer that Joe had. It was all sent with the DIC form.

I decided to call the VA to find out what exactly they wanted. I was made aware that they were looking for a letter from a doctor stating that Joe's cancer was related to his service. I went to work trying to obtain what they were looking for. Two weeks went by, and I received a follow-up letter from the VA saying my claim was denied because I didn't send them the proof they were looking for. I was completely shocked; two weeks was not enough time to compile what I needed. Plus, all I could think was, how could they deny something they know is an issue?

I called Rosie for guidance on the latest VA development. She was always willing to help. She provided me with an attorney to handle my VA denial appeal. I had been having a hard time finding someone who would take my case. That attorney is still representing me now.

Rosie advised me of all the years of advocacy she and Le Roy had been doing. She informed me of the legislation they were working on trying to pass. I couldn't believe what was going on and what our veterans were going through. She made me aware of a press conference in Washington, D.C. she was having with Jon Stewart and John Feal. Then she asked me if I would be interested in telling my story at that April press conference. I immediately agreed. This wouldn't bring

Joe back, but if we could help save one person by telling his story, then it was worth it. That is where my advocacy journey started. That is where I found my new extended family.

The kids were excited about going on a road trip; it had been a while due to COVID. On our drive to D.C., I was contacted by a reporter who wanted to interview me when we arrived at our hotel. Shortly after we checked in, we met the reporter outside for the interview. That's when we first met Joe McKay from the FealGood Foundation; he was standing with the reporter when we got to him. He was so nice to us; he welcomed us as if we'd known him for years. He stayed for a part of the interview and then excused himself to go to CVS. When he returned, he had two bags of M&M's. He showed them to me and asked if it was okay to give them to Ava and Isabelle. Of course, not only was it okay, it was incredibly kind of him to do. That night I met a lot of people who were advocating for the legislation. We all met in the lobby of the Hilton to talk. I was trying to remember everyone I was introduced to.

The next day was the press conference. Rosie and Le Roy spoke, as did several members of the group, John Feal, and Jon Stewart. Senator Gillibrand from New York was there since she was a sponsor of the legislation. I could tell from my interaction with her and her staff that she was all in on this. She was going to do all she could to ensure our veterans and their families were taken care of.

That is also where I met Kim; she was a force. She had this advocacy work on autopilot. She had her folded American flag, her husband's dog tags, and his jacket; she was representing him beautifully. She came over to the girls and me to introduce herself. She immediately invited me to join her at other widow events she was planning on attending. I could tell her goal was to make me feel welcome and not alone. We shared a few short stories that day.

After the press conference, I was asked to participate in a CNN interview for the Jake Tapper show, alongside Jon Stewart. As wonderful as you think Jon Stewart is on TV, he is even more delightful in person. He welcomed us with open arms. He spoke to Ava and Isabelle as if he knew them. Isabelle loves acting, singing and dancing; so they had a lot to talk about on the walk to the CNN mobile studio van. I have a great picture sent to me from a Gillibrand staffer of them talking on that walk. Ava doesn't like to be in front of the camera; so she stayed opposite us off of the camera, while Isabelle sat on my lap. After that, more interviews were requested, and my journey grew.

Shortly after that press conference, Jon Stewart was starting the taping of his new show The Problem with Jon Stewart. He determined that his first episode of the show would focus on burn pits. His staff interviewed potential guests for the show and asked me to participate in the taping for the show. I was humbled and honored to be included on one of the panels. His staff was wonderful before, during, and after the taping. He has a fantastic group of individuals that work with him. The taping took place in New York City in July, in front of an audience. It was an experience I will never forget.

After this taping, I started participating in regular Zoom meetings with the other advocates from Burn Pits 360. I was included in emails and texts regarding next steps and what everyone was doing to gain additional legislative support. That's when I met Kevin and Tim. They, too, had already done so much advocacy work; I felt like a complete rookie! They had so many contacts with congressmen, senators, and local veteran's associations. Kevin's VFW work was extensive. They were all so welcoming, even though I knew the least out of everyone. I felt an instant connection with them. They, along with Kim, were so passionate about getting our veterans the help they had earned and deserved.

I started helping our cause in any way I could: sending emails, posting on social media, and making phone calls to congressmen, senators, and anyone else we needed to reach out to to gain support for the legislation. The kids started to become more familiar with everyone the more involved I became. I started to learn about what Kevin, Tim, and Le Roy were experiencing. My heart broke for what they had to endure.

The kids came to everything with me. On every trip to D.C., at every press conference, they were there. Isabelle always stood with me in front of the cameras, and Ava stayed in her position away from the camera.

In March 2022, we attended another D.C. press conference, as well as a hearing regarding the PACT Act for the Senate Veterans Affairs Committee. We walked the halls of Congress trying to speak with senators to tell them our stories and to try to convince them to support the PACT Act. We were escorted around by staff from the offices of Senators Gillibrand and Schumer. I was glad to spend time with Kim, Kevin, and Tim during that trip.

In May 2022, we went to the Rolling to Remember Rally, which had invited Burn Pits 360 to speak. John Feal and Jon Stewart were there, and I thanked them for making sure that no matter what amendments the politicians wanted to make, they always ensured that survivors remained included in the bill. I always felt that we were the easiest people to remove when politicians were trying to make compromises and save money. I mean, our veterans are deceased; what can they do now? They can't speak for themselves. That's part of why I started advocating. I was Joe's voice in his absence, a voice for those who could no longer speak and a voice for those who were so stricken with grief from their loss that they couldn't use their voices.

At the end of May, Rosie called me and said, "Senator Gillibrand is doing a quick press conference in her New York City office in two days. Do you think that you can go and represent Burn Pits 360?"

I said, "Sure, no problem."

I took Isabelle out of school early so that the three of us could attend. Ava is now homeschooled due to all of her horrible experiences in school while Joe was sick and shortly after. We took the train in, and the kids enjoyed that. Then we took a cab to Senator Gillibrand's office. Of course, Joe McKay met us there; the kids were very happy about that. We all really enjoy seeing Joe. The press conference aired on the evening news, and Senator Gillibrand and her staff were wonderful, as usual. She truly meant what she said and was always so genuine when she saw us. After the press conference, Joe drove us to Penn Station.

As I was meeting people, I started hearing about all of the illnesses, diseases, and VA gaslighting that everyone was experiencing. I started finding out things that I didn't know, like the fact that hypertension is a red flag for toxin exposure, as are fertility issues, both things that Joe experienced. What would annoy me the most was that we were never informed about these red flags. The Marine Corps, the DOD, the VA - nobody reached out to us and said, "You were exposed to these toxins and these chemicals. You need to monitor your health." No one was providing our veterans with information to help them. This was so disturbing to me.

Veterans endured the same circumstances as the 9/11 recovery site; it's the same toxic environment. They have a 9/11 health registry for anyone who was within a certain radius of the World Trade Center. Having been down there, along with my mom, I'm familiar with that registry, as I'm on it. They send out annual surveys, looking for health updates. They are trying to track people so that they can be proactive with people. I received more notification from them than Joe ever did from the Marine Corps, the DOD, or the VA about what he was exposed to. You're not providing people with the knowledge and the information that they need to be proactive instead of reactive. That is simply unacceptable.

Had we known, maybe we would have gone for annual toxicity screens to be able to monitor things better. Maybe we would have caught the cancer early. Maybe that would have helped; maybe not. Joe's cancer was very rare and aggressive. I don't know if it would have helped, but I would have liked to have the opportunity.

The Warfighter Bill changed names to the Honoring our PACT Act, and it had passed the House vote. It was heading to the Senate for a vote; we needed to ensure we had the necessary support to get it to pass. We were happy to be there pushing for support, but also seeing our family. It was always nice to be around Kevin, Kim, and Theresa because they just knew what we were going through. There is a bond built upon shared experiences. I was also grateful to see my friend Julie who I'd become close to during our advocating as well. She is an incredible woman who is also a veteran. We were all cautiously optimistic about the bill since it had passed the House vote, but the Senate hurdle would be difficult.

Advocating for the PACT Act, with the way the politicians change their minds, has been a lot of quick reaction. We have to be reactive to what politicians are doing. You know how fluid that is, and you know how it flips and flops all the time.

At the end of July, the PACT Act looked like it would be passed and heading to the President's desk for signature into law. It was a very exciting time. I was just so happy to know that our veterans would receive the healthcare and benefits that they earned, deserved, and needed to survive. Happy that survivors like us could finally receive the survivor's benefits that our loved ones earned and would be proud to know they left for us. I believed all of this would help with closure for so many.

When that didn't happen, what was supposed to be the celebratory press conference we wished we could have held turned into a call for action once again. The team pulled together, and the efforts to get the bill through the Senate again began. That's when the Firewatch on the Capitol steps was started. Unfortunately, we had to wait until that weekend to meet up with everyone, since Isabelle was still in camp. Kim, Tim, Kevin, and Theresa were already there or on their way, and I wished we could be there with them.

One of our advocates was able to put together a rally quickly in Philadelphia, since Senator Toomey was one of the Senators contributing to the bill's recent failure. The rally was set for Monday, August 1. I deferred to Rosie to find out where she most needed us, D.C. or Philadelphia. She asked me to go to the Philadelphia rally. My plan became to attend the Philadelphia rally Monday morning and then head straight to the Firewatch in D.C.

Monday came, which ironically was my and Joe's wedding anniversary. I spoke at the Philadelphia rally; Joe McKay was there and spoke as well. Then the girls and I got back into the car to head to D.C. to support the Firewatch. We were glad to see Kim, Tim, and Kevin when we arrived. It was late Monday; so, we stayed for a bit and then headed back to the hotel. I couldn't make the kids sleep outside. They had done so much to support me already.

We woke up Tuesday morning and headed straight to the Firewatch to hold signs, do interviews, and show our support. John Feal and Jon Stewart were there as well. Jon brought an entire crew from his show; some I had met during the filming of that first episode. They are an incredible group of people, and I'm so glad I had the opportunity to see them again. I still interact with some on social media, and I'm thankful for that. We were there all day. Senator Gillibrand and Senator Schumer came out in the afternoon to let us know they were putting the bill to the floor for vote again. They told us, "We're going to allow you guys in the gallery if you'd like to be in the gallery."

The girls and I definitely wanted to be there. It was a very surreal feeling, being escorted into the building by staffers from the offices of Senators Gillibrand and Schumer. They took anything that transmitted a signal from us, which included our phones and my Fitbit. I had to check my pocketbook as well. They instructed us before we entered and while we were in the gallery of very specific rules we needed to follow, rules such as, no talking and no showing emotion either in support of or opposition to any vote. We were told we could not cheer or show emotions after the final vote was read.

The senators were putting three amendments up for vote and then voting on the PACT Act. While they were working on the final amendment, Isabelle had to use the bathroom; so the ushers contacted a staffer to escort us. There was a group of about seven of us who took the bathroom break. When we returned, the staffer who brought us back escorted us to a different section than we had previously been in. We ended up being right next to Jon Stewart and his staff from The Problem.

By the time we were seated, the voting was almost coming to an end. Ava asked me if it was the final vote for the bill, but I wasn't sure. I couldn't imagine we had missed that much or that it had gone that quickly. A gentleman behind us heard us and said it should take about fifteen more minutes. I quietly asked the usher if it was the final vote for the bill, and he responded that it was. Then it was announced that the PACT Act had passed. I had no idea how I would feel.

We stood up to exit, as the ushers were trying to dismiss us in an orderly manner. The section Jon Stewart was in started walking out of their rows and up to exit. Jon came out of his aisle, which was across from us, and saw the girls and me. He looked at me and came directly over to me to give me a hug.

I don't cry that easily. There's nothing wrong with crying; it's just the way I am. However, when Jon came over to me and gave me that hug, my emotions just ran over. Tears started pouring down my face. I was relieved that our veterans would finally receive the care that they needed and deserved and that survivors like us would receive the benefits their loved ones had earned. Everyone would feel validated.

Looking back now, I guess I also felt that maybe this meant Joe didn't die in vain. His service and sacrifice meant something, and while this bill didn't save him, maybe it would save someone else. Maybe some other family wouldn't have to fight like we've had to to receive their benefits. It also meant Joe could rest easy knowing that his efforts would help the girls' future; after all, they meant the most to him.

I will be forever grateful to Jon for all he has done for first responders and veterans, but I will always remember what he did for me that day. Since he'd been through this before, he knew. He understood, and he just stayed there with me for a minute or two, to allow me to feel. I'll never forget that he did that for me.

Once we exited toward where we'd checked our belongings, we saw everyone else. We saw Kim, Tim, and Kevin; we all had big smiles on our faces. I saw Rosie, whom I hugged and thanked for all she had done. We were overjoyed.

We filtered out to a press conference Senator Schumer was having. Isabelle and I stood with Kim, who was holding her gold star flag and Gary's folded flag. She always shared those things with us. There was a great deal of press already set up and ready to record. They were snapping pictures and recording everything.

When Rosie said during that press conference, "Gina, now you and the girls will get your benefits," tears came to my eyes again as that sense of validation came back. Jon Stewart came by to stand near us and hugged us all. He was just as happy for us. We'll really miss seeing him; I'm glad I told him that when we were at the press conference.

Another person ended up right beside us during that press conference, and I'm grateful he did. Joe McKay is our fellow advocate from the FealGood Foundation, but so much more than that. He's our friend. When he saw us, he gave me a big hug, so genuinely happy for everyone. He was happy for the girls and me, that we would finally receive our benefits. The press caught that hug on camera. It is one of my favorite pictures because it captures the moment perfectly. It's one of joy and relief. He's a special man. He gives his all to anything he's involved in, and he cares about people. I'm thankful for him and his family, who understand that his advocacy work takes him away from them.

It was overwhelming. Thank God for Rosie and Le Roy, who had done this work for so many years, so many more years than I have. I'm thankful they started their foundation. It has brought purpose and family to so many people; it's certainly brought those things to me. Tim, Kevin, and Kim are family to the girls and me. I was glad we were all able to return a week later to watch from the White House as President Biden signed the PACT Act into law. What a beautiful, fitting celebration. I was finally able to hug and celebrate with my friend Julie as well; the girls and I were so glad we could spend time with her.

Now, what the PACT Act does for my family is to provide us with the presumption of eligibility. Joe's cancer is one of the twenty-three presumptive illnesses within the law; so, the VA will now presume that Joe's illness was a direct relation to his service. That was the very thing they had asked me to prove to them in the first and second denials; the PACT Act takes the burden of proof off me.

The second VA denial I received a few weeks before the Firewatch. That came after my attorney handling my appeal completed an extensive questionnaire that the VA had sent us looking for additional information. I was very thankful that I had hired him since it seemed a daunting task. When I read his response, I was even more thankful for him, because half the questions were items the VA was supposed to compile, not things I was supposed to provide them. That's the sad part. I think sometimes they make the process overwhelming for people so that they will just give up.

Lastly, before the denial letter came. I received another letter from a third-party medical company. They sent the same letter twice, and addressed them both to Joe. Within that letter, they basically said, "We're going to be doing a medical review. You don't have to attend any appointments now, but you may, at some point, have to attend an appointment. It's critical that you do so because it could affect your claim if you don't show up."

I ignored the first letter, casting it away to a side table with important papers. When the second one arrived, stating the same information, I had to do something. I called the company and said, "You do realize that Joe's deceased, right? Is it somewhere in your bio there? Because you're sending me a letter addressed to him about making appointments, which is not going to happen, ever."

And they said, "Oh, it's a standard form."

My response was simple, something along the lines of, "You may want to look into creating another form for deceased patients, as it's rather disturbing for families to receive these letters."

The second denial letter, which the VA said was based on its medical review of evidence, shifted the burden of proof back to me. This was the exact reason we fought so hard for our veterans and their families. We shouldn't have to prove something the government already knows is an issue.

The PACT Act removes that burden of proof for twenty-three illnesses and grants them presumption. Since we had John Feal, Jon Stewart, and Joe McKay to guide us, we were able to add the most amount of illnesses we could justify in the first bill, with the ability to add more as they would arise. We have appropriate dollar amounts to fund the claims, because to go back to add funds and illnesses is difficult.

Once our VA claim gets approved, it will make things a bit easier for us. It should mean health benefits and college funds for the kids, which are both so important. One of the things that was most important to Joe was that he took care of his family, and it'll feel really good to make that happen. It will feel good to be able to provide some things to them in his honor. It will allow me to stay home longer to take care of the kids. After everything they have been through, I feel it's most important for me just to be here for them. It's best that they have my attention when they need it most. I know he'd want that.

My plans going forward are to help educate people on the PACT Act, to help implement it and to disseminate information to as many people as possible to make them aware of their exposure. We'll follow the bill to ensure it is doing what it was intended to do: provide healthcare and benefits to potentially 3.5 million veterans and their surviving families.

I'm working with a wonderful doctor who has done a great deal of research for Burn Pits 360 and our veterans, to help discover toxin exposure and illness. He's currently working on a urological study of veterans. Due to Joe's involvement in all of his trials at a hospital that is also a research hospital, we had samples remaining there. I was able to have them sent to this doctor for testing and analysis to see what he can find in them. I'm hopeful about this research, hopeful that it will help others who were exposed to burn pits and toxins, furthering the proof of the illnesses they cause.

I'd like to find a way to ensure that cancer facilities make that connection between exposure and service when seeing our veterans. Some won't start out at the VA because they may not immediately connect the exposure to the illness, much like what happened to Joe. The facility that treated Joe sees a significant number of 9/11 first responders whose illnesses seem to be mirroring our veterans' illnesses. Let's face it: they were exposed to the same toxicity in both environments. We are missing a great opportunity to piggyback on that research, to make correlations between the two. More importantly, we are missing the chance to realize what treatments may work better on these types of toxin exposure cancers and illnesses. Perhaps correlating the two will provide them with better treatments.

Better, hopeful, purpose, family: these are words I find myself repeating frequently. I'd like to think we made things better for our veterans and their families, and we will continue to work to do better. I'm hopeful since I found my new family. They've helped me to feel validated, not to feel alone. They understand what we are going through without words being spoken.

I'm hopeful that our writing this book provides others with hope and validation like I found - hopeful that maybe it gives them inspiration while grieving. I found in my advocacy something that gave me purpose after losing Joe. It made me feel that even though I could not save him, I could perhaps save someone else in his honor. I keep speaking and writing so that perhaps someone else who is going through a difficult time will see that there is light at the end of the tunnel, especially when you find purpose. Find something that breathes life back into you. Sometimes it will take a bit to find, but don't stop looking for it, even when things look darkest.

We are all aware how tragic 9/11 was. I know first-hand; my mother and I were there. I almost lost my mother that day, but thankfully she survived. I still can't recall the route I took home that day. But if it weren't for 9/11, I wouldn't have met Joe. His unit wouldn't have been activated. It was a good thing that came out of a tragedy. Who would know that so many years later, we'd have something else good come from tragedy? Life just has a way of coming full circle sometimes, doesn't it?

Family, my blood family, has been with us through thick and thin. I know they will always be here, and they will not fail us when we need them. Through everything, they have shown me that. My new Burn Pits 360 family, they understand us; they appreciate us; they support us. We want the best for each other, and we all work toward a common goal and interest.

To Kevin, Kim, and Tim, we will always have each other's six. It doesn't matter that we all live in different states. It doesn't matter what we all have going on. We made a promise to each other to take care of one another and our families, and we will never break that promise. Find people like them. It will make all the difference, I promise.

FAMILY IMPACT TRIBUTE

## *by Isabelle Cancelino*

My dad died when I was five years old, a few months before I started kindergarten. I don't have as many stories about him as my mom or my big sister. They tell me stories about my dad that help me remember him: memories of how Dad used to tell stories and make everybody laugh. He would keep going and adding more details because everybody was laughing so much.

I'm like Dad that way. I love to perform. I've been with a theater group since kindergarten called Neat, and we put on two plays a year. Sometimes the plays have dancing in them, and I like to dance. I like costumes, and I'm really good at doing different kinds of makeup. I like watching YouTube makeup tutorials and trying out what I see. Once, I got so much green makeup on me that it took three makeup wipes to get it off!

People say I look like my dad, too. I even got glasses last year. Dad wore glasses, too. But mine are pink. That's my favorite color. People say I look like my sister Ava, too, but I don't think so. Our hair is different, and we like different things.

My dad was really nice. He used to watch shows about building things. But when I woke up and I came out to the living room, he changed it to my channel. We watched Disney together. Now, I like Nickelodeon and the Disney movie Zombies. But he didn't mind changing the channel for me. He liked watching my shows because he knew I liked watching with him. He introduced me to Star Wars. At first, I thought I would be scared, but I ended up really liking it. Our favorite one to watch was The Empire Strikes Back. We started collecting Star Wars Pez dispensers, and we would line them up in front of the TV. We can't keep them there anymore because our new dog would eat them!

We used to play games together, too—sometimes just us and sometimes with Ava and Mom, too. We liked to play Go Fish. It's in my memory box now because we didn't want to play it anymore after Dad died. Dad used to play the Wii with me, too. We would play bowling. He used to play his Xbox by himself, but when I wanted to play, he'd change the game and put me on his lap as he sat in his big leather chair. He'd help me use the controller and "let" me play.

Dad was the fun parent. He was always the one who would say yes to things. He used to build forts with me, like pillow and blanket forts. But he liked things to be clean. He always used to tell me to pick up my toys. We have these bins where the toys are supposed to go, and Dad would tell me I should give away some of my toys because I didn't keep them in the bins. But I wasn't going to give them away!

He was a good cook. The best thing he made was grilled cheese. He could make good spaghetti, too. He used to eat it by turning it around his fork. I tried to do that, too, but I don't do that anymore. I got a noodle caught halfway down my throat. I couldn't swallow it down, so I had to bring it back up. That was scary!

Dad loved to eat Captain Crunch for breakfast. I used to ask Mom if I could have some of his cereal because I liked to eat breakfast with him. He would also make us oatmeal with blueberries.

Dad had a sports car we used to call the hot rod. I really liked driving with him in that car. It was a lot of fun. I used to ask him if we could take the hot rod instead of the truck when we went out.

Dad, Ava, and I loved roller coasters. Before he died, we went to Hershey Park. I loved the roller coasters there. I like going fast. We also went to Disney twice before he died. We went to Chef Mickey's for breakfast where we met all the characters. They came up to our table and talked to us—all except Daisy. But we went outside and found her later. The roller coaster at Universal was the only one that scared me. It was the Harry Potter and the Forbidden Journey ride, and the dragon blew smoke in my face! I had my eyes closed. I was freaking out.

One of my favorite places to go was Splish Splash. It's a waterpark that's really fun. It's not that big, but I love going there. I remember going there with Mom, Dad, Ava, and my cousins Jacqueline and Hailey.

Dad was good at swimming. He could hold his breath for a really long time underwater. Once in the pool on one of our vacations, he was holding his breath for too long and a lifeguard said, "Don't do that! I thought you were drowning!"

Dad just thought, "I'm a grown man, and I can't go under the water in the pool? Okay."

I remember my dad teaching me how to swim. We don't have an in-ground pool; it's a circle pool. Dad got in there and helped me learn. He held me up and took me around. I was never scared when he was teaching me. He used to throw me around and I thought, "This is the life!" Now I can do three backwards somersaults and two front somersaults.

My dad would always try to help people. If he saw somebody who needed help, he would say, "Here, you can have this." He would give to people who needed it. That was my dad.

When my dad got sick, I would lay down beside him on the couch. I just wanted to stay by him and talk to him. Sometimes he would rub my feet. And sometimes I would fall asleep. I just liked being around him. He would call us on FaceTime sometimes when he was in the hospital. He didn't have any scary needles or tubes. It was just my dad's face, and he was always smiling. I was happy to see him.

I feel sad sometimes that I wasn't there when he died. I was sleeping over at my cousin's house. Mom called me so I could talk to Dad, even though Dad couldn't talk anymore then. Mom put the phone up to his ear so I could talk to him. When I came home, I found out that he died. I really wanted to talk to him one more time.

Now on his birthday or other special days, we go to the cemetery to see him. I saw other people putting stones on top of graves, and I thought I would do that, too. But then I stopped doing that. Now I just kiss my hand and put it on the top of the grave. Or I hug the stone. We don't stay long, but I tell him I love him.

It makes me happy to see some things in my house that my dad made. He was a good fixer and builder. We also have his police hat hanging in our house. I like seeing it there. I think, "What if my dad's right there?" I always think about that.

I used to think that maybe I wanted to be a police officer, but then I saw police officers doing their job and how dangerous that job is. Now I think that maybe I would like to be a teacher. Kindergarteners are really cute. I think I would like to teach them.

I also think about him when I cuddle my favorite stuffed animal. That's my pink bunny. She used to be bright pink. Her name is Uh-oh because I kept losing her. Once I lost her at a store, and I was not happy. I was crying hysterically. Luckily, somebody told me that she found the bunny. I still have her today.

I'm not always sad. I like to draw and color, sing,

dance, act, and play with my friends. I love bunnies. My favorite color is pink. I love gym class in school. I like to have fun and spend time with my family.

I have good friends at school. They are sweet people, and they make up fun games. Sometimes, it makes me sad when other people are talking about their dads. I feel left out. I have a great dad, and I am sad that he's not here with me anymore.

I like going places with my mom to talk to people about Dad and how he got sick. I'm not afraid to talk to anybody. I like staying in hotels and listening to music on the way. I like being in the car and going somewhere different. I like seeing all the new friends we made that are like family now. I like seeing people's pets. Rosie and Le Roy have a dog, and I love seeing their dog. Something I'll miss is seeing all of our Burn Pits 360 family now that the bill has passed.

What I want people to know is that if you lost somebody, don't give up. Sometimes you feel like you want to give up, but don't. You can always remember them, and you can still talk to them.

FAMILY IMPACT TRIBUTE
## by Ava Cancelino

I had a good childhood, great parents, and a big family filled with aunts, cousins, and uncles. I was always a happy kid. The only big loss I had ever felt was when I was six and my grandma passed. I was devastated, but I was so young I don't remember much of it now. Then, when I was in fifth grade, my Mom and Dad told me my Dad had to have surgery. It was out of the ordinary for him because he didn't get sick often, but I didn't worry. Soon enough one surgery turned into two, and two turned into three. My concern started to grow, but I still kept it in the back of my mind.

Sixth grade started, and that's when I realized something was really wrong and that it wasn't just a small surgery. My family would come hang out with me and my sister all the time, while my parents went back and forth from the city for 90% of the school

351

year. That June, when sixth grade ended, I really started to struggle. At the end of summer it got bad. My mind went to a really dark place, but I assumed I'd feel better over time. However, I felt the exact same. I didn't know what to do.

When seventh grade started, after school I spent most of my time in my room. I wanted someone to realize what was wrong. After all that time in my room, it became a routine for my Dad to come and hang out for a little. One day he came into my room trying to talk to me, asking questions about my day and just trying to make conversation, but I really wasn't having it. I kept answering back with "Mhm" and "Yeah" just to try and get him to leave so that I could be alone. All of a sudden, he stopped talking and just looked at me. I didn't look up. I just assumed he had enough and was going to leave, but then he asked, "Are you depressed?" I said, "What? No," with a nervous laugh to try and make it believable. He told me to be honest, but I denied it again. He eventually left, and I didn't think about it too much after.

Holidays were especially difficult with everything going on. I was always very close with my cousins. We had a decent sized age gap, but I never saw them as "older". They were my best friends growing up, and I always felt like I was treated the same. I never felt lesser, even if I was younger. But that Thanksgiving I spent the whole time in the back room of the house; it was the first time I wasn't bouncing around the house hanging out with everyone. I felt isolated.

Everyone was happy, and I still couldn't be. I didn't even truly know why. I was surrounded by family; why wasn't I happy? Even though I was isolating and probably seemed annoyed to everyone else, my family still came and said hello and hung out with me from time to time. My aunts and uncles would come and ask me how school was and such, and my cousins, as per usual, made me laugh. My birthday was a week later; we always had family birthday parties. It was my last birthday party I had before my Dad died. My birthday party came, and I had a good time. I felt better than I had. Christmas was the same, and I felt like I was on the right track again.

April was my sister's birthday and Easter. It also happened to be the month our dog passed away. We first found out he was sick in fifth grade, same as my Dad. He had been struggling for a while, and we all knew the time was coming soon. When the time came, we all loaded into the car to take him to the vet. When we got to the vet, Isabelle and I said our goodbyes to Max and left to wait in the waiting room. Eventually my Dad came out to get the car, and my Mom came out a little after. The entire car ride home was silent. A few weeks later, my cousin Jacqueline posted where she would be going to college since she was graduating that year. It was states away. A little later, my cousin Hailey, who was graduating the next year, posted she was going to college upstate, not too far, but I realized that now all my cousins, my best friends growing up, were leaving me.

At the end of May, we got the news that my Dad's cancer had spread and that we had no more treatments left to try. Me, my Mom, and my sister were in the hair salon. My Dad called my Mom to tell her. I could tell something was off; I practically forced my Mom to tell me what was going on. The next day at school I went to my guidance counselor to tell her what had happened. Due to everything that was going on, I was struggling; so, she was kept updated. I told her, "He's dying, and there's nothing else we can do. Isabelle is going to have to grow up without a Dad. She's only five. It isn't fair." I didn't know about burn pits yet; so, I didn't know how unfair it truly was. But her response to me was, "Ava, I'm so sorry; that's terrible. But how are you feeling?" I can't really remember exactly what she said; I blocked so much out that it's all blurry. But it was along the lines of that. I said that I was fine and I just felt bad for Isabelle. She told me, "You'll always have videos to show her, and she'll be okay." After talking, I left and went back to my day, trying not to cry, because if I cried in front of everyone I knew people would talk and I'd be humiliated.

When school ended, we were getting ready for a trip to Hershey Park, one of my favorite places. I was excited to go even though I knew my Dad wasn't going to be able to do anything due to how sick he was. The night before we were leaving, my mom and my sister were at my Aunt Alexis'. I was there for a little, but then I decided I wanted to leave early. So my Aunt

Denise drove me home and told me to text her if I needed anything. My Mom asked me to help my Dad pack; so, I went home and I asked if he needed help. He said, "Yeah, that'd be great." I didn't like seeing him sick, but I still helped. I don't know how much I really helped because no matter how many times I told him to sit down, he still insisted he could do it himself, even though I could tell it was difficult. It was just the kind of person he always was. Even if I didn't help him that much, I think he still appreciated that I spent time with him, and looking back, I'm kind of glad I did, too.

Three days after we returned from our trip to Hershey, my Dad was now in hospice care spending his last few days at home. Not a day went by without family coming over to say their goodbyes. One morning my Mom woke me up and asked if I wanted to be home when the time came. I don't think I realized how soon that time would be. I knew he was dying; it was clear. But the rest of his fight was so slow and painful. I didn't even want to see him. It wasn't even him anymore. The person who needed to be waited on 24/7 wasn't my Dad. It was a person his sickness had turned him into.

The night of July 16th, my cousin Jennie, my Aunt Daurene, and my Uncle Steven came over to say goodbye. My Mom had fallen asleep for a little since she had barely been getting any rest while taking care of my Dad. Before they left, my Aunt told me to wake up my Mom at midnight so she could give my Dad his meds. They left, and I locked the door behind them and went back to my room. Not so long after, it was midnight. I woke up my Mom and told her what time it was and that Aunt Daurene told me to wake her up. She gave me a slight nod to let me know she was awake and said, "Okay" and "Thank you." I went back to my room. I FaceTimed my friend Ava for a little while after, but then I hung up and said I'd call her later because I wanted a snack. She ended up being the first person I told when my Dad passed. Two minutes after I hung up, my Mom came into my room and asked if I wanted to be there when "they" came, meaning the funeral home.

Three years later, I'm sitting in the Capitol building surrounded by a bunch of people in similar situations watching a bunch of Senators decide if my Dad died for nothing. I was in one of the most talked about buildings in the country. Everyone was saying what an amazing experience this was and, "How cool is this?" As soon as the PACT Act passed, everyone was so emotional and so happy. I just wanted to leave; I was so tired. We walked out of the Capitol onto the lawn where there were a bunch of cameras set up with Senators and other survivors and families waiting to speak. My Mom and my sister got up to get into the camera area, and I stayed behind, out of the camera's view. I think I was just kind of blankly staring at everything because some woman behind me asked if I was okay. I gave her a slight nod and hoped this would be over soon. After everything started to die down, the lights started going off, and the cameras were put away. My Mom was finishing an interview, and I was waiting with my sister. My Mom's friend Joe came up to us and said, "Remember this moment; your Dad is so proud of you." I just nodded, which was probably rude given the situation, but I was so tired that I didn't know what to say. We walked back to where everything had been set up for the Firewatch, and I grabbed a lemon-lime Gatorade. I don't even like Gatorade that much, but my Dad did. Lemon-lime was his favorite.

One week later, we were at the White House watching the President sign the PACT Act into law. Sick veterans will receive the care and benefits they earned, and surviving families will receive benefits. It won't fix what's happened, but it's something.

*Love*

FROM THE MOMENT WE MET,
THAT WAS IT.

LIFE WITH JOE WAS FUN. WE
CREATED TWO DAUGHTERS
WHO ARE OUR PRIDE AND JOY.

AVA

ISABELLE

MAX BY MOM WHO
IS HOLDING AVA

MAX, AVA & ISABELLE
ON HALLOWEEN

THIS SCENE OUTSIDE MY BUILDING ON THE AFTERNOON OF 9/11 IS THE AFTERMATH OF THEATTACK ON THE TWIN TOWERS. IT'S THE CLOSEST I'VE COME TO EXPERIENCING THE EFFECTS OF A BURN PIT.

*Deployment*

JOE'S SLEEPING QUARTERS (WHITE CIRCLE) WAS NEAR A BURN PIT (WHITE SQUARE).

*Remembering Joe*

TOBY

BLUE

JOE WAS SO MUCH FUN TO BE AROUND.
EVEN THOUGH WE MISS HIM, WE REMEMBER
TO HONOR HIM BY ENJOYING THE TIME
WE HAVE WITH EACH OTHER.

*Living Joe's Legacy*

EVERY SURVIVOR IS A MESSENGER.

## ACKNOWLEDGEMENTS

Michael, Kathy, & Julia Santucci; Denise Santucci; Alexis, Jacqueline, & Hailey Galison; Daurene, Steven, Katie, & Jennie Scianimanico; Christine Santucci; Greg Hansen; Luke Germanokos & family, Dr. Jenifer Kramer; Gia Bauer; Bob Ganley; New York City Police Department; NYPD 105 & 110 Precincts; TD30; NYPD Counterterrorism Div.; NYPD employee relations; NYPD SBA; NYPD medical division; Memorial Sloan Kettering Cancer Center; Dr. Samuel Funt & his staff, especially Annie; Rosie & Le Roy Torres (Hope, too); Burnpits 360 veterans organization & all the advocates who became our family; Jon Stewart & the amazing staff at *The Problem with Jon Stewart;* Joe McKay; Julie Tomaska; Kerry Baker; Dr. Anthony Szema; Genevieve Doherty; Jennifer & Jake Grivas; Maryann & Bobby White; Brett Ruffo; the FitzSimmons family; the DeMaria family; the Saulpaugh family; Denise Barone; the Henriquez family; Donna Murphy; Kevin & Carrie O'Brien; Cherisse Quinn & family; Laura King; Amy Bermudez; Gina Santangelo; the Brooks family; the Dupont family; the Montiel family; Laurie Yuditsky; the Kirshman family; the Johnson family; the Hernandez family; the Accardi family; the Monahan family; Tom Miller; Sue Dillion; the DellAccio family; CKO Kickboxing Long Island (Christie, Frankie,

363

Krystal, Tyson); Joe Andreula; Watson & Koula Miller; Victoria Sanquini & all of the Staff at Neat acting studio; Valerie Pezzulo; Mark & Jeanne Marino; the security staff at my children's school; Isabelle's preschool; Dan Krueger; Thomas Hansen; Elyse Cruz; Dawn Plotnick; Cortney Campo; Lisa Holmes; Hope Morreale; Julieta Améndola; Steven Presaud; Kathleen McGrady; Julia Kohn; Rob Palomba; The New York Islanders; Cindi Sansone-Braff; Danielle Anatra; Robin, Philip, Joseph, & Irina Licitra; Carissa & little Danny Solares; Suzanne Russo; Dominick Fasano; the Gioffre families; Uncle Joe Gioffre; Aunt Gail & Aunt Barbara Cancelino; Gail & Tony Guglielmo; Deborah & PJ Miley; Senator Gillibrand & her staff; Senator Schumer & his staff; Congressman Ruiz & his staff; Congressman Garbarino & his staff.

I know there will be people that I miss on this list; please know that if that happened, I'm truly sorry. Just know this: we greatly appreciate you and everyone who supported us.

CONCLUSION
## *Keeping the Promise*

Not one of us would have chosen to become the advocates we are today if we had been given a choice. Trust us. We would far rather be hiking in the woods, traveling without thinking about oxygen needs, or waking up next to someone who's not here anymore. Sometimes you can't choose the tragedies that find you.

And those tragedies can find you even when you're doing the right thing, when you're doing something good. Kevin, Tim, Gary, and Joe were fighting the good fight and following orders when they were exposed to toxins. Kim and Gina were taking care of kids at home and keeping life together while burn pits were stealing their husbands.

None of us were doing anything to endanger us. We didn't deserve the pain, suffering, and loss that we've endured. But the question we've had to face is what we do with loss. What do we do once the unthinkable has happened? What do we do with the terminal diagnosis, with the irreplaceable absence?

Sure, we mourn what we don't have. But we can't stay there in that place of just feeling sad. We have to keep going, keep living. We have kids to raise and love. We have work to do. And we have each other.

Having each other has been an unexpected blessing and a joy. Normally, you don't get to pick your family. But we are family that has chosen each other. Knowing that someone who truly cares about you and knows exactly what you've endured is only a phone call (or FaceTime) away is worth so much. As Kevin says, "We are family through tragedy advocating for triumph."

That advocacy work bonds us together. We all care deeply, not just about each other, but about our great, big, extended military family. We are all in this together, and we want to make sure that each member of that extended family is okay, that each one has what he or she needs to be well, to keep going, to heal damaged bodies, and to take care of loved ones.

We are grateful for the passage of the PACT Act, not as a closed door but as an open one. With the passage of this important legislation, the real work begins. All of us have areas of special interest ranging from enacting further legislation to reaching out to homeless veterans to spreading the word about screening for toxins and getting proper care in time for it to make a difference. The encouragement and support we offer each other as a team and a family helps us keep going with this important work.

Thanks for listening to our stories. We're happy you took the time to get to know us and the people we love through these pages. Once you close this book, don't let that be the end of your interest in veteran issues. Find a way you can help by contacting one of the organizations you'll find in the acknowledgements, a group like Burn Pits 360 or the FealGood Foundation. Then offer whatever you have to give, donations or time or skill, to help them in their work.

Together, we can bring one small triumph at a time out of the tragedy of burn pits.

GROUP ACKNOWLEDGMENTS

Please, join us in heartfelt appreciation for Le Roy and Rosie Torres, founders of Burnpits360. It is because of their steadfast determination and unwillingness to allow an injustice related to toxic exposure that our stories, our becoming a family, and our writing this book even came to be!

To Jon Stewart, a genuine human being, who has cared for other human beings from 9/11 to Afghanistan to Iraq and other wars, operations, and conflicts. We thank you.

To John Feal and Joe McKay of the FealGood Foundation for all of the hours, press conferences, events, and so much more, and for bringing your heart and soul to this fight.

To Tim Jensen and Will Wisner from Gruntstyle Foundation for bringing boots-on-the-ground advocacy and Warfighters to rally our nation in support of veterans and their families all around our great country.

And a special thank you to Robbie and Sharilyn Grayson of Traitmarker Publishing. With your help this all became possible.

Please go to www.thepromisepactact.com to show your support for our American Patriots.

368

## ABOUT KIMBERLY HUGHES

KIMBERLY HUGHES, *a native of Chicago, is the mother of two and the widow of Army Major Gary Hughes, who passed away in the prime of his life.*

*When Gary fell ill, Kim found herself in a whirlpool of struggles that she would have to battle: losing a business, filing for bankruptcy, and proving her husband was a victim of toxic air exposure. She soon discovered Burn Pits 360, where she found hope, and reached out to founders Rosie and Le Roy Torres.*

*Eventually, her family left the only place they had ever called home and moved south. She began traveling, sharing her story, and empowering others. Along the way, she met Kevin Hensley, Gina Cancelino, and Tim Hauser. Together they helped make history.*

*Even though cancer stole Gary's life, Kimberly became resilient—not only for her own family but ultimately for many others.*

*Now that the PACT Act is law, Kim advocates for veterans, their families, and survivors. She continues to advocate for the implementation of the PACT Act, encourages early onset testing, and shares information that will spare others from the painful experiences that she and her family had to suffer.*

## ABOUT KEVIN HENSLEY

KEVIN HENSLEY *operates from a highly developed sense of justice. But on deployment, Kevin had to let one big transgression go. The burn pits right beside where he slept and worked were making him sick. Back home, Kevin paid daily for his exposure to the pits. Breathing and swallowing became difficult.*

*Towards the end of his twenty years of service, his situation became dire. Tests revealed hundreds of polyps in his airways and damage to his lungs. As Kevin's health worsened, his debt mounted when treatment remained uncovered. He learned to keep massive notebooks of every test result and procedure to litigate for his treatment with a VA that seemed determined not to acknowledge the source of his illness.*

*With the passage of the PACT Act, Kevin will finally be able to put those notebooks away and receive treatment without losing anything more. He can continue to help other veterans keep government representatives from breaking protocol. After all, enforcing regulations is what he does.*

## ABOUT TIM HAUSER

TIM HAUSER *was a high school student who liked photography, art, track, and cross country. Growing up in Ohio, Tim biked to nearby Lake Erie with his friends or went there with his family. He enjoyed spending time outdoors swimming, running, fishing, or lining up a shot with his camera. When he joined the service, he took every opportunity to find some fun or adventure.*

*But when he got home from months of deployment abroad, he couldn't even run a mile before the lack of air made him stop. A biopsy back home revealed that, after just a few months of toxic smoke exposure, the bottom of his lungs had turned hard and diseased, a change that it would take decades of hard chain-smoking to approximate.*

*Tim spoke for decades to other veteran patients in waiting rooms, doctors in the VA, and people close to him about what the burn pit smoke had done to his lungs and health. With the passage of the PACT Act, Tim wants to help homeless veterans find medical care and a path back to stability. Having come near to homelessness himself because of his health, he wants to serve those less lucky than him.*

## ABOUT GINA CANCELINO

GINA CANCELINO'S *husband Joseph was a Marine who spent his entire six-month deployment in Iraq, sleeping adjacent to both a jet-fuel-ignited burn pit of refuse and barrels filled with burning human waste coated in lye and also ignited by jet fuel. Fourteen years after returning home, Joseph was diagnosed with a rare, aggressive form of cancer: cancer he would die from two and half years later because of his exposure to toxins from burn pits. At no time during or after his deployment was he ever notified of the potential damage to his health those burn pits could cause. No one advised early testing and intervention, something that might have saved Joseph's life.*

*Following the loss of her husband and the realization that other veterans and their families could be devastated like her own, Gina began advocating for the PACT Act. Her ability to passionately yet articulately express her grief, sadness, and frustration over the lack of resources being applied to this growing tragedy led her to Burn Pits 360 and a new type of family. Little did she know that her advocacy and support as well as her voice at press conferences, on CNN, on radio, and in newspaper interviews would be returned to her and her daughters through their deep and lasting relationships with other advocates.*

*Now that the PACT Act is law, Gina and her two daughters will receive the service-connected death benefits that Joseph earned: benefits they had been denied. Gina is also focusing on the PACT Act implementation and education within the veteran and survivor communities with the hope that this knowledge will lead to early detection for some and closure for others. She is determined to spread the importance of screenings and early detection so that our veterans can have the opportunity at life that Joe was denied.*

**988**

**SUICIDE &**

**CRISIS LINE**

*Portions of the profits from*
*The Promise will be donated*
*to Veterans organizations.*

thepromisepactact.com